ROUTLEDGE LIBRARY EDITIONS:
SOVIET SOCIETY

Volume 9

I0105302

HEALTH CARE IN
THE SOVIET UNION
AND EASTERN EUROPE

HEALTH CARE IN
THE SOVIET UNION
AND EASTERN EUROPE

MICHAEL KASER

Routledge
Taylor & Francis Group

LONDON AND NEW YORK

First published in 1976 by Croom Helm Limited

This edition first published in 2025
by Routledge
4 Park Square, Milton Park, Abingdon, Oxon OX14 4RN

and by Routledge
605 Third Avenue, New York, NY 10158

Routledge is an imprint of the Taylor & Francis Group, an informa business

British Library Cataloguing in Publication Data
A catalogue record for this book is available from the British Library

ISBN: 978-1-032-86028-2 (Set)
ISBN: 978-1-032-88076-1 (Volume 9) (hbk)
ISBN: 978-1-032-88080-8 (Volume 9) (pbk)
ISBN: 978-1-003-53610-9 (Volume 9) (ebk)

DOI: 10.4324/9781003536109

Publisher's Note
The publisher has gone to great lengths to ensure the quality of this reprint but
points out that some imperfections in the original copies may be apparent.

Disclaimer
The publisher has made every effort to trace copyright holders and would
welcome correspondence from those they have been unable to trace.

HEALTH CARE IN
THE SOVIET UNION AND
EASTERN EUROPE

MICHAEL KASER

CROOM HELM LONDON

First published 1976
© 1976 Michael Kaser

Croom Helm Limited
2-10 St John's Road, London SW 11

ISBN   0–85664–193–4

Printed in Great Britain by
Lowe & Brydone Printers Limited, Thetford, Norfolk

CONTENTS

ACKNOWLEDGEMENTS

Over the past twenty years occasional *ad hoc* studies in the field of health economics, commissioned by the World Health Organization,[1] its Regional Office for Europe[2] and Stanford Research Institute[3] made it clear to the author that little published work was available either in the West or the East on what is a vast and distinctive mechanism of health care. This book endeavours to present a comprehensive and comparative survey of the health services of seven East European countries as they are in practice, for which the sparse official data has had to be supplemented not only by much documentary research but also from personal communications in the countries concerned, for which the author wishes to record his thanks. A study-tour of health services, with interviews at the Ministries of Health of the USSR and of the Ukraine in 1961, had afforded a number of initial insights into operational features of the Soviet system;[4] further visits to the USSR were made in 1965, 1973 (the Semashko Institute and the Institute for Health Information, both of the Ministry of Health) and 1975. Earlier visits to the GDR (1964, 1968) had included discussions of social policy economics at research institutes; further consultations with health authorities were obtained between 1969 and 1974 in Bulgaria, Czechoslovakia, Hungary, Poland and Romania.

The pattern of statistics characterizing a health-care system employed in the book owes much to that set up for world-wide comparability by Dr M. Rosner and Mr J. Deering, then of the Stanford Research Institute, for that Institute's project covering one hundred countries. The data which the present author then compiled ended in 1968, and Mr Andrew Seton of Wolfson College, Oxford (under funds from the Social Science Research Council) has added those for more recent years. The brief histories of pre-war health services with which Chapters 3, 4, 6, 7 and 8 open draw upon a study by Dr Milan Hauner (of St Antony's College, Oxford) on social infrastructure between the two wars, which forms part of the present author's collaborative research on the economic history of eastern Europe since 1919, also supported by the SSRC.[5] In that history a summary of the present book will constitute a chapter in Volume III which treats of economic organization in 1950-75.

The author expresses his appreciation to all those whom he had the opportunity of meeting in the countries concerned, as well as to those in Oxford (where the bulk of the research was undertaken) who kindly gave advice or the help of bibliographic and other facilities.

2 *Health Care in the Soviet Union and Eastern Europe*

1. M. C. Kaser, 'Observations on the likely economic efficiency of the malaria eradication programme' (report to WHO Malaria Eradication Division, 1958), subsequently published in R. Barlow, *The Economic Effects of Malaria Eradication*, Ann Arbor, Mich., 1969, pp. 145-67; 'Health Planning as Part of the National Development Plan' for WHO Expert Committee on Public Health Administration (1960); and 'Health Economics and the Classification and Articulation of Activities and Expenditures in Standardized National Accounts' for Inter-Agency Working Party on Costs and Sources of Finance of Health Services (1965)
2. M. C. Kaser, 'The Evaluation of Public Health Programmes: Research Experience in the United Kingdom' for WHO Regional Office for Europe Working Party on the Evaluation of Public Health Programmes (1972), published in revised and extended form as 'Choice of Technique' in M. Perlman (ed.), *The Economics of Health and Medical Care*, London, 1974, pp. 510-27
3. Health Planning Research Program, Stanford Research Institute: No. 11, *Romania*; No. 45, *Hungary*; No. 80, *Czechoslovakia*; No. 83, *Bulgaria*; No. 87, *USSR*; No. 88, *GDR*; and No. 89, *Poland*, Menlo Park, Calif., 1970-1
4. M. I. Roemer, 'Highlights of Soviet Health Services', *Milbank Memorial Fund Quarterly*, Vol. XV, No. 4, October 1962, pp. 373-406
5. Chapter 2 by M. Hauner, in M. Kaser and E. A. Radice (eds.), *The Economic History of Eastern Europe Since 1919*, Vol. I, Oxford University Press (forthcoming)

1 THE REVOLUTION IN HEALTH CARE

I. Postwar convergence within Eastern Europe

The nine per cent of the world's population with whom this book deals benefit almost without direct charge from a completely comprehensive health service. Before the accession of Communist Party governments — sixty years ago in the case of the USSR and thirty for the other six countries — compulsory social insurance ensured cheap medical services for the majority of the urban employed, but little had been done for farming, the predominant occupation of the region. Those below and above working age, housewives and the unemployed were, by and large, as ill-provided for as the peasant or farm labourer: high infantile mortality and short life-expectancy were the concomitants. In a series of autobiographical short stories, a Soviet physician, Mikhail Bulgakov, has described his experiences in running a rural clinic in Russia in 1917-18.[1] In one year he saw 15,613 patients, 43 a day including Sundays, and admitted 200 inpatients helped by a feldsher and two midwives. Conditions would not have been much different in rural Bulgaria, Hungary, Poland, or Romania between the two wars, although higher standards generally prevailed in Czechoslovakia and Germany.

The communist-directed administrations assured in the first place free and sufficient services to industrial workers, either by developing existing social insurance, transferred to trade-union jurisdiction, or by preferential access at the workplace, and it took time for rural deficiencies to be remedied. Even today only a minority of agricultural manpower is employed by the state, whereas the postwar nationalizations had put almost all urban workers on a public payroll at the time when national health services were being organized. Farmers in collectives (and, continuing in Poland, on individual holdings) were, in the main, not automatically covered until the sixties. When such cover was assured the way was open to declare free health care a 'civic right' and enactments were almost everywhere made in the past decade.

The first session of Comecon's standing commission on health, held in Moscow in October 1975, could hence survey a comprehensive service of health care covering some 360 millions from cradle to grave. Had it met a decade earlier, significant gaps would have been revealed, chiefly in provision for the rural population, but access to free services has been made general by recent legislation, particularly that of the USSR of 1969, Poland of 1971 and Hungary of 1975. Entitlement through insurance, as was general prior to the present socialist administrations, continues — and is the basis of the present scheme in the

3

German Democratic Republic (GDR) — although the Soviet government took medical care out of the social insurance scheme in the mid-
thirties. It then incorporated health-service finance into the central
budget and allocations for capital and recurrent needs into an overall
planning system, the 'material-balance' procedure of the Five-Year
Plans, of which the First was launched in 1928 and the Tenth in 1976.
When Comecon (the Council for Mutual Economic Assistance) was set
up in 1949 all the other members were preparing five-year plans; in
1976 they were also beginning a new quinquennial round with health
services that had become fully comprehensive. Procedures for forecast-
ing the calls of the health services on economic resources and for inter-
locking appropriations with the production and other social sectors
were initially developed by the USSR and were applied by the other
members of Comecon early in their use of socialist central planning.

This book must therefore begin with consideration of Soviet practices, both because they have been taken over in all the states here
analysed and because their history extends over double the period of
the others. But the book is also a complement to *Health Care in the
European Community* (1975) by Alan Maynard and as such conforms
to its structure — a chapter of international comparison and one on
each country. The justification of a matching volume lies in the division
of Europe into two political groupings at the end of the Second World
War, a consequence of which was the establishment of separate economic agencies. On the Western side, the Organization for European
Economic Cooperation evoked the creation in the East of the Council
for Mutual Economic Assistance, but the former remains a forum for
inter-governmental consultation, within which it is the European
Economic Community that, since 1958, has sought integration of its
members' social as well as economic objectives. Comecon, on the other
hand, from the start grew increasingly more homogeneous in a process
of which three features are salient. Inescapably the first is a political
identity: Communist (or Workers') Parties control not only the governments, some of which are nominally coalitions with other parties in a
patently subordinate status, but virtually all economic and social organizations. Because a uniform framework of domestic and foreign policy
is imposed by the political structure, Comecon is not therefore as
intrinsically necessary to socioeconomic harmonization among its members as is the Common Market to Western Europe. A quarter-century
elapsed between Comecon's creation and the establishment of its
Commission on Collaboration in Health Protection, but similarities of
the system evolved within the 'socialist commonwealth', as it came
officially to be termed. The interaction within its defensive alliance, the
Warsaw Treaty, has recently been formulated by a Western commentator, who sees the Treaty as 'an instrument of socialist consolidation: it

derives its substance as much from the social system of its members as from the purposes and obligations set out in the treaty'.[2]

A second feature which has, with almost equal pressure, promoted integration within Comecon was the establishment of the Common Market itself. Comecon was endowed with a Charter (1960) and 'Basic Principles of the International Socialist Division of Labour' (1962) which respectively furnished a procedure and criteria for integration to counter the expected deterioration in Comecon's gain from trade with Western Europe. The then Chairman of the USSR Council of Ministers, Khrushchev, in 1962 took as exemplar objectives of supranationality in the EEC to urge upon Comecon 'a unified planning organ, empowered to compile common plans and to decide organizational matters'.[3] Romania, as the member most in need of rapid development, objected to a scheme of specialization which could have narrowed its prospects, and positive steps fostering integration were largely deferred until a new drive began in 1969. This was crystallized in a 'Complex Programme for the Further Extension and Improvement of Cooperation and the Development of Socialist Economic Integration', formulated at the Comecon Council Session of 1971. The new phase in economic collaboration gave impetus to the harmonization of social policies and Ministers of Health decided at a conference in Budapest in 1974 in favour of a formal entity within the organization.

The final characteristic of Comecon relevant to the present study is the political conflict between the USSR and China, which induced Comecon to redraw its frontiers along ideological lines: Albania was dropped as a member at the end of 1961, Mongolia was brought in during the following year and Cuba joined in 1972. For the sake of parity with Maynard's book, treatment here is restricted to the present European members of Comecon. Comparisons are in any event more meaningful within a single continent sharing the same historical influences; the inclusion of the economically underdeveloped members of Comecon, i.e. Cuba and Mongolia, would have involved an excessively broad spread of data on health conditions and documentation on health care institutions. A work dealing with socialist health systems under Communist Party governments of coverage beyond the East-West European context would properly have to consider China. There, a trend contrary to the Soviet has been promoted, basing the provision of health care, like the generation of all goods and services, on 'self-reliance': devolution was thus urged on the Chinese province and commune where the Soviet rule has been centralization.[4] By late 1975, however, emphasis seemed to have been withdrawn from local self-sufficiency as exemplified by the 'barefoot doctors', and more of a common model might be emerging.

II. The structure of each country-study

The social legislation enacted from country to country of Europe from before the First World War, together with the mutual insurance offered through friendly societies, cooperatives and trade unions, makes the point of historical departure parallel in the East as in the West of the Continent: each chapter opens with a survey of the institutions, policies and laws which eventuated in the present comprehensive free services. The chapter on the USSR is the lengthiest, not only because its socialism has run for nearly sixty years but because there are certain continuities in focusing health-care primarily on the factory which come from pre-revolutionary experience. The landmarks in legislation and coverage are briefly indicated for the other countries.

Six topics are chosen for analysis: the sections are similarly titled for ease of cross-reference and within each an attempt has been made to set down as full a statement of the relevant facts and figures as available documentation allows. The research has thus brought between two covers as much information as a Western reader is likely to find of interest. Since national descriptions have been the prime objective in the compilation, international comparisons are not made in the chapters on individual countries, but a very wide range of statistics is cited to enable quite detailed confrontations to be made with the particular features of any other national system for which corresponding data may be available. Tables are grouped at the end of each chapter to facilitate comparison.

The first section of each chapter specifies demographic experience: the need for health care is evidently variant with the age-structure of the population; the tempo of population growth itself determines in part the extent to which a health service must budget to keep up with sheer numbers of clients or may husband resources to intensify provision. It is equally patent that the protection of child-health today affects the productive capacity of a group which, twenty years hence, will have a population approaching 415 million. It is also relevant that their citizens will show a median age (i.e. that which divides the age distribution into equal parts) rising over the next two decades from 30 to 33 (see Table 1.1). The increase in the proportion of the elderly against that of children must already begin to evoke different patterns of disease and care.

The following section of each chapter identifies present-day needs in so far as they are apparent from the state of health. The available statistics of mortality and morbidity are presented, a compilation in itself of interest since the countries concerned are reticent on the publication of social statistics; the USSR, in particular, has not published comprehensive statistics on health conditions for forty years. Enough indications can nevertheless be gained for all countries for some valid conclusions to be drawn on the changing incidence of disease and injury. As might be expected, the increasing industrialization of the countries, fostered by centralized economic planning, has led to a trend of the morbidity pattern away from that associated with agrarian communities to that of highly urbanized societies. If (as in Table 1.4 for 1967) comparisons are made with France and the United Kingdom as representative of the EEC group, tuberculosis, though much reduced since the fifties, inflicted as much as seven times the United Kingdom mortality in Poland, but in Bulgaria and Czechoslovakia was about the same as in France, which in turn was still triple the United Kingdom level. On the other hand cancer deaths closely approached the levels of France and the UK only in Czechoslovakia, Hungary and the GDR, with half those rates exhibited in the USSR, Poland and Romania. The pattern of heart disease was remarkably similar in those eastern and western countries considered, but the incidence of motor accidents was, as might be expected, much lower in Eastern Europe.

After a description of the administration of health services which, in the distribution of function between central and local authorities, may be of interest as a survey of comparative government, the contribution is estimated of insurance, taxation and personal payments to the finance of the health service. The resultant development in the delivery of health care and the utilization of health resources is charted. A survey for a conference in 1975 by a Czechoslovak health economist stressed that 'most socialist countries have utilized Soviet practice on standards of expenditure on the health service and have adapted them to local conditions'.[5] It seemed for this particular reason important to describe first the Soviet system, with chapters on other Comecon members following, and to summarize in this introductory chapter the essentials of the common planning system.

Soviet planning procedures have not incorporated health outcomes in the way that they have set targets for outputs of tangible goods, but over the past decade health economists in the USSR have developed a considerable corpus of research. The public launching seems to have been by the nonagenarian economist Stanislaw Strumilin, who had in the early twenties begun work on the economics of education. In an article of 1966 he pointed out that the prolongation of life-expectancy since the 1917 Revolution had by 1964 represented the addition of 5 million to the workforce.[6] The estimate was raised to 10 million (for the period 1940-65) by M. P. Roitman of the Semashko Institute of Public Health Administration, Moscow.[7] Both studies were of the same type as research in 1965 by the Czechoslovak Ministry of Health showing that from 1950-62 the value of every incremental unit of outlay was matched two-fold by the product of the additional work-lives created by the decline in mortality.[8] In the Soviet Union of the First Five-Year

Plan such a general evaluation has been used to justify the switch to the
so-called 'industrial principle', that is, preferential treatment for industrial workers. The then leader of the trade unions, M. I. Kalinin, so
addressed the VIIth Congress of Health Departments in 1930: 'When
we assure the worker a whole range of privileges and advantages in the
field of medicine, we do not do it because he is the hegemonic power,
but rather because he is the most necessary and decisive productive
factor in our society. Consequently the interests of the self-mainten-
ance and the development of society compellingly force us to pay most
attention to workers.'[9]

Conversion to a money measure has been studied in the USSR mainly through losses of work-time due to sickness or injury absence.
Writing for a broad readership in the newspaper for the medical profession, A. V. Sergeev confined himself to the generalization that the
average of 13 days a year absence 'cost thousands of millions of roubles',[10] while A. E. Shakhgel'dyants compared such absences as
percentages of man-days worked in 1965:[11]

GDR	5.37	France	6.02
Czechoslovakia	4.28	Yugoslavia	5.80
Poland	3.71	Norway	4.60
USSR	3.21	Austria	4.56
		FR Germany	4.43

A variant of this manpower budget approach deducts employment in
the health service (over 5 million in the USSR in 1970) as a further cost
to offset benefits from health care. Neither he nor M. I. Sharkov and
E. I. Sheinova[12] attempted macroeconomic quantification, but the
latter provided a monetized method. They estimated the average value
of a working-life at 2,000 roubles annually, although it is not clear to
what definition that refers.[13] The 1960 values of the two national
accounting aggregates published by the USSR Central Statistical Office
— global social product of 328,000 million roubles and net material
product of 145,000 million roubles — show a dividend by a 120 million
workforce of 2,730 and 1,210 roubles respectively; the Western concept of gross national product (estimated at 188,000 million roubles)
yields a dividend of 1,570 roubles.[14] A worker aged 20 who is completely disabled costs society the 80,000 roubles which an able-bodied
life would have provided plus the 18,000 roubles pension he would be
paid. Pensions of employed persons are calculated according to degree
of loss of ability (the 100 per cent incapacity group cited is Group I),
as distinct from discretionary pensions *ad personam (personal'ny*

pensioner) and retirement pensions (under the state-guaranteed schemes of the trade unions and of the collective farms).

Among microeconomic analyses undertaken in the Soviet Union, which may be cited as typical, was one in a Novosibirsk factory where the reduction in work-time lost through illness represented 0.2 per cent of the average cost of production; in the year examined (1964) this represented 31,500 roubles, to which would be added a saving 13,300 roubles in payment of sickness benefit.[15]

The Soviet planning system (and with it the similar procedures used elsewhere in Comecon) has from the start been well suited to the incorporation of health outcomes as a target for maximization under the constraints of planned inputs of manpower and capital and of available technology (as itself developed under plans for skill-enhancement, research and new investment). The index of health outcomes applied (though not as yet widely for planning) is the percentage of the population who did not suffer illness or injury during the course of the given year.[16] Wider measurements have not yet been adopted (although there has been discussion of them[17] in the two principal institutes concerned of the USSR Ministry of Health in 1973) accompanied by research into the evaluation of individual treatments, such as the clinical evaluation of therapies (efficiency), the utilization of resources applied (efficiency) and the resultant health outcomes (effectiveness).[18] Because they are not commensurate, they cannot be fitted into a central planning system and no health administration as yet aggregates the assessments of particular services or therapies in a manner usable for forward planning.[19]

Rather, the Soviet-type planning system is attached to 'indicators' which can be attained by the application of capital and recurrent inputs with a certain technology. As 'material balances' of expected production and planned distribution in physical units, their use dates from 1920 in the USSR, although they did not become the fundamental tool of planning until the First Five-Year Plan. Consistency is effected by a process of iteration (the 'method of successive approximations', in the Soviet phrase), by altering projected production or consumption where the first draft showed inadequacy or superfluity, and by carrying each change through the derivative inputs and outputs.[20] The Soviet parallel in health planning is of indicators of the network of services as surrogates for production, while norms of utilization serve for the 'technology' relating inputs to 'indicators'. Not all figure in the formal text of the health plan — the so-called 'confirmable' targets — as approved by the Council of Ministers of the USSR or of the Union Republics, but those that are include the numbers of hospital beds, physician services, pharmacies, beds in sanatoria and rest-homes, etc. Other ratios — 'accountable' indicators — are compiled in the Ministry of Health in the framework of the confirmed plan.[21]

Norms of utilization applied to convert resources to the indicator of provision include bed occupation rates in hospitals, mean consultations per day in polyclinics or by house-visiting physicians, professional staff per unit of pharmacy turnover — to name but a selection. The parallel financial plan is compiled once the indicators of provision have been specified down to the supplier of the service itself. The centralized financial system establishes, for example, wage rates of medical staff differentiated according to the function occupied, education, length of practice in the health service and location of the respective health facility, and norms per hospital bed on scales of the different specialties, the type of hospital, the price zone for consumables and the mean rate of bed occupancy.[22] Since these procedures have become fairly standardized and their detail is not germane to this book, the country chapters do not examine individual variations.

The material basis for the services is also compared (at the end of the present chapter) in estimates of the consumption of pharmaceuticals *per capita*, converted into a standard Western currency (conventionally the United States dollar). Each country, as part of a programme of economic self-sufficiency, has sought to develop its supplies for the health services, rather than rely on imports, a policy nevertheless modified by the prominence of trade in such products among Comecon members. In addition to specialization within Comecon, some members make a substantial impact on world markets.

Sutcliffe's definition of health services for the York University conference of 1970 incorporated 'hospital care, services of physicians, dental care, drugs and public health facilities', but left the precise production boundary uncertain, as still subject to controversy. He rightly stressed the need 'to include health activities within branches of government other than health, e.g. medical care for the armed forces and the school health service'.[23] These are included in the present study as far as official reporting permits, for there are substantial services in all Comecon countries outside the Ministry designated that of Health. Each of the Ministries of Defence operates a military medical service, which is, however, excluded from all published statistics.

Perhaps the most significant element of international economic comparison is the finance of the health service and the call thereby made on national resources. Many models are available[24] but application has been constrained by the statistics published. A number of estimates have had to be compiled by manipulating those statistics, but for all seven countries shares of national income, proportions of government health outlay devoted to capital investment and sources of aggregate finance have been, at least tentatively, identified.

In the absence of full national or cross-country studies, the collection and analysis of official data has occasionally had to be accompanied by informal information about some aspects, particularly of finance, which have drawn little attention — e.g., it is a rare book which mentions, for example, *sub rosa* payments in the health service.[25] Some Western research has appeared and more is known to be under way on the Soviet system, but very little seems to have been compiled on the other east European states, and even in Eastern Europe no international analysis has been published. Comecon's creation of a Standing Commission on Cooperation in Health Protection may well foster such cross-country research, but, for the present, this book is the first comparative survey of a distinctive mechanism for health care covering more people than any other in the world.

III. Population trends as a factor in health care

With virtually everyone now entitled to free health care, the services must be prepared to combat the total morbidity of the population and to adjust to demographic change. Over the last quarter of the century, there will be (on the projections of Table 1.1) exactly 100 million more people in the seven countries of east Europe; many fewer of the 459 million population will be children, and many more in retirement, and those of working age as the twenty-first century begins will only be 45 million more numerous than in 1975.[26] With relatively fewer in the productive age-groups it will be all the more important for the health services to operate cheaply, and it is an achievement that they have hitherto been functioning at lower cost than in the West. An ageing population is moreover at greater health risk and can scarcely be expected to show the very low mortality rates now reached. As Table 1.2 indicates, the crude mortality rate for the group of states was small enough in 1974, but it was rising from a nadir of as little as 7.7 per 1,000 in 1966 (7.3 in the USSR, 9.2 in the rest of Eastern Europe). Except in the GDR, where births are now fewer than deaths and the population is declining, birth rates are remarkably uniform (18 ± 2 per 1,000). Infantile mortality has also been reduced to a uniformity characteristic of most advanced societies: if the extremes of the GDR (low) and Hungary and Romania (high) are excluded, the 1974 rates were in the twenties per 1,000. The reductions since the Second World War are more telling: the 1974 rates as a percentage of those in 1945[27] were 16 in the GDR, 21 in Bulgaria and Czechoslovakia, 24 in Romania, 26 in Poland and below 29 in Hungary (where some of what would elsewhere be stillbirths count as neonatal deaths); in comparison with 1940 (in the absence of a 1945 figure), the decline in the USSR was to 14 per cent. Since infantile mortality is something of an inverse surrogate for the level of health in a community at large, its reduction to a quarter or one-fifth over three decades is a key indicator of the success of the services concerned.

Still greater uniformity at a high standard is to be seen in the expectation of life. The latest available data (Table 1.3) are all within three years of 67 in the case of men and 72 in that of women. The increases in expectancy since before the Second World War[28] are also most marked: taking males, it was 22 years in the USSR, 19 in Poland, 18 in Hungary, 14 in Bulgaria, 12 in Czechoslovakia and 9 in the GDR; for both sexes the rise was 27 years in Romania.

The leading causes of death, as would be expected at such longevities, are diseases of the circulatory system and cancer. The first group, as Table 1.4 indicates, accounted for 45 per cent of deaths in Bulgaria, Czechoslovakia and the GDR, for relatively more in the USSR (48 per cent) and Hungary (52) and for fewer in Romania (41) and Poland (36 per cent), which — with Bulgaria — have the lowest degree of urbanization.

The pattern of mortality from cancer is fairly similar, causing 15 per cent of the deaths in Bulgaria, the GDR and the USSR, relatively more in Poland (16), Hungary (19) and Czechoslovakia (21), and fewer in Romania (13). Conversely infectious diseases persist in Poland and Romania (5 and 3 per cent respectively), are barely over 1 per cent in Czechoslovakia, less than half a per cent in the GDR and are midway between these extremes in Bulgaria and Hungary at 2 per cent. No data are published for the USSR but their continuing importance may be imputed from a comparison of new cases of specified communicable diseases per 10,000 population in 1972 with the GDR:

	GDR	USSR
Infectious hepatitis	11.7	19.4
Scarlet fever	47.3	12.9
Typhoid and paratyphoid	0.1	0.8
Acute poliomyelitis	—	0.02
Diptheria	0.0	0.02

Whereas, however, all the ten notifiable diseases in the USSR shown in Table 2.10 have shown a decrease since 1960, four out of the twelve in the corresponding Table (5.5) on the GDR have shown an increase.

IV.   Health care services

As everywhere, the health service is highly labour-intensive and a Soviet analyst has stated that in the late sixties the Soviet service was increasing in this respect faster than the national average for the production of tangible goods (i.e. net material product). In 1970 80 per cent of outlays for the Soviet service was on manpower, which totalled over 5 million (of which 0.67 million medically qualified and 2.12 million medium-qualified). The following comparisons may be made with the British National Health Service, since both are comprehensive and mainly supported from public funds.

	USSR (1970)	England and Wales (1971/2)
Employment as percentage of total population	2.1	1.6[a]
Labour costs as percentage of health-service outlay	80	69
Percentage occupancy of hospital beds	87[b]	80
Mean length of stay per hospital bed	15[b]	13
Physicians per 10,000 population	27	13
Direct (personal) charges as per cent of pharmaceutical prescriptions	30	5
Capital expenditure as per cent of all health-service outlay	5	10

a   United Kingdom
b   Urban areas only, as being more comparable to United Kingdom

There are now over one million physicians in the seven Comecon states (the 1974 total was 1,030,000 against 568,000 in 1960[29]). The physician numbers of 1973 (from the same sources as in Table 1.5) show 27.9 per 10,000 population (21.3 if the more labour-intensive USSR is excluded) or double that in the European Community (13.9 in 1970-2), although dentists at about 4.2 were not much more numerous than in the European Community (3.6 in 1970-2).[30] The number of pharmacists per 10,000 population is much greater in Comecon (2.56) rather more than half that in the European Community (4.6); the East-West disparity is narrower within Europe alone, since Comecon excluding the USSR had 3.32 pharmacists per 10,000 population in 1973.

Not all countries separate medical (or fully trained) nurses from statistics of medium-trained medical personnel but the following ratios of nurses to the total number of physicians (i.e. not only those serving in hospitals) are given in later chapters:[31]

USSR	(1973)	1.50
Bulgaria	(1973)	1.41
Czechoslovakia	(1972)	1.50
Hungary	(1973)	1.26
Poland	(1974)	1.87
Romania	(1968)	1.27

The comparable ratio for the European Community in 1968-72 was 2.17. Hospital bed numbers in relation to population had reached parity in the two groups of states: 106 per 10,000 inhabitants in Comecon and 102 in the European Community.[32] Table 1.5 shows quite a wide variation among Comecon members, only two (GDR and USSR) exceeding one hundred beds per 10,000 inhabitants, while the average without the USSR was 85. In terms of the utilization of those beds, Hungary was well in the lead in Comecon, as the following data show:[33]

			Annual occupancy (days)	Mean stay (days)
Hungary	(1973)		327	15.0
USSR	(1970)	urban	319	14.9
		rural	295	12.6
Bulgaria	(1973)		307	14.8
Romania	(1974)		306	11.8
Poland	(1974)		304	14.9
Czechoslovakia	(1972)		290	14.4

If Soviet and rural and urban hospitals are accounted separately, as is the Soviet practice, the range is 19 days' occupancy around 309, which is almost exactly the average in the West. Noting that 310-day norm, a Soviet author draws attention to diversity of Western experience (from 302 days in Japan to 331 in the Federal Republic of Germany) and quotes a recent recommendation of the USSR Ministry of Health that urban hospitals should operate at between 330 and 340 days and rural between 300 and 310.[34] It is noteworthy that a recommendation made in 1959 on the basis of morbidity surveys in five Soviet cities (11.7 per cent sample of the population, 22.1 per cent in four of the towns) in 1955-6, suggested that 11.5 to 12.5 hospital beds were required per 1,000 urban inhabitants to eliminate refusals for hospitalization,[35] when the actual rate was 7.6.[36] That level was reached for both urban and rural areas in 1973 (11.4 beds per 1,000). That sample survey found a shorter period of hospitalization (12.1 days) than recorded in the national returns, though it could not have been a wide discrepancy since the 1958 urban average was 12.6 days. But as the text-table above shows, the period had by 1970 lengthened to 14.9 days. The average for the European Community (1969-72) was 15.3 days[37] but the range was 5.3 days each way, whereas the spread between Comecon countries was much narrower around exactly the same figure (15.2 ± 3.35). Czechoslovakia at 8.0 beds per 1,000 population in 1973 had not obtained the norm of 9.4 which its Ministry of Health has set as an 'ideal'.

Statistics of outpatient consultations are not readily comparable. In the USSR in 1965 there were 9.7 consultations per inhabitant in urban polyclinics and in 1970 1 screening or periodic health check for every 2.4 persons.[38] Statistics quoted in subsequent chapters showed 5.9 outpatient consultations per inhabitant in state polyclinics and practices (with a significant addition to be made if private practice data were available) in the GDR in 1968; 5.7 per inhabitant in Poland in 1973 (other than in the school health service); 6.9 in Romania in 1971; 10.2 in Czechoslovakia in 1968 (also excluding the school health service); 5.4 in Hungary in 1972; and 5.0 in Bulgaria in the same year.

At the other extreme, a comparison might, finally, be in order with China. Estimates for 1966 put the number of physicians with 'Western' medical education at 150,000 or 2.1 per 10,000 population; with 30,000 physicians in Comecon statistics, the ratio was 2.5, against Comecon's contemporary range from 14.6 in Romania to 23.9 in the USSR. But, geographically at least, more apposite comparisons might be made with Comecon's sole Asian member, Mongolia, and the Soviet Union Republic nearest to, and having some ethnic affinities with, China, that is, Kirgizia. The following ratios per 10,000 population emerge for 1965-6:[39]

		China	Mongolia	Kirgizia
1.	Graduates of Western medicine			
1.1	Physicians and stomatologists	2.5	13.5	19.1
1.2	Pharmacists	0.3	0.2	1.5
1.3	Medium-trained personnel	6.9	..	58.8
2.	Practitioners of Chinese medicine	6.9	..	..
3.	Hospital beds	5.4	91.0	91.1

The practitioners of Chinese medicine were the forerunners of the 'barefoot doctors' greatly encouraged during the Cultural Revolution (having a 3 to 6 months' training period), but whose significance was apparently being reduced in 1975; they had counterparts in herbal naturopaths in both Mongolia and Kirgizia, of whom some certainly continue to be consulted outside the official health services.

V.   The finance of health care
By no means all health care is financed 'indirectly' (to use Abel-Smith's term), but as Table 1.6 shows, taxation is the overwhelming source of

funds in the USSR and Bulgaria, whereas it contributes less than half in the GDR and Hungary.

The table relates, for lack of information, only to legally-sanctioned expenditure, some private payments being made *sub rosa* to physicians or other personnel for the assurance of a desired service. It also separates expenditure which is part of social and private consumption from that (mainly by state enterprises and cooperative farms) which is embodied in production costs. The distinction, familiar in national accounting methodology, has an advantage in comparable presentation for Comecon, because no information on such outlays seems to be available for Bulgaria, the GDR and Hungary. In countries for which it is derivable, however, its ratio to the principal sources of finance is trivial save only in the USSR, where it adds one-sixth to the main outlays. The paradox that so much health care provision is furnished through the services within enterprises or collective farms is explicable by reason of the finance of the services by the local health authority. The host organization supplies only the building and its upkeep, heating and cleaning.

Social insurance is a major channel of finance in the GDR and Hungary and a substantial one in Czechoslovakia and Poland; no more than 1 per cent is so funded in Bulgaria and Romania. Private payments are only really large in Romania, Poland and Czechoslovakia, though their volume has been declining over time; they are significant in Hungary and the USSR, but in the one case being due to a small share of high retail cost of prescriptions plus much self-medication, and in the other due to a full payment of outpatient prescriptions at a lower aggregate retail cost. To make some composite pattern for the east European group as a whole, Table 1.6 weights shares of expenditure by population (implying that, with comprehensive care to all residents, the per-person service is roughly comparable): rounded to indicate roughness, about seven-tenths of finance are derived from taxation or public sector profits, and two-tenths through social insurance premiums. These fall in most countries only on the employer, but in the GDR the employee contributes 10 per cent of earnings up to a (fairly low) maximum and in Romania 2 per cent of earnings.

An East European author at an international conference in 1975 sweepingly stated that 'operations . . . and medicaments during hospitalization are fully free of charge for the patients'[40] and, while such a statement is true for almost every hospitalization in a Comecon state, it is still not strictly accurate. Non-entitled inpatients in the GDR, Poland and Romania have to pay for both treatment and medication, and an intermediate group in Romania (cooperative farmers) pay reduced charges. The requirement on non-insured persons to pay in Hungary was repealed in July 1975.

Prescribed pharmaceuticals for ambulatory care were wholly free in Hungary until 1952, in Poland until 1953 and in Bulgaria until 1956. Full direct payment has to be made in the USSR, Bulgaria and Romania; there are large reductions in Hungary and Poland, where respectively only 15 and 30 per cent of the retail price is paid, and the 'handling charge' in Czechoslovakia is so modest (1 kčs for up to two items on any one prescription) that it aggregated a mere 2.7 per cent of prescription value in 1972.[41] Prescriptions are fully reimbursed to insured persons in the GDR. All pensioners have free prescriptions in Poland, as do a certain number in Romania and everywhere medication for maternal and natal care is free, as are prescriptions for specified diseases (the communicable group, tuberculosis and diabetes generally) and public-health prophylaxis. Abortion is not charged for in Soviet and Polish institutions, but payment is required in other countries, either at a flat rate at a low level in Bulgaria (5 leva) and Romania (30 lei) and at a high rate in Hungary (1000 ft, which in purchasing power is some ten times that of the Bulgarian fee and still further above the Romanian), or graded according to the income of the woman as in Czechoslovakia (200 to 800 kčs). Consultation for the contrary purpose, the treatment of infertility, is everywhere free, as is pre- and post-natal care. A major social transformation has been effected in hospitalizing virtually all confinements, which, also, are without charge. The related social development, raising to near the maximum participation in gainful employment outside the home (though 'out-work' still plays a certain role in Romania), has been matched by the accordance of free medical treatment for children at least up to 3 years of age and by the organization of a school medical service. In principle, where, or for the period that, there was no comprehensive service, children of non-insured aged between 3 and 7 were not covered but their inoculation has everywhere been without charge (as in some cases also before the Second World War).

Private practice is legal in the USSR under licence that the consulting room is properly equipped, but it is discouraged by penal taxation. A licence is granted in Czechoslovakia to retired physicians and medically-qualified dentists while lower-qualified dentists may run a private surgery for conservative and prosthetic operations only. Private practice is both legal and reimbursable from the Social Insurance Fund in the GDR. In Hungary a physician in full-time employment in a state-owned facility can obtain permission to practise privately out of hours, for 1 hour a day after his stint of 8 hours; a retired physician may practise without a limit of time.

Bulgaria and Romania have outlawed private medical practice (although Romania allows group dental practice), while at the other extreme 2,000 physicians in the GDR and over 4,000 in Hungary operate a private practice; Poland has about a quarter of its physicians in private practice. Group practice in medical cooperatives is subject to inspection for adequacy of facilities, and to control of fees, by the Ministry of Health. A partner in such a practice is limited to 3 hours a day after a stint of 7 hours in the public service. Until the extension in 1974 of social insurance to private farmers − the bulk of the rural population − health care cooperatives financed by the local inhabitants were standard, but they have now been absorbed into the government system.

The 'professorial privilege' of private consultations for the top rank of specialists is conceded in Czechoslovakia, Hungary, Poland (where though officially limited to private consulting rooms, it extends informally to the hospital itself) and Romania.

No 'pay-beds' are tolerated within state hospitals in any Comecon country, although clinical professors enjoy the attribution of certain beds, except in the USSR and Bulgaria. Private hospitals (the majority of them run by religious communities) are, on the other hand, an integral part of the health service of the GDR, where they provide service on direct payment and under contract with the Social Insurance Fund. Fee-paying hospitals were advocated in the USSR in 1966, though the proposal has not been taken up officially. Fee-paying outpatient facilities were opened during the sixties in the USSR and Romania.

Prices of pharmaceuticals have remained generally stable over the past decade, but the rapid replacement of specialities is said to have concealed price rises, especially as each new item was generally costed to incorporate research outlay. Some reductions did, however, take place as costs declined. Thus wholesale prices were reduced by 5 per cent in the USSR in July 1967 and by 18 per cent in January 1968 in Hungary. In neither case was this passed on to consumers, and the change was reflected in a rise in turnover tax in the USSR and a cut in the subsidy in Hungary. When a major group of pharmaceuticals was cut by 31 per cent in Poland in December 1970, it was, on the other hand, at the expense of producers' profits, their margins declining correspondingly. The same was true of the substantial price cuts of January 1968 in Bulgarian pharmaceuticals, although that of June 1971 was chiefly on imported specialities and on domestic antibiotics (which had reached a certain over-supply). Retail prices for health care products have been kept constant over a long period in the GDR, although wholesale prices have fluctuated − downward by 3 per cent in 1964-8 and upward by 7 per cent in 1968-70.

Among other current costs catering outlays are low by international standards. Meals served to patients (except, by account, in the more luxurious closed-access hospitals) are very poor in quantity, quality and preparation. In part this was deliberate policy while consumer standards in healthy life were being held back in favour of government expenditure for rapid industrialization. Better nutrition in hospitals would have induced pressure against discharge; in countries where a significant or total charge is made for outpatient prescriptions poor standards of food are a disincentive to seek admission to hospital where pharmaceuticals are free. Patients quite frequently have to tip orderlies to get what is available (peculation in the kitchen is not uncommon) and refrigerators in wards are frequently used for the storage of perishables brought in by patients' relatives. The report on fulfilment of the 1971-5 Soviet Plan stated (as noted in Chapter 2) that catering standards had been improved in general hospitals and would be bettered in the next plan period (1976-80) in maternity homes, children's hospitals and 'other specialized hospitals' (by which psychiatric hospitals were almost certainly meant). As resources are generally no longer needed to increase the coverage of services, more finance can be allocated to qualitative aspects, and the Hungarian Plan for 1976-80 made a priority point of better quality of care.

The very low current costs hitherto achieved by keeping down salaries are also decreasingly accessible as labour shortages force up salaries. It is often remarked that the very high share of women in the medical services of Comecon countries (72 per cent of physicians in the USSR, for example) has an element of concealed wage-discrimination. Two substantial rises were accorded to Soviet medical staff in 1964 and in 1972, and one was given in Hungary in 1970, with a further rise said to be imminent.

Reference has already been made to the high provision of physicians in each of the health services and, save in Romania, the annual addition (net of retirements, death and emigration) has everywhere exceeded 3 per cent, at least triple the demographic increment.

Percentage increase in physician numbers in Comecon states (end-year)
1960 to 1973 and 1974

	1973	*1974*
USSR	78	85
Bulgaria	57	63
Hungary	63	68
GDR	76	84
Poland	84	89
Romania	31	34
Czechoslovakia	55	62

Source: Comecon Secretariat, *Statistical Yearbook, 1974*, p. 442; *1975*, p. 434

On balance the trend of health service costs will have been upward, the rise in the manpower components and in rates of pay exceeding reductions in cost of pharmaceuticals. Trends in building costs have not been published but as Table 1.7 shows, these are a small component of overall outlay. Countries fall into two groups: the USSR, Poland and Romania where government outlay is only to a small degree devoted to investment in health facilities (5 or 6 per cent in the early seventies) and Bulgaria, Czechoslovakia and Hungary where around triple that share is reported. The capital contribution of state enterprises and cooperative farms adds proportionately more to the low-level group than to the others. No data are published on the GDR, but in the sector including health, education, welfare and culture, the proportion put to capital expenditure conformed to that of the lower group.

Two classes can also be perceived in shares of national income (Table 1.8). Because only Hungary officially estimates an aggregate corresponding to the gross national product (GNP) commonly adopted in the West, the safest criterion is Comecon's own usage of net material product (NMP). All NMP data, save in Romania, are published in absolute terms and the percentage therein of health care expenditure puts the USSR, Bulgaria and Romania together among the small spenders (some 3.5 per cent). For comparisons with the West, estimates of GNP have to be made, although the components are available from the published statistics of Czechoslovakia and Poland as well as officially from Hungary. The same categories are exhibited as for NMP (which falls short of GNP by the value of services such as administration, the armed forces, health, education, housing and personal service). The USSR, Bulgaria and Romania show closely similar shares at a mere 2.4-2.8 per cent of GNP, Czechoslovakia, Hungary and Poland are intermediate at 4.8-5.1 per cent, while the GDR shows a high share at 5.8 per cent. Only Ireland in the European Community spends as little as 5 per cent of GNP on health, the shares for other EEC states 1971-2 being 5.1 for the United Kingdom, 5.5 for Denmark and France, 5.8 for the Federal Republic of Germany, 6.0 for Italy and 6.7 for the Netherlands.[42]

Comparisons within Comecon of the provision of pharmaceuticals is much more hazardous because of wide divergence in price ratios. The value of sales in domestic retail prices has been identified with only a modest need for estimation, and country totals are shown in column (1) of Table 1.9. The structure of retail prices greatly differs, however, from those in Western countries (as may be demonstrated by a product-by-product comparison by the present writer for Czechoslovakia and the United Kingdom), although in two countries (as Chapters 7 and 8 show) the Ministry of Health has calculated its own 'exchange rate' to world prices (which, because of varying incidences of indirect taxation, are manufacturers' prices). An implicit exchange rate of the same nature can be constructed from estimates of production adjusted for imports and exports (Table 1.10). Column (5) of Table 1.9 sets out the results of such conversions to world prices, giving the GDR double the consumption *per capita* of the next highest users, the USSR and Hungary. There must be considerable reservations about the ranking of the USSR, for the underlying data use a published index of pharmaceutical production which can only be impressionistically adjusted from a gross value of output to a gross value-added basis. As a pharmaceutical industry expands, it produces proportionately more of its basic materials (substituting for medicinal plants or imports): the gross value of output double-counts transfers within the industry from basic-producing enterprise to finished-good manufacturer. The other Comecon countries may be more accurately ranked on the dollar basis. Poland is fairly close behind Hungary in *per capita* consumption and well ahead of Czechoslovakia (subject to the *caveat* on the dispersion of its price-relativities) and Romania. Bulgaria is well at the bottom of the table, but its fast-expanding pharmaceuticals industry brought its consumption by 1974 to the level of Czechoslovakia in 1968.

An alternative exchange rate (column (6) of Table 1.9) comes from GNP comparisons in dollars and in national currencies, but the ratios of prices of all goods and services mean little in practice when the home currency cannot be freely converted either into foreign goods or within the availabilities of domestic goods.

Finally, Comecon's own 'transferable rouble', a collective unit of account which is not actually used in any transaction, provides some relationship for foreign-traded goods. The ranking is similar to that into dollars at a pharmaceutical exchange rate, as apposition of columns (7) to (5) shows, but the USSR is much reduced in order, possibly because the uncertain valuation of production does not affect the outcome, but also perhaps because relatively fewer pharmaceuticals produced in the USSR are traded (and hence affect the rate to the 'transferable rouble').

There is, however, no doubt about the dominant position of the Soviet Union as Comecon's principal producer of pharmaceuticals (64 per cent in 1968 if the estimates of Table 1.10 are correct). But it accounts for only 9 per cent of Comecon's pharmaceutical exports, most (38 per cent) being sold by Hungary, which sells abroad 70 per cent of its production (though only 7 per cent of Comecon aggregate output). Bulgaria sells, mostly to the USSR, relatively more (76 per cent) of its production, but accounts for less than 2 per cent of the group's total manufacture. The GDR and Poland are the two biggest producers after the USSR — 12 and 10 per cent respectively — but consume the bulk at home. Czechoslovakia and Romania each make 3 per cent of Comecon's output, but the former exports twice as much as the latter. On balance, Comecon is a net exporter of pharmaceuticals to third parties ($51 million in 1968, the equivalent of 2 per cent of its aggregate manufacture). Mutual deliveries within the group represented in that year 11 per cent of production but this is certain to grow as further specialization is promoted under Comecon's *Complex Programme for Further Economic Integration* adopted by a 'summit meeting' in 1971.

REFERENCES

1. Collected under the title *A Country Doctor's Notebook*, trans. Michael Glenny, London, 1975, p. 107
2. D. Holloway, 'Foreign and Defence Policy', in A. Brown and M. Kaser (eds.), *The Soviet Union since the Fall of Khrushchev*, London, 1975, p. 59
3. Cited in M. Kaser, *Comecon: Integration Problems of the Planned Economies*, London, 1967, 2nd edn, pp. 106-7
4. See references in Chapter 9, fn. 15
5. J. Penkava, 'Financing of Health Care in Eastern Europe', paper read to the International Institute for Public Finance, Nice, 1975 (mimeograph), p. 13
6. S. Strumilin, *Vestnik ekonomicheskoi nauki*, No. 5, 1966, p. 28
7. M. P. Roitman, *Metodika izucheniya ekonomicheskoi effektivnosti likvidatsiya ryada zabolevanii*, Moscow, 1970, cited by V. V. Golovteev, P. I. Kal'yu and I. V. Pustovoi, *Osnovy ekonomiki sovetskoi zdravookhraneniya*, Moscow, 1974, p. 12
8. Penkava, op. cit., p. 11
9. Quoted in G. A. Batkis and L. G. Lekarev, *Teoriya i organizatsiya sovetskogo zdravookhraneniya*, Moscow, 1961, p. 55
10. A. V. Sergeev, *Meditsinskaya gazeta*, 26 November 1971
11. A. E. Shakhgel'dyants, *Ekonomichesky effekt snizheniya zabolevaemosti s vremennoi utratoi trudosposobnosti*, Moscow, 1969, cited Golovteev *et al.*, op. cit., p. 11
12. M. I. Sharkov and E. I. Sheinova, 'The Economic Significance of Workers' Health Protection', in *Stroitel'stvo komunizma v SSSR i sotsial'no-gigenicheskie problemy meditsiny*, Gorky, 1964, p. 312, cited Golovteev *et al.*, loc. cit.
13. Ibid., p. 12
14. Net material product and gross national product (there defined) from Table 1.8, linked to 1960 on official index 1970 = 100 (NMP = 50 and global social product = 51); global social product value from *Narodnoe khozyaistvo SSSR v 1973 godu*, Moscow, 1974, p. 57. 1960 workforce from F. A. Leedy, 'Demographic Trends in the USSR', in US Congress Joint Economic Committee, *Soviet Economic Prospects for the Seventies*, Washington, D.C., 1973, p. 433
15. Golovteev *et al.*, p. 61
16. Yu. Lisitsyn [transliterated as Y. Lisitsin], *Health Protection in the USSR*, Moscow, 1972, p. 41
17. Especially A. Williams, 'Measuring the Effectiveness of Health Care Systems', in M. Perlman (ed.), *The Economics of Health and Medical Care*, London, 1974, p. 363; R. J. Lavers, 'The Implicit Value of Forms of Hospital Treatment', in M. M. Hauser (ed.), *The Economics of Medical*

Care, London, 1972, p. 191

18. M. Kaser, 'Choice of Technique', in Perlman, op. cit., p. 510
19. B. M. Kleczkowski, 'Planning and Evaluation of the Community Health Care Programme', *Santé publique*, 1971, pp. 259-78 and, for a comparison of health plans, S. Litsios, 'The Principles and Methods of Evaluation of National Health Plans', *International Journal of Health Services*, Vol. 1, 1971, pp. 79-85 and *The Evaluation of Public Health Programmes*, Report of a Working Group, WHO Regional Office for Europe, Copenhagen, 1973
20. M. Kaser, *Soviet Economics*, London, 1970, pp. 151-2
21. L. G. Tarasova, L. M. Lemenev, *Rukovodstvo po planirovaniyu khozyaist-venno-finansovoi deyatel'nosti khrozraschetnoi apteki*, Moscow, 1972, p. 23
22. Penkava, op. cit., p. 12
23. E. M. Sutcliffe, 'The Social Accounting of Health', in Hauser, op. cit., p. 240
24. From B. Abel-Smith, *Paying for Health Services* (Public Health Papers 17), WHO, Geneva, 1963, to Sutcliffe, op. cit., pp. 244-56
25. E. R. Weinerman, *Social Medicine in Eastern Europe*, Cambridge, Mass., 1969 and M. Kahn, 'Vue d'ensemble des problèmes de la santé en Europe orientale', in 'Aspects de la santé publique en Europe de l'Est', *La Documentation Française*, No. 275, 9 January 1976, p. 6
26, USSR (rise from 143 to 175 million) from F. A. Leedy, in *Soviet Economic Prospects for the Seventies*, Washington, D.C., 1973, p. 477, and East Europe (rise from 55 to 68 million) from P. F. Myers, in *Reorientation and Commercial Relations of the Economies of Eastern Europe*, Washington, D.C., 1974, p. 446, both US Congress Joint Economic Committee. 1966 East European total projected to 2001 (for which a figure was provided for the USSR) on 1991-6 rates given
27. V. Srb, *Demografická příručka*, Prague, 1967, cited by Penkava, op. cit., except for USSR, from *Narodnoe khozyaistvo SSSR 1922-1972*, Moscow, 1972, p. 40
28. *Breviar de statistică sanitară, 1971*, Bucharest, 1972, p. 302.
29. Comecon Secretariat, *Statistichesky ezhegodnik, 1975*, Moscow, 1975, p. 434
30. European Economic Community, *Report on the Development of the Social Situation in the Community in 1973*, Luxemburg and Brussels, 1974, p. 215, cited by A. Maynard, *Health Care in the European Community*, London, 1975, p. 263
31. Tables 2.16, 3.8, 4.10 and 7.18 and text of Chapter 8. Comparison with Maynard, loc. cit.
32. Table 1.5 and Maynard, op. cit., p. 264 (his data in preference to those of the EEC *Report*)
33. Following chapters of this book, except Romania (*Breviar*, op. cit., pp. 175, 181) and USSR (V. V. Golovteev, P. I. Kal'yu and I. V. Pustovoi, *Osnovy ekonomiki sovetskogo zdravookhraneniya*, Moscow, 1974, p. 89)
34. Golovteev in ibid., p. 80
35. I. D. Bogatyrev, 'Material Referring to the Establishment of Standards for the Necessities of Curative-prophylactic Assistance to Inhabitants of Towns', *Santé publique* (Bucharest), No. 2, 1959, p. 52 (there is a misprint of 100 for 1000, apparent from the context); his later work is cited in Yu. Lisitsyn, *Health Protection in the USSR*, Moscow, 1972, p. 39 and in *Health Planning and Health Economics in Countries of Eastern Europe*, WHO Regional Office for Europe, Copenhagen, 1971 (a compendium of abstracts of publications, 1965-69)
36. I. I. Rozenfeld', *Osnovy i metodika planirovaniya zdravookhraneniya*, Vol.

III, *Planirovanie potrebnosti zdravookhraneniya vo vrachebnikh kadrakh*, Moscow, 1961, p. 66

37.   Maynard, op. cit., p. 264
38.   Respectively, B. V. Petrovsky (ed.), *50 let sovetskoi zdravookhraneniya, 1917-1967*, Moscow, 1967, p. 78; O. A. Aleksandrov and Yu. P. Lisitsyn, *Sovetskoe zdravookhranenie*, Moscow, 1972, p. 63
39.   Chinese data from V. W. and R. Seidel, 'The Development of Health Care Service in the People's Republic of China', *World Development*, July-August, 1975, p. 543; Mongolia from Comecon Secretariat, op. cit., pp. 442-4; Kirgizia from *Narodnoe khozyaistvo SSSR, 1972*, pp. 684-7, except that number of pharmacists was computed pro rata to that of pharmacies (1.1 per cent of Soviet total). Other recent sources on China are L. A. Orleans, *Every Fifth Child*, Stanford, Calif. and London, 1972, and 'China's Experience in Population Control', *World Development*, loc. cit., pp. 507-12; V. W. and R. Seidel, *Serve the People*, Boston, Mass., 1974; F. Avery Jones, 'A Visit to China', *British Medical Journal*, November 1975, pp. 1105-7; and J. S. Horn, *Away With All Pests*, London and New York, 1974
40.   Penkava, op. cit, p. 4
41.   Ibid., p. 8
42.   Maynard, op. cit., p. 257

TABLES

1.1 Demographic projections affecting health needs of Comecon states in Europe

	Population (million)		Per cent of children		Per cent retired [b]		Median age	
	1974	1996	1971	1996 [a]	1971	1996	1971	1996
USSR	252.06	295.5	30.9 [c]	25.7 [d]	6.1 [c]	11.2 [d]	29.5 [c]	31.5 [e]
Bulgaria	8.68	9.6	22.6	20.5	9.9	14.7	33.4	36.8
Czechoslovakia	14.69	16.6	23.0	23.2	11.5	11.8	31.8	33.4
GDR	17.17	15.9	23.2	16.2	15.7	14.5	34.4	39.0
Hungary	10.46	10.7	20.3	18.6	11.7	14.3	34.2	38.7
Poland	33.69	40.3	26.2	23.2	8.6	11.4	28.4	34.1
Romania	21.03	25.3	25.6	24.5	8.8	11.7	31.1	31.7
Total of above	357.78	413.9	..	..	..	..	30.0	32.5
Total excluding USSR	105.72	118.4	..	..	..	..	31.4	35.2

1.1 (cont)

Source: 1974 population: *UN Monthly Bulletin of Statistics*, September 1975, Table 1; 1976 G. Baldwin, *Projections of the Population of the USSR and Eight Sub-divisions by Age and Sex*, International Population Reports, Series P-91, No. 24, US Department of Commerce, Bureau of the Census, Washington, D.C., June 1975, pp. 6, 10 and 24; P. F. Myers, 'Population and Labor Force in Eastern Europe; 1950 to 1996', in US Congress Joint Economic Committee, *Reorientation and Commercial Relations of the Economies of Eastern Europe*, Washington, D.C., August 1974, pp. 430, 434; projection series B (assuming constant gross reproduction rates) has been used, except in Table 2.5 (series C)

a   Aged 0 to 14
b   Aged 65 and over
c   1970
d   1995
e   The source gives an estimate only for the year 2000. A slightly different projection (F. A. Leedy, 'Demographic Trends in the USSR', in US Congress Joint Economic Committee, *Soviet Economic Prospects for the Seventies*, Washington, D.C., 1973, p. 468) shows a lower dependency ratio in 2000 than in 1996 but 82 per cent of the 1996-2000 increment is 35 and over. An earlier projection by Baldwin (same title, International Population Reports, Series P-91, No. 23, March 1973, p. 4) provides a basis for interpolation between 1990 and 2000

1.2 Vital Statistics for Comecon States

	Abortions	Births	Deaths	Natural increase	Infantile mortality	Gross reproduction rate
	1965	*1974*	*1974*	*1974*	*1974*	*1970-5*
USSR	25.7	18.2	8.7	9.5	27.8	118
Bulgaria	14.1	17.2	9.8	7.4	25.5	98 [a]
Czechoslovakia	7.5	19.8	11.7	8.1	20.4	115
GDR	2.6 [b]	10.6	13.5	2.9	15.9	102
Hungary	21.1	17.8	12.0	5.8	34.0	95
Poland	7.4	18.4	8.2	10.2	23.7	102
Romania	58.6	20.3	9.1	11.2	35.0	127

Source: Abortions from H. P. David, *Family Planning and Abortion in the Social-ist Countries of Central and Eastern Europe*, New York, 1970, p. 20, except for USSR (see Ch. 2, Section III); vital statistics from Comecon Secretariat, *Statistichesky ezhegodnik* (hereafter: *Statistical Yearbook*) *1975*, pp. 13-14; gross reproduction rates from Economic Commission for Europe (ECE), *Economic Survey of Europe in 1974*, Part II: *Post-war Demographic Trends in Europe and the Outlook until the Year 2000*, United Nations, New York, 1975, p. 165

a   1972
b   1964

NOTE: 1965 was approximately the peak year for legal abortion. Abortions and vital statistics are per 1000 population, mortality of children under 1 year is per 1000 live births and the gross reproduction is the number of females that will be born to 100 women during their reproductive lifetimes at the year's age-specific birth rates. The Hungarian definition of a live birth is stric-ter than in other Comecon countries, so that the infantile mortality is higher.

1.3 Life expectancy at birth in Comecon states: actual and projected

	Males		Females	
	1970-5	*1995-2000*	*1970-5*	*1995-2000*
USSR	66.5	69.5	74.3	76.5
Bulgaria	68.6 [a]	71.6	73.9 [a]	75.7
Czechoslovakia	66.9	68.7	73.3	74.7
GDR	70.0	72.0	75.3	77.5
Hungary	66.9 [b]	66.0	72.6 [b]	72.1
Poland	67.2	71.8	73.2	76.4
Romania	65.1	71.2	69.5	75.0

Source: ECE, op. cit., p. 164, except for Bulgaria and Hungary actual, from
   Comecon Secretariat, *Statistical Yearbook, 1975*, p. 14

a   1969-71
b   1972

1.4 Causes of death per 100,000 population in Comecon states in 1967

| | Infectious diseases | | Malignant neoplasms | Cardio-vascular disease | Respiratory disease | Diseases of digestive organs | Congenital deformity | Accidents, poisonings, and violence | | All causes |
| | All | Of which tuberculosis | | | | | | All | Of which motor accidents | |
ICD	A1-43	A1-5	A44-59	A70, 79-86	A87-97	A98-107	A127-129	AE138-150	AE138	(rounded)
Bulgaria	19.5	14.0	136.1	402.1	141.0	24.6	4.9	51.2	13.2	900
Czechoslovakia	16.2	11.1	211.1	461.1	86.7	42.3	8.3	78.3	17.4	1010
Hungary	27.6	23.0	201.7	552.6	50.2	43.3	10.3	74.8	9.5	1070
Poland	38.1	31.7	128.6	279.8	51.2	33.8	9.2	55.7	9.4	780
Romania	31.9	22.6	117.7	385.8	171.0	44.2	9.3	53.7	..	930
GDR (1969)	15.8	11.9	220.8	396.4	98.2 [a]	40.3 [b]	8.8	57.4	..	1427
USSR (1971-2)	..	..	129.6	404.0	..	..	..	..	..	837
France	19.5	13.1	207.3	370.7	63.2	66.2	7.5	89.0	27.1	1100
United Kingdom	8.3	4.3	226.4	580.6	130.5	30.2	9.8	48.5	14.9	1130

Source: *Breviar de statistică sanitară, 1971*, Bucharest, 1972, pp. 291, 296-7, except for USSR from Tables 2.6 and 2.7 and for GDR from Tables 5.3 and 5.4 (which are both on different revisions of ICD)

[a] 480-486 and 490-493 in Table 5.3
[b] 531-533, 540-553, 560, 571 and 580-584 in Table 5.3

1.5 Indicators of civilian health care facilities in Comecon states in 1974

	Per 10,000 population			Thousands			
	Hospital beds	Physicians [a]	Dentists [a]	Pharmacies	Pharmacists	Sanatoria beds	Rest-home beds
USSR	116	31.5	4.0	24.9 [b]	57.8	490	336
Bulgaria	84	25.1	4.1 [c]	1.0	2.9	12.5	78.1
Czechoslovakia	79	26.4	4.2	1.3	5.9	66.3	12.8
GDR	109	22.7	4.5 [c]	1.4	3.0	23.7	102
Hungary	79	24.5	2.9	1.4	4.0	2.4	78.7
Poland	75	21.5	6.1	3.6	14.4	33.2	495
Romania	89	15.8	0.3 [c]	1.8	5.6	38.1	95.6

Source: Comecon Secretariat, *Statistical Yearbook, 1975*, pp. 443-40; for *per capita* ratios in text, population from pp. 11-12

a Including stomatologists
b Of which over 3,000 in hospitals (1970 data from *Bol'shaya sovetskaya entsiklopediya*, 3rd edn, Vol. 2, Moscow, 1970, p. 138
c Stomatologists only

1.6 Estimated sources of finance of legally-sanctioned expenditure on health care in Comecon states

Millions of national currencies and percentages

	Social and private consumption				From production costs of socialist enterprises	1970 population (millions)
	Govern-ment	Social insurance	Direct (personal)	Total		
	(1)	(2)	(3)	(4)	(5)	(6)
USSR: 1968	8089	580	386	9055	1433	242.76
Per cent	89	7	4	100	16	
Bulgaria:						
1960	124.4	0.3	5.8	130.5	. .	8.49
Per cent	95	—	4	100	. .	
1973	385.9	0.6	16.0	402.5	. .	
Per cent	96	—	4	100	. .	
Czechoslovakia:						
1958	5460	432 [a]	588	6480	125	14.33
Per cent	84	7 [a]	9	100	2	
1973	15402	5125	1427	21954	. .	
Per cent	70	23	7	100	. .	
GDR: 1968	3175	3109	230	6514	. .	17.06
Per cent	49	48	3	100	. .	
Hungary:						
1968	6469	6238	801	13508	. .	10.34
Per cent	48	46	6	100	. .	
Poland:						
1965	18009	3631	5641	27281	229	32.53
Per cent	66	13	21	100	1	
1973	42919	8062	10013	60994	716	
Per cent	70	13	16	100	1	
Romania:						
1968	5965	56	1378	7399	120	20.25
Per cent	81	1	18	100	2	
East Europe (excluding USSR):						
Per cent [b]	69	20	11	100	. .	103.00

Source: Tables 2.20, 3.10, 4.14, 5.9 and 5.10, 6.15, 7.21 and 8.15, except the 1958 entry for Czechoslovakia, which is from B. Abel-Smith, *Paying for Health Services*, WHO, Geneva, 1963, pp. 58, 75

a Medical care only; not comparable with 1973
b Weighted by population in col. (6)

NOTE: Expenditure on spas is included; direct (personal) expenditure on health care products includes non-prescription items. Social insurance outlays are for health care alone (i.e. including sickness benefit, resorts, etc.). Although some components from tables in other chapters are rounded estimates, they have not been further rounded in this table, which is nevertheless a collection of estimates.

1.7 Capital component of government health-service outlay in Comecon states

		Percentages			
USSR	4 (1960)	5 (1970)	5 (1973)
Bulgaria	16 (1960)	19 (1970)	15 (1973)
Czechoslovakia	9 (1958)	11 (1968)	13 (1973)
GDR			5 (1973) [a]
Hungary		14 (1968)	
Poland	10 (1960)	8 (1967)	6 (1971)
Romania		7 (1968)	

Source: Tables 2.24, 3.10, 4.14, 6.15, 7.16 and 8.15, except for Czechoslovakia 1958, Abel-Smith, op. cit., pp. 71, 75

a   Investment outlays on social and cultural purposes (excluding on research and development and on housing) (1,720 million M), when aggregate government outlay for these purposes was 35,932 million M (*Statistical Yearbook, 1974*, pp. 45, 311)

NOTE: Expenditure on spas is included.

1.8 Health expenditure as percentage of net material product and gross
national product in Comecon states

			Thousand million currency units			Percentages	
			Health (1)	NMP (2)	GNP (3)	NMP (4)	GNP (5)
USSR	(roubles)	1968	9.06	253.8	324.3	3.6	2.8
		1970		289.9	376.6		
		1973		337.2	..		
Bulgaria	(leva)	1968		8.56	..		
		1970		10.07	14.50		
		1973	0.403	12.15	16.84	3.3	2.4
Czechoslovakia		1968		275.2	309.3		
	(koruny)	1970		312.3	377.6		
		1973	22.0	364.5	430.7	6.0	5.1
GDR	(marks)	1968	6.51	98.1	113.5	6.6	5.7
		1970		108.7	133.8		
		1973		126.7	155.3		
Hungary	(forints)	1968	13.5	245.0	277.5	5.5	4.9
		1970		277.3	332.9		
		1973		360.3	433.2		
Poland	(zloty)	1968		691.1	783.4		
		1970		749.2	906.2		
		1973	61.0	1064.8	1265.4	5.7	4.8
Romania	(lei)	1968	7.40	200.0	266.2	3.7	2.8
		1970		230.2	328.7		
		1973		323.4	454.1		

Source: Col. (1) is col. (4) of Table 1.6 to three significant figures. Col. (2) is
from national *Statistical Yearbooks* except for Bulgaria (direct communication) and Romania (from I. Spigler, *ACES Bulletin*, Vol. XIV (1972), No. 2,
p. 26); the GRD value is at 1967 prices, but these do not appear to have
changed significantly between 1967 and 1973. Col. (3) is from, or derived
from, official estimates by the national statistical offices, for the USSR that
by F. W. Dresch *et al.* for SRI, cited in US Congress Joint Economic Committee, *Soviet Economic Prospects for the Seventies*, Washington, D.C., p.
124, and for Bulgaria, GDR and Romania from T. Alton *et al.*, in US Congress Joint Economic Committee, *Reorientation and Commercial Relations of
the Economies of Eastern Europe*, Washington, D.C., 1974, pp. 302-3 which
also provided the indexes for 1968-70 in current US dollars

1.9 Approximate estimates of pharmaceutical consumption *per capita* (prescribed or bought over the counter) in Comecon states in 1968

	At retail prices in national currencies	Exchange rate to:			At world prices	At retail prices	
		US dollar		transfer-able rouble	in US dollars	in transferable roubles	
	(1)	(2)	(3)	(4)	(5)	(6)	(7)
GDR	62.70	4.00	4.39	5.50	15.70	14.30	11.40
USSR	3.80	0.52	0.61	1.20	7.30	6.20	3.20
Hungary	340.00	47.20	23.69	40.00	7.20	14.30	8.50
Poland	399.00	64.00	23.65	40.00	6.20	16.90	10.00
Czechoslovakia	108.00	25.00	12.76	18.00	4.30	8.50	6.00
Romania	106.00	25.20	16.24	17.50	4.20	6.50	6.10
Bulgaria	2.62 [a]	0.97	1.49	1.50	2.70	1.80	1.70

Source: Col. (1) is domestic sales as shown in Chapters 2-8 divided by mid-1968 populations. Col. (2) is 'pharmaceutical' exchange rates calculated by national agencies for Poland and Romania or, for other countries, dividend of col. (1) by col. (5). Col. (3) is implicit conversion rates for GNP to dollars in Alton, in *Reorientation and Commercial Relations of the Economies of Eastern Europe*, Washington, D.C., 1974, pp. 302-3 and for the USSR by Dresch *et al.* for SRI in *Soviet Economic Prospects for the Seventies*, Washington, D.C., p. 124 (both US Congress Joint Economic Committee). Col. (4) is rates to the transferable rouble (the unit of account of the International Bank for Economic Cooperation, Moscow) agreed by the Standing Commission (of Comecon) on Currency and Financial Questions, 18 October 1973, cited by H. Matejka, *Annals of International Studies* (Geneva), Vol. 5, 1974, p. 176. Col. (5) is col. (4) of Table 1.10 divided by mid-1968 populations. Cols. (6) and (7) are dividends of col. (1) by cols. (3) and (4) respectively. Cols. (5) to (7) are rounded to one place after the decimal point

a   4.35 leva in 1974

NOTE: Population estimates used (million) GDR 17.08, USSR 238.3, Hungary 10.26, Poland 32.31, Czechoslovakia 14.36, Romania 19.72 and Bulgaria 8.37 (total 340.4)

1.10 Production of pharmaceuticals in Comecon states in 1968

Millions of US dollars at world prices

	Production (1)	less Exports (2)	plus Imports (3)	Consumption (4)
USSR	1596	29	173	1740
GDR	293	51	26	268
Poland	238	56	20	202
Hungary	174	122	22	74
Czechoslovakia	74	17	5	62
Romania	73	9	7	71 [a]
Bulgaria	43	33	13	23
Total	2491	317	266	2440 [b]

Source: Author's estimates based on national statistics

a The comparable cover and valuation for Table 1.9 is US $82.7 million
b US $7.20 *per capita*

2 THE USSR

I. Legislation and policy

A century ago Tolstoy, in *Anna Karenina*, had Levin reluctantly oppose, as many landlords did, the attempts of the then new local authorities to furnish rudimentary social services: 'for the three thousand square miles of our district, what with the deep slush when the snow starts melting, our snow storms, and the pressure of work at busy seasons, I don't see how it is possible to provide a public medical service.' In the nineteen-fifties, Tendryakov wrote his short story *Potholes* around the fruitless attempts to get an injured man with internal haemorrhage from his village to the local hospital, thirty kilometres distant: 'We couldn't get the lorry through in the daytime, so we'll never manage it at night.' 'We couldn't do it on a horse either. He'd be so shaken up that he'd probably die on the way.' True to its foundation under 'the dictatorship of the proletariat', the Soviet government for half a century looked more to the factory than to the farm. Not until the enactment by the Supreme Soviet on 19 December 1969 of 'Principles of Legislation on Health Care' was the system put on an unequivocally national basis. Article 4 then declared that 'citizens of the USSR are supplied with free professional medical care, available to all; such medical care is furnished by the state agencies for health protection'.[1]

The last decade has brought the villager close to equality with the townsman, after a discrimination which began with industrialization and farm-collectivization in the First Five-Year Plan (1928-32). Peasants are finding their incomes are now close to those of wage-earners (88 per cent of average earnings in 1973), can migrate freely within the USSR and have access to social services which — practical delays apart — are on a par with those in urban areas. As recently as 1960 the mean income of a collective farmer was only 63 per cent of the worker's wage; between 1932 and 1975 he had no right to settle outside his home farm, and it was not until 1966 that full secondary education was made compulsory in rural areas.

In differentiating the provision of both health and education, the Soviet government from the nineteen-thirties to the nineteen-sixties can in some respects be interpreted as selectively continuing Tsarist policies. Peter the Great envisaged that those taught in his new schools would 'go forth into the church or the civil services, be prepared to wage war or to practise engineering or medicine'.[2] A strict economic rationale made for the attachment of clinics to the state-sponsored factories which his Westernizing policies created. As early as 1717, a 'cottage hospital' (a nearly literal translation of *izba dlya skorbyash-chikh*) was attached to the Izhorsk factory, while the hospitals of the Ekaterinburg factory (1728) and in the Minusinsk region (1730) were contemporary with the first large military hospitals, the Army Hospital in Moscow (1706) and the Naval Hospital in St Petersburg (1715). Later in that century both state and private factories set up their own hospitals, and in Kolyvana (Siberia) a training establishment was started to staff them. Although there had been a few small civilian hospitals before Peter (two in Moscow in the seventeenth century), health care provision began in Russia from a factory-based service.

For the century after Catherine's accession, Russian industry languished, and, with it, incentive to train or care for its workers. More specifically, whereas in Peter's day ascription to factory work was restricted to Crown serfs in state enterprises, the subsequent and extensive manning of private plants by gentry-owned serfs, patently diminished concern for labour.[3] Speransky's 'Rules for Enlightenment' (1803) in educational reform had their parallel in M. Ya. Mudrov's reorganization of clinical teaching after 1809 in Moscow University, and in his tenets that the physician's prime concern was the patient rather than the disease and prevention rather than cure. The crushing of the Decembrists in 1825 was a new setback for such social progress as was emerging, crystallized in the quip of Tsar Nicholas I 'that the police were to educate the public and the schools to discipline them'. His Minister of Education frankly avowed that 'to teach the whole nation to read and write would do more harm than good'.[4]

Serf emancipation (1861) was a new turning-point, and a precondition for industrial development based on free and mobile manpower. The fiscal, legal and educational reforms of 1864 were matched by a law of 1866 which required factory owners to provide hospitals with a capacity of one bed for every 100 workers employed; despite much evasion, in particular by small factories, the tradition of medical service through the place of work was re-established. Concurrently, nevertheless, general access services began to be developed under the local *zemstva* (from 1864); permeated by sentiments of democracy and populism in general, and of social medicine (notably under the leadership of the Pirogov Society) in particular, social need was first introduced among the determinants of health provision. Religious and other charitable foundations had never assumed the services for the sick which they had in Western Europe, and municipal services were confined to Moscow and St Petersburg.

Private demand was quantitatively trivial because in a two-class society of gentry and serf it was generated only by the few with the capacity to pay. The nineteenth-century *Notes of a Physician* observed 'Medicine is a science dealing with the treatment only of the rich and

free. In relation to everyone else, it is merely a theoretical science dealing with how they would be cured if they were rich and free.'[5] The
burdens laid upon the emancipated peasantry — they paid redemption
dues between 1862 and 1905 to compensate landlords for loss of
labour and land — precluded a free-for-service basis with regard to some
four out of five of the Tsar's subjects. The 'investment demand' for
health care continued and was strengthened after the 1905 Revolution
by the preponderance of employers on the board of control of the
compulsory industrial sickness insurance scheme of 1912 (*zakon o
bolnichnykh kassakh*), an industrial injuries compensation law having
earlier been promulgated (1903). The novelty of the last half-century of
Tsarism was provision against social need.

One constituent is evident in the title of the journal *Arkhiv sudebnoi
meditsiny i obshchestvennoi gigeny* (founded 1865), linking 'forensic
medicine' with 'social hygiene'. The prevalence of crime was part of
'the lack of moral development of the common people, the diffusion of
syphilis, drunkenness, etc.'.[6] Law and order would be protected by
more schooling and better health. The second trend was that fostered
by the Pirogov Society, the Society of Russian Physicians (founded
1885) and promoting the concept of preventive medicine not only of
N. I. Pirogov himself (a surgeon, 1810-81) but of S. P. Botkin (1832-
89), a clinician who pressed for centralized anti-epidemic services, and
of G. A. Zakharyn (1829-97), whose 'dispensary method' (surveillance
with medical-record linkage) became a keystone of the Soviet system.
Priority for prophylaxis, another tenet of the Soviet health service,
goes back to Mudrov, who observed 'It is easier to prevent an illness
than to cure it, and I hold that this is the physician's paramount duty.'[7]

The Provisional Government which followed the February Revolution of 1917 embraced the 'industrial principle': its decree of July 1917
on social insurance extended the coverage of the 1912 law and put the
provision of medical care as a charge on enterprises (a 2 per cent levy
on payrolls), excluding those with special schemes (notably the civil
service and railwaymen) and the vast majority of the population, the
peasant and the farm worker. The Soviet government, in power after
the October Revolution, applied insurance to all who worked under
contract (thus bringing in the professions, but still leaving out the peasantry) and required that beneficiaries receive all types of prescribed
treatment and medicine free of charge. It re-enacted the provision of
the 1866 law that every factory should endow its sickness-insurance
fund with one hospital bed for each 100 workers, and added (in the
decree of 27 November 1917) one maternity bed for every 200 female
staff.[8]

The Second Programme of the Party (1919) enshrined three principles for the health service 'generally-accessible, free and qualified

treatment and medication'. Entitlement to free medicine other than that provided in hospitals was withdrawn in 1935 and the Third Party Programme (1961) spoke of its reinstatement by 1980. The target has been dropped for the time being, but by 1975 70 per cent of prescriptions were without payment by patients, being either issued in hospitals and the like or for specified diseases for which free prescription is authorized. The requirement of general accessibility was implemented by lifting the formal insurance qualification in 1936, but it took 50 years for the health service to be as readily accessible to the rural as to the urban worker. Membership of a trade-union social insurance scheme until 1935 gave to the insured and his family free general and specialist treatment, including oculist and dentist, free hospital care, and free medication and prostheses.[9] In 1929/30, the cost to the Social Insurance Fund for medical care to insured persons was approximately equal (334 million roubles) to that of sickness benefit paid out (358 million roubles), and together were near the government's outlays on health services (888 million roubles).[10] With the creation of a unified Commissariat of Health in 1936, which took over these medical provisions, social insurance benefits were restricted to dietetic, convalescent and recuperative treatment and social-security payments (sickness, maternity, retirement, widows and orphans).

The administration of Soviet medical care has from its very inception been affected by the currents of political pressure and change. The earliest months, until the nationalization of industry in July 1918 which ushered in 'War Communism', were of fragmentation. Medical-sanitary departments were attached to each relevant People's Commissariat with a unifying focus on worker self-management. The All-Russian Federation of Medical Workers (Medsantrud) was partly a Bolshevik front against the Pirogov Society (transformed into the All-Russian Union of Professional Physicians), but partly a vehicle for the autonomous operation of health services. When, after conflict between the 'medical-sanitary departments' (coordinated by a Council of Medical Collegia) and the 'Pirogovists', the threat from the right was liquidated in 1918, the syndicalists, like their powerful counterpart, the railwaymen's trade union committee (Vikzhel), presented an opposing force from the left. The same observation might be made of Medsantrud as Carr's *History of Soviet Russia* makes of Vikzhel: 'It recognized no political authority and no interest other than the professional interest of the railwaymen . . . it demonstrated beyond possibility of contradiction the need for new forms of control, more rigid, and more centralized.'[11] Each syndicalist group was soon neutralized, and centralization came at about the same time in 1918. A significant dispersal of services was tolerated in the health departments (*zdravotdely*) of other Commissariats, notably in that of Rail Transport (which to this day runs its own health care system), but a People's Commissariat of Health of the Russian Republic (RSFSR) was established in July 1918, the world's first such ministry. The Ministry of Health in the United Kingdom was set up in the following year, and can claim to be the first to cover an entire nation: as other Soviet republics were created — beginning with the Ukrainian in March 1919 — they were endowed with their own health commissariats and no all-Union Commissariat of Health was created until the Constitution of 1936.

The smaller, 'closed-access' health services run by commissariats for their own staffs built up somewhat better provision than was generally available, particularly because the RSFSR Commissar of Health, N. A. Semashko, required priority to be given to measures against the epidemics which inevitably accompanied hostilities. Lenin's often-quoted remark of the time was put as a battle strategy: 'Either lice will defeat socialism or socialism will defeat lice' (1919), but prophylaxis soon re-emerged as a key concern (1924). On the unification of preventive with curative services in 1925, a start was made on health care for rural areas, and the fundamental unit of the Soviet system, the 'block' or micro-district (*uchastok*), was established within the lowest administrative level. In the urban areas the date was significant for introduction of the dispensary method; the rural system continued that of the *zemstva*, viz. a general practitioner (or medical assistant) cared for patients locally (facilities with 2 to 10 beds were common) and only in very serious cases referred them to district or regional hospitals. Resources were then too few adequately to implement the programme, but it began an open-access service parallel with those under the several production authorities (with some special attention to miners under a scheme of 1921) or through local 'commissions for labour health and for living conditions' (*kotiby*), which supplied a 'medico-industrial' service.

The appointment of a new Commissar for Health, M. F. Vladimirsky, in early 1930 took place as Stalin consolidated his autocracy after the 'Year of the Great Change'; the second Soviet revolution was beginning with the Five-Year Plan. Vladimirsky's slogan 'Face to Production' crystallized the new determination to industrialize the country at any cost and to make health 'a battle task of the working class and Party'.[12] His policy, laid down by a Party Central Committee resolution of 18 December 1929, marked a clear priority for the industrial health service. A history of the role of the Party in the health system rightly terms that resolution 'an extremely important Party document', the essence of which was 'to improve medical services for workers in industrial centres and with first preference for such branches of industry as mining and metallurgy'.[13] The factory 'health post' became the principal channel of care, the number rising from one to four thousand in the first six months of 1932 alone, linked to a much denser hospital service, over 2,000 new hospitals being opened over 1928-32. In a radical reorganization of training, pursuant to a decree of June 1930, medical schools were separated from universities and 24 new schools were created (1929-35), studies were reduced to four years, and graduates were required to serve a probationary year (under qualified guidance) in a health care institution; medical schools were transferred from the Commissariat of Education to that of Health. In October 1932 a further decree required the institution of a State Institute of Experimental Medicine, which was forthwith set up by 'shock-work construction'.[14] So rapid was the development of the infrastructure of medical research that 223 research institutes were in being when the USSR was invaded by Germany in 1941.

The campaign to convert peasants into collective farmers in the period of the First Five-Year Plan set the villager behind the townsman in civil rights, since, as earlier noted, a collective farmer had no internal passport and hence could choose neither residence nor occupation. By a decree of January 1930 he became entitled to certain treatments in urban hospitals, but by the same decree each farm was made largely responsible for its own health care. Agrarian overpopulation was tapped for the industrial expansion, mainly through a recruitment agency for collective farms, and massive migration and urban overcrowding rendered essential more intensive public health measures. Although a start had been made by a decree of February 1927, 'On the Sanitary Organization of the Republic', a comprehensive network of sanitary-epidemological stations was begun in 1932.[15] A unified State Sanitary Inspectorate was created in 1933. A distinctive service of this period were medical 'flying squads', deployed against epidemics, to undertake investigative and treatment campaigns in ill-supplied areas or to furnish on-the-spot care in rural districts at harvest time.[16]

Some of those flying squads were more to service the 'collectivizers' than the 'collectivized', but there was a doubling of rural hospital beds in the period of the First Five-Year Plan,[17] the costs being borne by the state or collective farm concerned. With recovery from the havoc wrought by collectivization, the 'Three Good Years' of 1934-6[18] saw increased priority for health care and a reorganisation which commuted (as already indicated) workers' insurance into a budget-financed service. G. N. Kaminsky took office as RSFSR Commissar of Health in 1934 and became the first All-Union Commissar in 1936. The Commissariat of the Russian Federation had exercised a certain tutelage over the Commissariats in the six other republics (which in turn had health commissariats in their eighteen constituent republics): Semashko, writing after his retirement as Commissar, spoke explicitly of them as 'subordinate authorities'.[19] Centralization not only had its own economies,

but made for somewhat stronger competitiveness with other departments for projects in the Plan and for supporting finance.

The Second World War brought further centralization. All civilian
health services were put under the Commissar of Health (G. A.
Miterev), including those for evacuation (under a Chief Administration
for Evacuated Hospitals, run on military lines), for civil defence and in
territory regained after enemy occupation. Research coordination was
enhanced by the setting up in 1944 of the USSR Academy of Medical
Sciences.

This unification ceased at the end of the War — a separate administration was set up for war invalids' hospitals and the other services
returned to their former subordination — but the first postwar Minister,
E. I. Smirnov, launched an attack on the 'industrial principle'. In 1947
hospitals were combined with municipal-service polyclinics (though
from 1949 each had its own budget), and many factory 'health posts'
were shut down, as well as other small institutions under independent
control. Health care services were put on open-access on a local basis
(the 'uchastkovoi principle'), extending the dispensary method to
general physician-prophylactic institutions; nomenclature was standardized within the health services and the sanitary and anti-epidemic services were brought together.

Stalin's death in 1953 came only just in time to lift the threat over
some members of the medical profession on the basis of an alleged
'Doctors' Plot', according to which eight (Jewish) physicians were
accused of murdering eminent patients. The Party Politburo's call to
the populace, in its announcement of his death, was followed by an
economic policy directed rather more towards the consumer, including
substantial reductions of retail prices. The non-hospitalized patient
benefited modestly from the latter in cuts of some pharmaceutical
prices and particularly by the abolition of the dispensing charge (which
reduced the over-the-counter cost by 15 per cent).[20]

After a brief tenure of the health portfolio by A. F. Tretyakov,
1953-4, M. D. Kovrigina, the first woman to occupy the post, restored
the industrial orientation. Priority access of industrial workers to
hospitals and the reopening of factory 'health posts' made the worker
the focal recipient of care, but for the first time since collectivization
the farmer benefited from occupational priority. From 1953 all rural
services were grouped under the authority of the Chief Physician of the
district; hospital and resources were increased for both these hospitals
and the medical-assistant service in villages. The provision of buildings,
including accommodation for medical personnel, remained at the
charge of the collective farm.

Khrushchev's liquidation of the Industrial Ministries in May 1957
tilted the balance against the 'industrial principle': factories and

construction enterprises were handed over to regional economic agencies, the boundaries of which coincided with the provincial authority for the health service. Greater planning authority was given to Union-republican authorities, of which a Ministry of Health was one. The reorganization involved the transfer of sanatoria from industrial ownership to that of the trade unions (1959). When S. V. Kurashov became Minister in January 1959 he soon promoted a decree (January 1960) allocating more funds for new municipal hospitals, for reconstruction of existing facilities and for opening new pharmacies especially in rural areas. Whereas in 1959 there were 14,500 inhabitants for each urban pharmacy and 15,500 for each rural, by 1968 there were respectively 13,000 and 9,800. Many polyclinics were separated from hospitals in 1960 when a network of specialized polyclinics was also authorized, but re-unions were effected in 1967 under a new Minister. Because the focus moved towards the territorial health service (and partly because, as in the contemporary NHS in the United Kingdom, economies of scale were expected), big district hospitals of 600 beds began to be built. The Minister died in August 1965, leaving to his successor, B. V. Petrovsky, a first draft for the codification and universalization of 1969. They were outlined in the Minister's report to the Supreme Soviet of June 1968, which was forthwith implemented in a decision of the Party Central Committee and Council of Ministers of 5 July 1968 'On Measures for the Further Improvement of the Health Service and for the Development of National Medical Research'. The formal Law of 1969 completed the legislation.

Although the universalization of the service is properly to be regarded as a measure improving social welfare – and with it went increased allocations of funds and a 20 per cent rise in pay for medical personnel (1972) – the supply side of provision was also undergoing change. There had been in 1965 major reforms in economic management, sponsored by Kosygin in industry and Brezhnev in agriculture. The first gave profit a higher place in the objectives of enterprises, making it more rational for them to concentrate on productive activity and to shift the cost of fringe benefits to other budgets. The second assured agriculture equality with industry in governmental esteem, although it was Khrushchev in his last three months of power who put through a law bringing collective farmers into a state-supported social insurance scheme. Assurance of equal treatment in the health service was part of Brezhnev's policy towards agriculture and the comprehensive legislation of 1969 may be seen in conjunction with a decree of 1968 fixing priority on the very large hospital in the 1,000-bed range. Some of 1,500 beds and one of 3,000 were put up and the small dispersed services in factories and farms alike came further under critical review.

The Law of 1969 did not eliminate the departmental structure of the Soviet health service, but, under Article 9, other ministries and corresponding organizations can run their health services only with permission from the USSR Council of Ministers. Substantial services were, and continue to be, provided by the Ministries of Transport, Civil Aviation, Defence and Internal Affairs, but the USSR Ministry of Health is given the function of coordinating their services. Such departmental services can be traced back also to the Tsarist period, for health care was provided by all the predecessors of these ministries (Transport, War and Internal Affairs) as well as by Education, Agriculture and Crown Domains.[21] A textbook of 1969 claimed that 'all medical-sanitary establishments in the country operate on a common plan and common methodology, are interlinked and serve common aims'.[22] The law also introduced some 'patient participation' by embodying (according to the Chairman of the health committee of the Soviet of the Union, when introducing the legislation) 'greater participation of social organizations, including trade unions, in the improvement of the health services'.[23] Finally it introduced two legislative innovations in medical ethics. It required thenceforward a professional oath from medical students on graduation, which the Minister, Petrovsky, commended as 'raising still higher the prestige of this noblest of professions'. It also laid down that persons who are without special training could not practice medicine or engage in pharmacy. The prevalence in the European regions of folk and gypsy medicine and of shamanistic or lamaistic practice in the Asian parts has much diminished and may primarily have been in the legislators' mind, but homoeopathy is quite extensive and fears were expressed at the time that its continuance was endangered. There are seven homoeopathic pharmacies in Moscow alone.

II. Demographic pattern

The official estimate of the Soviet population on 1 January 1975 was 253.3 million; only two censuses have been conducted since the Second World War, that of 15 January 1959 showing 208.8 million, and that of the corresponding date in 1970 241.7 million. The rate of increase, as Table 2.1 shows, has been declining: over the two decades 1950 to 1970 the average natural increment was 1.5 per cent, but that comprised a peak quinquennial rise of 1.8 per cent in 1955-60 and a low of 1.0 per cent in 1965-70.

Demographic experience has, however, widely varied within the country. For the twenty years to 1970 mean rates in Central Asia and Kazakhstan, Islamic in culture and still predominantly rural, were 3.1 and 3.5 per cent respectively, whereas in the Baltic republics, incorporated into the USSR only during the Second World War and with a history and religious composition like that of Western Europe, the rate was as low as 1.0 per cent. The republics of the Slavic majority, of Russian Orthodox tradition, have experienced low and declining rates of population growth. Byelorussia, wholly occupied during the Second World War and demographically devastated, showed a mere 0.8 per cent annual increase over 1950-70, while the Ukraine, which also had hostilities over its entire territory, showed 1.3 per cent. The Russian Federation also exhibited less than the Soviet average and, at 1.2 per cent annually over 1950-70, its share of the Soviet population dropped from 56.8 to 53.8 per cent. Russians, whether dwelling within the Russian Federation or in other Union Republics, were down to a bare majority of the Soviet population at the 1970 Census, as Table 2.2 shows.

The long-standing and universal availability of health services throughout the USSR has brought uniformity into death rates, and the variation by region or nationality is chiefly due to the wide gamut of birth rates. For the country as a whole and for most, though not all, regions lower growth rates have been the consequence of a significant decline in fertility, as Table 2.1 shows. In the longer run the country's crude birth rate in 1960 was 35 per cent below 1950 and fell by a further 30 per cent in the next ten years. The birth rate in the Russian Federation was as low as 14.6 per 1,000 in 1970 but was 23.4 per 1,000 in Kazakhstan and 33.4 per cent in the four Central Asian republics. The death rate was much more stable over time and less dispersed by region. From 9.7 per 1,000 in 1950 it reached a nadir a decade later; its subsequent rise, as Table 2.1 indicates, to 8.7 per 1,000 in 1973, is due to the ageing of the population, not to any overall regression in mortality experience. The range in crude mortality rates in 1970 was from 6.0 per 1,000 in Kazakhstan and Central Asia, through 8.7 in the Russian Federation, to 10.1 in the Baltic Republics.

The continuing urbanization of the USSR was demonstrated by an intercensal rise (1959-70) of the population living in towns from 100 million (48 per cent) to 136 million (56 per cent) in 1970 and to 151 million (60 per cent) on 1 January 1975 (official estimates). The tendency for these to live in large conurbations (where health conditions and hazards approximate those in similar aggregates in the West) is sharply demonstrated by the rise in the population registered at the census in cities (from 83.0 million in 1959 to 116.3 million in 1970) rather than in areas defined only as urban districts (from 17.0 million to 19.7 million); the former was a 40 per cent intercensal increment, whereas the latter, at 16 per cent, coincided with the mean increment of the total Soviet population.

The Government's demographic policy has gone through three phases, which may be dated by legislation on abortion. It was allowed gratis from 1920 to 1936, the preamble initially conceding it 'to moral survivals of the past and the difficult economic conditions of the present'.[24] It went hand-in-hand with the 'glass of water' concept of sexual intercourse and the ease of marriage and divorce. Intense urban overcrowding, which resulted as the first two Five-Year Plans created jobs and attracted workers to towns without providing anything like sufficient new house construction, was a major factor in increasing abortions in the early thirties, when, in the larger cities at least, the abortion rate exceeded that of births. Abortion was prohibited in 1936, the woman as well as the practitioner becoming liable to criminal prosecution; family allowances (though starting with the third child) and other pro-natalist measures (notably the 1944 *ukaz* instituting the Orders 'Heroine-Mother' and 'Glory to Motherhood' and the 'Maternity Medal') also characterized the ensuing two decades. By 1954 non-hospitalized, principally illegal abortions had reached 80 per cent of the known number of abortions. The review of all policies after the death of Stalin (1953) included a revision of that on abortion. The woman's legal responsibility was repealed and after 1955 abortion was permitted on her request if the operation were carried out by a physician: by 1966 only 16 per cent of abortions were effected outside a hospital.[25]

The legalization of abortion was part of an attenuation of the pro-natalist policy (and included such *minutiae* as withdrawal of the free bus and tram travel to which the holders of the 1944 orders of motherhood had been entitled). It was, however, inspired more by greater explicit concern for the social problems of unwanted pregnancies. An enquiry published in 1968 found that the reasons given for abortion by married women with children were (with percentage of respondents in parentheses) the cost of a further child (37.8), the obstacle it represented to improving the family standard of living (36.2), poor living conditions (28.7), unwillingness to make 'the personal sacrifice' (27.3), the fact that the wife as well as the husband was at work (21.1), that no pre-school facilities were locally available (18.5), the difficulties of raising children (11.8), the fear of another confinement (5.9); other factors were only 2.6 per cent of those questioned.[26] A survey of 1971 (4,000 questionnaires) in a largish city (Kalinin), two smaller towns (Kimry and Torzhok) and in villages showed that most abortions were occurring in the 20-34 age group, and somewhat more frequently in towns than in the country. Only about 50 per cent of women who considered pregnancy undesirable were using contraceptives. 47.3 per cent of women questioned in rural areas and 33.4 per cent of those in Kalinin underwent abortions because they wanted no more children at all. Compared with 1959, inadequate housing and pre-school facilities were less frequently cited as reasons, but 6.5-6.8 per cent of answers mentioned the husband's alcoholism, which had not figured significantly in the earlier sample.[27]

Statistics relating to the health services and conditions of cities exceeding 1 million inhabitants are put together in Table 2.3. Such cities are much better endowed with hospital beds than is shown on average for the USSR (with the exception of Novosibirsk, the new industrial and academic centre of Eastern Siberia) and tend to show more favourable rates of infantile mortality (with two exceptions in non-Russian republics, Tashkent and Baku, and one mixed but predominantly Russian city, Kuibyshev). Since the census, two other cities have joined the 'million-plus' group and the number of Soviet citizens living in such conurbations has risen from 8.7 per cent to 10.0 per cent over 1970 to 1975 and to 9.1 per cent if the ten towns of 1970 are compared. The period saw, however, a new policy restricting industrial development in the largest towns, the reiteration of objectives formulated as early as the thirties (but respected more in the breach than in the observance), and promoting the development of small towns (over which an outcry emerged in the late sixties following revelations of the unemployment that existed because of inadequate job opportunities, mainly for women).

The ratio of females to males (high as a result of heavier male deaths during the Second World War) had by 1970 largely righted itself, as Table 2.4 shows, although a certain disparity persists in rural areas.

Virtually no problem of illiteracy now remains: at the 1959 census 98.1 per cent of urban women and 97.5 per cent of rural women were literate; at the 1970 census the respective figures were 99.8 and 99.4. Among men only 0.1 per cent illiteracy was found in towns in 1970 and 0.4 per cent in villages. The residual illiteracy in rural women was chiefly concentrated in areas of predominantly Moslem tradition, but the ethnic diversity of the USSR, exhibited in Table 2.2, no longer introduces differentiated problems into health care.

A factor more relevant to the long-run effects on the birth rate has been stated to be infertility consequential on abortion: one panel sample showed that between 12 and 16 per cent of women who underwent an abortion in the first year of marriage were thenafter infertile. The same enquiry showed that of 100 women in each cohort-year of marriage, 19.1 had an abortion in the honeymoon year (while 49.5 bore a child) and 28.1 in the second year of marriage (24.1 giving birth). At later cohort-years, abortions much outnumbered births: 28.1 (9.7) in the third year, 32.0 (9.4) in the fourth, 23.9 (5.7) in the fifth and 10.4 (4.6) in the sixth.[28] Until very recently no contraceptive pills were produced, officially because the Ministry of Health preferred to recommend intrauterine devices (of which a million were manufactured in 1968), in view of possible adverse side-effects.[29] The pill is, however, now becoming available and a member of a health study-tour to the Ukraine in 1974 was told (in the gynaecology clinic of Kharkov Polyclinic No. 20) that, though intrauterine and other mechanical devices were advised before the first abortion, contraceptive pills were available at a cost of 23 kopeks per month.[30] He was told that among the 25,000 girl students whom the polyclinic served there were about 900 pregnancies annually, of whom 600 deliver.

The gross reproduction rate is still high: 120 females would be born to 100 women during their productive life-spans if the 1972 set of birth rates by age of mother remained in effect. On the assumptions that it would continue to decline, though modestly, and that, because of the ageing of the population (to a more normal configuration after the 20 million premature deaths of the Second World War), the death rate would rise somewhat, the United States Bureau of the Census has computed the data in Table 2.5.

The median age would rise from 29.5 in 1970 to 34.0 in the year 2000, and the dependency ratio (the number of persons under 16 and over the nominal retirement age of 55 for women and 59 for men per 1,000 persons between those ages) would decline from 850 to 804. Because the effect of the Second World War, when very more men than women died, would have worked through by death of survivors, the number of males per 100 females would be more normal at 91.4 against the 1970 85.5. Even in the Ukraine, so severely hit by wartime deaths among its men that there were only 82.5 per 100 women in 1970, there would be, on the same demographic assumptions for the USSR as a whole, 89.2 in the year 2000. In health terms, the incidence of sex-specific diseases would have been normalized, although less obstetric and paediatric care would be required; the increase in the proportion of those beyond retirement age — from 15 to 20 per cent — would involve more geriatric and long-term care.

III.   Health conditions

Study of Soviet health conditions is rendered inordinately difficult by the inadequacy of published statistics. There are still no systematic comprehensive series on mortality or morbidity but scattered statistics which began to appear at the start of the seventies broke the almost total secrecy which had ruled for nearly forty years. Tables 2.6 and 2.7 relate to leading causes of death. Cardiovascular diseases accounted for 35.5 per cent of all male deaths in 1967 and 1968 (39.1 per cent on an age-standardized basis) and 53.6 per cent of all female deaths (50.9 per cent standardized), while deaths from malignant neoplasms accounted for 16.4 per cent of mortality in 1968.[31] The crude rates for mortality from cardiovascular diseases rose from 291 per 100,000 males and 385 per 100,000 females in 1967-8 to 345 and 454 respectively in 1971-2. The increase in cancer deaths can be seen from the following rates per 100,000 population.

1960	116	1965	124
1961	118	1966	124
1962	119	1968	127
1963	119	1971-2	130
1964	120		

Source: 1960-6: V. V. Golovteev, P. I. Kal'yu and I. V. Pustovoi, *Osnovy ekonomiki sovetskogo zdravookhraneniya*, Moscow, 1974, p. 51; 1968-72, *Vestnik statistiki*, No. 12, 1973, p. 83

Malignant neoplasms affecting the stomach, the leading cause in 1968, at 42 per 100,000 population, had declined to 40 in 1971-2, and those affecting the female sex organs from 16 to 12 per 100,000. On the other hand those affecting the larynx, bronchi and trachea — commonly spoken of as lung cancer — rose from 12 to 22.[32]

Soviet silence is particularly acute, when comparisons are in mind with Western European experience, on deaths due to accidents. Soviet newspapers report air and railway incidents only when foreigners are involved and only one recent statement has been found about road accidents: these in the Russian Federation in 1969 were 16,000 (with 66,000 injured) which at a population of 128.7 million implies a rate of 12.4 per 100,000 population. Overall mortality by age-group is shown in Tables 2.8 and 2.9, that for children being shown separately for comparison with data available for the sixties.

Morbidity statistics are equally exiguous and it was only in 1970 that the Soviet statistical yearbook (for 1969) included a table on the incidence of communicable diseases (Table 2.10).[33] All the diseases reported in the statistics exhibited a decline between 1960 and 1968, but hepatitis (which includes post-immunization and post-transfusion cases) has shown a slower decrease than the other major causes of illness. Malaria, with an incidence by now very low thanks to a major postwar DDT campaign, was still claiming around 300 new cases a year in 1968.

The absence of extensive morbidity series precludes judgement on the appropriateness of the Soviet medical service to meet the demands on it. Ryan echoes many commentators in remarking how 'the Soviet pattern of deployment of medical personnel differs markedly from that in the West and is undoubtedly wasteful by our standards' but adds that 'the current morbidity pattern in the USSR creates certain demands that, fortunately, have become comparatively insignificant in this country with its higher standards of nutrition and housing which reflect, in part, higher disposable income per person'.[34]

Of this morbidity pattern he singles out tuberculosis which is unlikely to reach the insignificance shown in the United Kingdom until 1985-90: new tuberculosis hospitals with 300-600 beds each are still being built, one authority considering it desirable for there to be two hospital beds and one sanatorium bed per 1,000 urban population.[35] These norms are much higher than those proposed by another authority at the same time: G. A. Popov, the Deputy Director of the Department of Planning and Finance of the USSR Ministry of Health, recommended 1.2 hospital beds and 0.2 sanatoria beds per 1,000 for tuberculosis, within a total provision of 13.2 hospital beds and 3.02 sanatoria beds.[36] Popov's own study for the World Health Organization tabulates morbidity registered on first consultations in the Kazakh city of Aktyubinsk in 1966-7, which, per 1,000, put communicable diseases at 123.8, parasitic diseases at 11.7, injuries at 59.5, poisoning at 2.2 and industrial and occupational diseases at 1.6. National data are available for the principal communicable diseases (Table 2.10), and the Aktyubinsk morbidity incidence of 5.6 per 1,000 first consultations for neoplasms and 43.7 for diseases of the circulatory organs may be compared with mortality data cited above and the following percentage distribution of admissions to urban hospitals.[37]

	1955	1965
Rheumatism (all types)	4.6	3.0
Cerebro-vascular lesions	11.7	6.5
Hypertension	4.3	4.1
Stomach and duodenal ulcers	1.3	0.9
Nephritis and nephrosis	7.8	6.2

The Aktyubinsk sample of causes for first physician contact included 7.7 for rheumatism, 14.6 for metabolic affections and allergies, 5.8 for mental disorders and 43.0 for diseases of the nervous system; diseases of the sexual organs were 47.3 for females and 2.5 for males, 33.9 for skin diseases and 68.2 for those of the digestive organs. Affections of the sensory organs constituted 25.7 for sight and 220.0 for the ear, nose and throat (ENT), of the respiratory organs 74.9, of the kidneys and urinary tract 11.9 and of the bone, muscles and joints 54.4. A sample of hospital admissions published in 1970 showed that for every 1,000 urban residents there were 18.0 admissions for respiratory complaints, 17.9 for those of the digestive organs, 9.9 were for infections and parasitic diseases, 8.1 concerned diseases of the nervous system and sensory organs and 7.9 were for those of the circulatory system. Another localized report of cases treated by the Kiev Emergency Medical Service Centre, reported by a visitor in 1974, stated that 78 per cent of calls were for unexpected illness (e.g. cardiac arrest), 'often caused by seasonal changes', 12 per cent were for road accidents and 10 per cent for other causes; 75 per cent of cases were fully treated on the spot, requiring no hospitalization, and only 3 per cent of cardiac cases died before reaching hospital. Case reports have formed the basis for estimating the rates of abortion at 12.1 per 1,000 population in 1955 and 33.7 in 1965 (against live births, as normally reported, at 25.7 and 18.4 per 1,000).[38]

Alcoholics form a risk group to which special services are provided. Since 1967 treatment for a diagnosed alcoholic is obligatory, although the patient may be required to pay. One report assigns up to one-quarter of the attendance at a psychoneurological dispensary as alcoholics, although drug-addiction (termed 'narcomania' in the USSR) is said not to be a cause of serious concern.[39] Similarly, although the first psychoneurological dispensary dates from 1925, as late as 1960 psychoneuroses were adjudged of 'low morbidity'.[40] Subsequently the gravity of psychiatric illness has come to be more fully appreciated and a 'norm' has recently been set at 25 beds per 10,000 population, against the 7 to 10 hitherto adopted.

On statistical reporting, it may be noted that with effect from 1 January 1970 the USSR Ministry of Health adopted the Eighth Revision of the International Classification of Diseases, Traumas and Causes of Death established by the WHO in 1965 (a 17-classification list). It had first embraced an international classification in 1965 (the Seventh Revision of the WHO Classification), earlier using a national grouping, the previous revision of which had been its fourth in 1952.

Much is written of Soviet studies of a 'health index', viz. the percentage of people who did not fall ill during the given year. A sample taken in certain Moscow factories in 1965-6 showed an index of 25 to 30 (defining 'illness' as a consultation at a health facility). An earlier enquiry in the same city in 1953 showed an index of 14 for infants in their first year of life, whereas one in Kaluga taken in 1964-6 showed the same age-group at 26.9. The latter was cited as illustrating the 'constantly rising' level of health, but precisely comparable data are not apparently published, as equally for the assertion that 'numerous statistical studies, including those conducted with due regard for the effects of living conditions (work, income, rest and recreation, etc.) reveal no great distinctions in the state of health of the different social groupings'.[41]

For epidemic diseases qualitative or impressionistic information is easier to come by than is quantitative. The experience of the severe epidemic of the El Tor cholera strain in the summer of 1970 is said to have 'demonstrated the broad potential of our system of health care and of sanitary-epidemological services'[42] but statistics for morbidity during the epidemic, which reached Soviet Central Asia in 1965 and the southern USSR in 1970, do not seem to have been published. It was sufficiently serious for the Kara-Kalpak and Khorezm regions in 1965 and the cities of Astrakhan, Volgograd, Ulyanovsk and Odessa in 1970 to have been isolated from all travelling and for tourists to be summarily sent homeward by the militia.[43] A public warning on the cholera danger was issued in April 1971 when the previous year's rapid spread was attributed to 'serious breaches of hygiene in the accommodation and living conditions of hundreds of thousands of citizens' in the southern districts. Officials attributed part of the trouble to the influx of tourists without permits (*putëvki*), the trade union or other authorizations for a stay in holiday rest-homes and sanatoria; many paying hotel rooms are reserved for foreigners and those not fortunate enough to obtain a permit take what is termed in the USSR a 'wild' holiday, camping or privately renting a sleeping place in what are already overcrowded resorts. One report in another (non-health) context, accusing the local population of profiteering, noted the use of large packing cases as sleeping units. Mortality from El Tor cholera has elsewhere been only of the order of 1 per cent of cases and the speed with which the Soviet health authorities reacted to the outbreak may well have resulted in a rather lower rate.

Mass immunization has all but eliminated poliomyelitis and diphtheria and greatly reduced the incidence of whooping-cough. Anti-measles vaccination was introduced in 1969 and was expected to be completed in three years. Smallpox (of which there was an outbreak in 1960, checked by the vaccination of 7 million people in 7 days) and plague have been eradicated, but the rates of acute intestinal disorders, measles, influenza and leptospirosis are still high. A survey by the Institute of Cardiology demonstrated that 4.5 to 5.5 per cent of the adult population was affected by arterial hypertension and that the incidence of ischaemic heart disease was serious.

There is still a significant problem of hospital infection, notably by staphylococci and by Gram-negative organisms; control is chiefly attempted through the use of small wards (4 beds is the standard), frequent disinfection and bacterial sampling and the ritual of gowning and masking (though physicians and nurses wear their own everyday clothes). In operating suites, dressings and instruments are autoclaved but in other parts of the hospital syringes etc. are sterilized in hot-air ovens, virtually no disposables being used throughout the country; reliance for disinfection is chiefly on phenolics for dirty situations and chlorine compounds for the clean. The severe restriction of patient visiting (normally one period a week) reduces transmission across the hospital boundary.

By contrast, food-carried diseases are comparatively well checked by intensive verification of food handlers, waterworks and pre-school staff, who undergo clinical and radiological examination on recruitment and then annually. In one reported survey an examination of 27,000 faeces from workers in these categories yielded only 18 isolations of shigella and salmonella (none being *s. typhi* or *s. paratyphi*).

IV. Health service administration

Under present arrangements there are five groups of health institution in the USSR. The first are general cure and prophylaxis hospitals (*bolnitsy*), in some cases united with polyclinics, panel surgeries (*ambulatorii*), polyclinics, dispensaries (*dispansery*), health posts (*zdravpunkty*), military hospitals (*gospitali*), sanatoria and pharmacies. The second are maternity homes, with ante- and post-natal clinics, children's hospitals, children's polyclinics, creches, children's convalescent homes (*doma rebënka*) and medical services to camps, schools and other educational establishments. Public health services constitute a third group, the sanitary-epidemiological (*sanepid*) stations and health education units. A fourth group comprises medical services for rural areas — *raion* hospitals and rural physician, feldsher and midwife 'blocks' (*uchastki*); while factory health services are the final classification, organized into 'workplace districts', each comprising between 1,500 and 2,000 industrial workers, the factory medical officer having charge also of any industrial hospital and sanatorium operated for those workers. Dispensaries (for follow-up treatment with record linkage, the active participation of the patient, and survey of the local social circumstances causing the condition) are notably for tuberculosis, venereal disease and alcoholism.

Fry's comparative study of the Soviet, United Kingdom and United States health services distinguished three 'discrete administrative levels' for care in the USSR — first-contact care, specialist care for the ambulatory, and hospital services — and sees the *uchastok* (which he translates as 'block territorial and neighbourhood area') as the unifying element and the polyclinic as the physical site providing the two first sets of services.[44]

Each of the fifteen Union-Republics has its own Ministry of Health, and each is divided into ordinary administrative areas of *oblast* and *raion*, within which the general medical service is subdivided into the block (*uchastok*). About one-fifth of all invalids receiving medical care are hospitalized (i.e. in the *statsionarny* as opposed to the *ambulatorno-poliklinichesky* service). General hospitals are usually of 200-250 beds, or of 400 to 600 and since 1949 their classification for plan norms has been by bed capacity. The average population coverage of each *uchastok* is as follows:

Urban:	one per 3000
Rural:	one feldsher-midwife post per 400-1000
	one physician block per 6000-15000 (depending on density of population)

Source: O. A. Aleksandrov and Yu. P. Lisitsyn, *Sovetskoe zdravookhranenie*, Moscow, 1972, pp. 61, 119

The peak visiting days at polyclinics are Sundays and public holidays, and many polyclinics have all specialists on duty on these days. Home visiting is the responsibility of the block physician (*uchastkovy vrach*) or nurse (*uchastkovaya sestra*). The 'general medicine' (*terapiya*) department of the district polyclinic includes the 'home doctor' (*domashny vrach*) who is the nearest equivalent of the general practitioner. The demand for home visits is compared to that at polyclinics in Table 2.11, the latter excluding paediatric polyclinics because the generalists (*terapevti*) do not treat child patients or maternity cases, for whom specialists must be called upon.[45] The head of an urban block (*uchastkovoi ordinator*) is responsible for prophylactic services and those first aid posts (*punkty neotlozhnoi pomoshchi*) which are part of polyclinics (providing both casualty reception and home visits outside clinic hours). In larger towns the emergency treatment station (*stantsiya skoroi meditsinskoi pomoschi*) is an independent unit.

Hospitals are also separate units, but staffing is frequently linked with the local polyclinic. A hospital physician sharing his time is either on the double-team system (*dvukhzven'evaya sistema*), spending 2.5-3.0 hours in bedside visits (having 12-15 beds in his charge) and the rest of his time in the polyclinic, or on the rotation system (*cheredovanie*), with 25 beds in his charge, alternating daily on in- and outpatients.

The 'medico-sanitary sections' in factories were rapidly developed from the beginning of the thirties and are responsible not only for general therapy of workers but also industrial accidents, labour safety and prophylaxis. Current standards provide for three categories of provision, viz. a medico-sanitary section in enterprises with more than 4,000 workers (2,000 in the coal, oil, oil-refining, ore-mining and chemical industries); a health post staffed by a physician in enterprises with more than 800 workers (500 in the above-mentioned industries and in non-ferrous metallurgy); and a post staffed by a medical assistant in enterprises with more than 300 workers. In the seventies still smaller enterprises began to be endowed with their own posts on a shared basis.

Ante-natal services start with visits by a medical auxiliary (*patrona-*

zhnaya sestra) to the expectant mother's domicile to check the physical and hygienic conditions of the dwelling; the mother should attend for medical examinations and, especially for first-births, courses to prepare her psychologically and physiologically for the birth. These services are ordinarily provided by the maternity home or ward, and there are virtually no home deliveries.

Since 1954 the sanitary-epidemiological stations have taken over the work of the sanitary inspectorates (whose operations cover four main branches — housing and communal services, food, industry and schools). In rural areas the sanitary-epidemiological station is a department of the *raion* hospital but its head, who is *ex officio* the deputy chief physician of the hospital, is also responsible to the *oblast* sanitary-epidemiological station.

As was noted at the end of Section I, the 1969 Law left intact the health care institutions outside the general health system but required the former to operate only under permission from the Ministry of Health: 4 per cent of beds are in hospitals of departments other than the Ministry of Health and such departments operate 3 per cent of the hospitals, 6 per cent of ambulatory and first-aid units and polyclinics and 8 per cent of public-health stations (Table 2.12).

Collective and state farms operate their own hospitals, but no separate statistics appear to have been published. The additions to the stock in 1973 have been found by Ryan for services controlled by the Ministry of Health (the 'main health service' in his term)[46] to which the *Statistical Yearbook* adds those data 'below the line' in Table 2.13. Collective and state farms operated 54 rest-homes and sanatoria in 1973 (22 in the Russian Federation) on an inter-farm basis, with 4,167 participant collective farms and 265 participant state farms.[47] Table 2.13 shows that the general health service provided less than half of the beds in new units in urban areas and just over a quarter of those in rural. Ryan draws attention to the significant proportions of beds put into buildings not designed as hospitals and observes that 'willingness to rely on such second-rate accommodation can be linked with the heavy emphasis on qualitative indices which pervades Soviet health service planning and, more specifically, with the stated objective of increasing the ration of hospital beds to population'.[48] But, he adds, Soviet Government policy since 1967 has been that inpatient facilities at enterprises should be no smaller than of 400 beds; he cites the Minister of Health for condemning 'tenacious local tendencies . . . squandering resources and irrationally deploying medical staff, equipment and apparatus' in small units.[49]

Some of the 'closed-access' facilities are, on the other hand, especially well-equipped and furnish a higher standard of care for those who are employed by the government department concerned. At the highest

level, senior state and party officials are entitled to use a modern hospital in Moscow, colloquially termed the *Kremlovka*, and all scientists
with the rank of Academician, Corresponding Member of the Academy
or with a higher doctorate have their own special polyclinic in the
capital city. Closed-access shops (*zakrytie rasprediteli*), special sections
of stores, or separate shops serving only permit holders usually have
foreign pharmaceutical specialities and scarce Soviet preparations on
sale.

A Union-Republican Minister of Health did, nevertheless, observe
in 1969 that 'our medicine today is at a sufficiently high level to render
qualified care to all the people, regardless of the sphere of the economy
in which they work'.[50] His implicit critique was of the better-equipped
units to which access is by employment under one ministry rather than
another or in a senior post rather than a junior.

Collective-farm hospitals are probably at the other end of the equipment scale. The farm pays for the construction of buildings (frequently
by its own labour) which the Ministry of Health — financing through
the local authority — staffs and supplies in current materials. The process of merging collective farms — effected in waves in the early fifties
and early sixties — has strengthened farm finances in the assurance of
better-quality premises, and hospital building reached a peak in 1967
when farms added 11,000 beds to their stock. The average for 1956-65
had been 7,800 and for 1971-3, 5,000.[51]

Some uncertainty surrounds the subordination of the special psychiatric hospitals, which led Amnesty International to enunciate the
principle that 'no one should, because of allegations of mental illness,
be deprived of legal, medical or procedural safeguards which would be
available to him if he were well. Anyone accused of an offence or
suspected of mental illness must be legally able to influence all deci-
sions affecting him.'[52] Its 1975 report on the subject quoted a Soviet
legal text which put such hospitals under the direct administration of
the Ministry of Internal Affairs,[53] and stated that there are nine such
hospitals in the USSR (Kazan, Sychyovka, Leningrad (the 'Arsenal'-
naya'), Chernyakhovsk, Minsk, Dnepropetrovsk and Orël being long-
established and two more, Blagoveshchensk and Kzyl-Orda, opened in
1972).[54] On the grounds that Article 37 of the *Fundamentals of
Corrective Labour Legislation* (1969) provides that procedure for
medical care for prisoners be jointly determined by the USSR Ministry
of the Interior and the USSR Ministry of Health, the Amnesty International report concluded that special psychiatric hospitals were under
the former[55] (and would hence figure under 'departmental services' in
Table 2.12). On the other hand, the Serbsky Institute of Forensic
Psychiatry, Moscow, which conducts many of the examinations which
result in confinement in such special hospitals, is, according to its

Director, under the Ministry of Health.[56] The units in that Ministry's jurisdiction comprise psychiatric hospitals (in 1965 3 per cent of which had fewer than 75 beds but 26 per cent had over 600 — and the biggest, the Krashchenko in Moscow, over 2,000); 'colonies' (having some 5 per cent of psychiatric beds); psychoneurological dispensaries (serving 4 to 8 urban *uchastki*); and consulting rooms (*kabinety*, serving one or two *uchastki*).[57]

Institutions run by the Ministry of Health are dually subordinated to the Executive Committee of the *oblast* in which they are situated and the Union-Republican Ministry of Health. The USSR Ministry of Health issues 'methodological instructions' to the Union-Republican Ministries, which are formally subordinate only to the Union-Republican Council of Ministers. The Academy of Medicine and the publishing enterprise Megdiz are subordinate to the USSR Ministry of Health. A medical council advises at each administrative level and the ministries have *collegia* (mainly, if not entirely, of departmental heads). The line of authority in planning runs from the USSR Gosplan (with the participation of the Union-Republican Gosplans) to the USSR Ministry of Health and thence to its subordinates, in terms chiefly of the norms described in Chapter 1.

V.   Health-care facilities

Table 2.14 brings together the main statistics of health resources for 1960-74. The rate of growth of physician numbers, of 85 per cent over 14 years, has not only been remarkably rapid, but steady at 4.5 per cent a year, as might be expected of a system which plans service by physician numbers and controls the intake of all medical schools. 'Physicians' cover not only the medically qualified but both those dentists (*stomatologi*) who would have the equivalent of the United States 'Doctor of Dental Surgery' or 'Doctor of Medical Dentistry' and dentists or 'dental doctors' (*zubnye vrachi*) who are trained in specialized secondary schools. Whereas in 1965 there were 25,000 of the former against 44,000 of the latter, the 'stomatologists' overtook the 'dental doctors' in 1974 (52,000 against 50,000).

Table 2.15 separates physicians by specialty, and the criticism is made that specialization is too narrow: by and large a physician in one branch does not attempt diagnosis or treatment for a disorder of another branch: the *therapevt* is a first-reference classifier rather than a general practitioner.

Despite these increases, numerous difficulties are experienced in physician supply. Poor living and working conditions, inadequate facilities, and the lack of senior personnel and medical supplies contribute to the high turnover rate of physicians in rural areas despite a regulation that for counting years of service, one in a rural post counts for 1.2

years in an urban zone. For 35,900 medical positions in the rural areas of the Russian Federation in 1966, for example, there were only 20,100 physicians; i.e. only 56 per cent of the positions were filled. Measures are being taken to open medical schools in deficitary areas in the hope that the students so attracted will remain in the locality. Even if the distribution in total number of medical staff is correctly made, the absence of a general practitioner in favour of specialization makes for difficulties. In Sverdlovsk and Moscow oblasts in 1968, for example, there were, respectively, 567 and 421 physicians not working in the specialties for which they were trained, although there were shortages of such specialists in these areas.

Pluralism has always been common under the pressure to fill posts. A further 97,100 physicians would have been required in 1964 to fill all available positions on a full-time basis, i.e. the equivalent of one post in every six was dually held. In a number of rural areas (where the turn-over in rural physician posts is triple that of urban), physician posts have to be filled by feldshers (medical assistants or auxiliaries) and nurses occupy feldsher positions; by contrast, due to preference for working in the better urban conditions, many feldshers work as nurses in town hospitals and polyclinics. The numbers of these 'medium-trained medical staff' are set out in Table 2.16. Extensive use is, as shown, made of feldshers, who were introduced into Russia by Peter the Great in the seventeenth century. The initial post-revolutionary reaction to halt the use of 'second-class doctors' was soon abandoned and, as Table 2.16 shows, their numbers rose by 56 per cent (excluding midwifery) during 1960-73, or by 1 per cent annually less than physicians. The trend contrasts with their decline (and replacement by fully-qualified physicians) in the other East European states where they are employed. Feldshers are even more frequently women (75 per cent) than are physicians (72 per cent). During the 13 years shown in the table, the number of medical nurses (virtually all female) per physician (excluding dentists) was fairly stable at around 1.6 but each nurse has on average only 2.5 hospital beds in 1973 against 2.8 in 1960.

The 1966-70 Plan of an increase of hospital beds to 2,680,000 was not quite fulfilled at 2,666,000. The 1971-5 Plan called for the improvement of rural health services to levels nearer those obtaining in towns and of environmental sanitation in both urban and rural areas; its target of 3 million was fulfilled at 3,008,000 and one of 3.3 million was set for 1980. The Directives of the XXVth Party Congress for the 1976-80 Plan made particular mention that catering norms had been improved in hospitals in 1971-5 and that further increases would be made in 1976-80 in maternity homes and in paediatric and other 'special' hospitals and wards.[58]

The classification of hospitals is shown in Table 2.17 and indicators of capacity use are collected in Table 2.18. The decrease in the load on rural hospitals has been remarkable. In 1953 their general beds were occupied for 358 days, their surgical beds for 313 and their paediatric beds for 354. By 1958 the overall rural mean had dropped to 318,[59] and by 1966 to 285 (as the table shows), but was climbing again by 1970.

The distinction between urban and rural hospitals, however, has decreasing implications for the actual hospitalization of urban and rural residents as more of the latter are accepted by urban hospitals. The percentage of admissions of rural residents rose, for example, as follows (using the titles of Table 2.17):

	1955	1965
Provincial	33.9	46.9
Town	8.9	11.6
Hospitals for rural districts located in urban areas	40.3	52.9
Specialist	12.2	13.5
Maternity homes	8.0	13.3
Inpatient dispensaries	36.2	43.3
Research institutions	16.4	18.2
Teaching hospitals	15.2	12.8

Source: B. V. Petrovsky (ed.), *50 let sovetskogo zdravookhraneniya*, Moscow, 1967, p. 100

The Ministry of Health network of dispensaries exceeded 3,700 in 1971, of which 1,373 were for tuberculosis, 772 for venereal and dermatological diseases, 269 for cancer and 247 for psychiatry and neurology. Over 9.5 million adults and adolescents attended dispensaries in urban areas in 1965 (1.12 mn for hypertension, 0.71 mn for rheumatism and 0.62 mn for stomach and duodenal ulcers). Screenings and periodic health checks in that year included 10.48 million workers in industrial enterprises, 5.2 million workers in food, sanitation, child care and health care institutions, 2.81 million apprentices and students and 22.20 million schoolchildren, the total number in 1971 was 101 million. In 1971 the 3,509 emergency aid posts treated over 55 million incidents of sickness or accident. No overall statistics of annual contacts with health care institutions seem to be published. There were 47,289,000 hospital admissions in 1965 (of which over 20 million were rural residents), 1,185.7 million consultations in urban polyclinics (126.4 million by rural residents), and 104.6 million home visits. Including emergency treatments, there were 9.7 consultations per

urban inhabitant (against 6.5 in 1940, 7.7 in 1950 and 8.7 in 1960).[60]
Some indication of the intensity of service can be seen in the lists
below:

	Urban population	Rural population
	Physicians needed per 10,000 population (in- and outpatients)	Physician contacts in outpatient services per person per year
First group (basic medical care)		
Therapeutic (including infectious diseases)	6.6	1.02
Paediatric	3.5	0.77
Obstetric-gynaecological	2.7	0.60
Surgical	2.7	0.69
Tuberculosis	2.0	0.21
Dermato-venereological	0.9	0.13
Ophthalmological	0.9	0.10
Neurological	0.8	0.09
ENT	0.7	0.10
Dental	3.7	0.74
Total for group	24.6	4.45
Second group (service to special categories)		
In pre-school institutions	0.5	..
In schools	0.7	..
For working adolescents	0.4	..
At factory health posts	1.0	..
For physical culture	0.3	..
Total for group	2.9	..
Third group (ancillary services)		
Laboratory	1.0	..
Radiology	1.5	..
Physiotherapy	0.4	..
Pathological anatomy	0.3	..
Other	0.3	..
Administration	2.0	..
Total for group	5.5	..
TOTAL FOR ALL GROUPS	33.0	..

Source: I. I. Rozenfeld', *Planirovanie potrebnosti zdravookhraneniya vo vrache-bynkh kadrakh*, Moscow, 1961, pp. 143, 164

Number of outpatient facilities in USSR in 1965

Urban physician blocks	29443
Urban child care blocks	31091
Polyclinics	18702
Emergency care stations	2439
Dental-care polyclinics	535
Dentist surgeries	24788
Dental prosthetic workshops	5753
Enterprise health posts	
— with physician	6168
— with medical assistant	25396
Health centres in large enterprises	1196
Dispensaries	
— tuberculosis	1724
— alcoholism	..
— venereal	632
— cancer	273
— psychiatric	213
— physical culture	210
— accident	166
— goitre	52

Source: B. V. Petrovsky (ed.), *50 let sovetskogo zdravookhranenie*, Moscow, 1967, pp. 77-89

VI. Finance of health care

The compilation and classification of the finance of health care on an internationally comparable basis was shown to be difficult enough with the cooperation of the governments concerned in Abel-Smith's classic report to the World Health Organization.[61] The Comecon member whose officials collaborated in that study was Czechoslovakia and the data then published are used in Chapter 4. Even Maynard's access to the insurance and national authorities in EEC countries did not permit a uniform or everywhere comprehensive breakdown, although a group of French authors at the Institut de Documentation et de Recherches sur les Maladies (INSERM) have shown how complete may be a matrix of costs and finance by individual health care sector.[62] This and the following chapters adopt the broad distinction used by Abel-Smith between capital and current costs and direct and indirect finance. The term 'direct' covers fee-for-service payments as well as purchase of health care items by persons ('households' in the INSERM study, 'beneficiaries in Maynard). Indirect finance can be separated — as in Table 2.19 — into government, social insurance and other (which in Comecon member states comprises allocations from operating budgets or from profits by state and cooperative enterprises and by collective farms). Government finance is predominantly through the Ministry of Health, although other Ministries furnish some capital and current outlay, usually on behalf of their staff. The Unified State Budget aggregates budgets at all lower territorial levels which, in the Soviet Union, are balanced — that is, shortfalls from or excesses above a planned expenditure are respectively made up to, or deducted from, locally accruing revenue.[63] It is hence local expenditure which is entered in the calculations below, local revenue having been adjusted to the corresponding aggregate value of outlay and not in any sense being earmarked to health (or any particular) expenditure. Furthermore, where a fee-for-service payment is made to a budget-financed institution (*uchrezhdenie*), it is separately entered and transferred to the supervising authority: it does not affect the public-funded budget. A recent instance occurred of a foreign tourist, injured in a road accident and hospitalized in a small provincial town, prevented from making an ex-gratia payment for the free care he had received 'because the hospital had no budget-head under which it could be received'.

The complexity of the sources and methods of derivation of Tables 2.20 and 2.21 show how scarce are Soviet published data on the composition of finance. It is by no means certain that anything like these tables are compiled by the Soviet financial agencies themselves: methodological texts show that macroeconomic distributions of finance between the public and personal purses are not a matter of analytical interest. The year 1968 happens to be one for which relatively full statistics are available. It is the latest year cited in a 1972 book on pharmacies which contains much information on prescription and non-prescription ('over-the-counter') pharmaceutical sales, and is covered in a 1970 collection of local budgets not, it would seem, yet republished.

In that year 9.1 per cent of official-sanctioned payments (others are discussed below, but cannot be evaluated as a magnitude) for health care was derived from the Unified State Budget, within which 13 per cent was expended centrally and the remainder what is termed 'locally', although this includes all outlay by Union-Republican Ministries of Health. By 1970 this proportion seems to have fallen to nearer 10 per cent, since 'almost 90 per cent' was said to have been spent locally.[64]

The extensive system of social insurance (operated through the trade unions) and of collective farmers' insurance (a joint agency of the state and collective farms), inaugurated in 1964, is all but unrelated to the finance of health care: its two contacts with the health service, which is wholly financed by the government from general taxation, are by payment of charges for resort cures and dietetic needs and prosthetics. Approximately 80 per cent of patients in sanatoria and rest-homes have either the full charge (between 100 and 200 roubles for a 24-day stay) or 70 per cent thereof paid by social insurance. In the health field, but not included as health care outlay, the insurance allows sick pay at a rate of 100 per cent of normal earnings for occupational injury or disease, and for any sickness or injury where the insured has more than 8 years' service; the range for shorter-service insured is from 50 per cent of normal earnings at less than 3 years to 80 per cent for 5 to 8 years' service. Those under 18 benefit from a 60 per cent rate irrespective of service.

Pharmaceuticals prescribed for inpatients are financed from the hospital budget without charge to the patient, but all others have to be paid for at the (controlled) retail price. Exceptions are those prescribed for childbirth and early infancy (including vitamins), and certain other chronic diseases, notably tuberculosis, schizophrenia and epilepsy, and vaccinations against smallpox, diphtheria, poliomyelitis and certain other diseases, which are free. Prostheses are normally paid for by the invalid but the social insurance makes a contribution in certain circumstances (such outlay amounted to 1.05 roubles per person in 1965).[65] The social insurance also pays for dietetic meals in public restaurants, factory canteens or special 'dietetic restaurants' by making available, on a physician's prescription, vouchers of entitlement to such meals gratis or at a discount. The restricted variety and irregular state of retail food supplies and the queueing and shortages affecting public catering make this dietetic provision virtually essential for proper medical care. Insurance also finances resort stays at spas, by the seaside and in other holiday areas. Like similar expenditure in Czechoslovakia, the GDR and Poland such 'cures' are not necessarily either prophylactic or therapeutic, but they are included for the sake of international comparability with Comecon.

Enterprises make a contribution both to capital and current costs of health posts, polyclinics and hospitals on their premises, the latter only being provided by large plants (as noted above). The sum of enterprise contributions to health services (including capital costs incurred by collective farms for facilities in their area) constitute column (5) of Table 2.19: the dip in 1965 was attributable to takeovers from collective farms. Enterprises also subsidise creches and kindergartens for dependants of their staff, the worker usually paying a standard 10 roubles per month (but with a sliding scale of reduction in relation to income) and the balance of costs (about 60 roubles per month per child) being met by the enterprise. Some creches are also run by the local authority, but no creche outlays are included in either Table 2.19 or 2.20.

The free supply of all prescribed pharmaceuticals was promised in the *Third Programme of the Communist Party* (the Second, as noted in

Section I, was of 1919) passed by a Party Congress in 1961 and covering social and economic measures to be implemented over the ensuing two decades. Official reference has not been made to this proposal since the changes of government of 1964; Table 2.21 estimates that free prescribing (i.e. for inpatients and the cases noted above) represented 42 per cent of the country's pharmaceutical consumption. The present writer was told by the USSR Minister of Health in 1975 that the current share was 70 per cent and the 42 per cent share follows from the application of that percentage to 1968 sales. No official statistics are available on private payments for health care. These may be classified, on the one hand, as direct payments for local-authority polyclinics in which payment is required and for legal private practice, and, on the other hand, as illegal expenditure in private practice (and especially for domiciliary care).

The autonomously financed medical institution (*khozraschëtnoe lechebnoe uchrezdenie*), more generally known as a 'paying polyclinic' (*platnaya poliklinika*) is administered and financed by the local-authority health department like any other free facility. Payments per visit are on a scale of 1 rouble, 1.50 roubles and 2 roubles, for which the patient may make appointments with a panel of specialists; except in cases of urgency, a week's delay is usual between registration and interview. No numbers of such polyclinics have been published but there were recently 10 in Moscow which has a population of 7 million; assuming that only the urban dweller purchases such aid and that there are rather more per head in the capital than in other cities where they are located, there are probably 130 such facilities throughout the USSR, viz. numerically insignificant against the free facilities but nevertheless an outlet for those who claim to find in them more personal professional attention. A proposal was voiced by two physicians in 1966 that fee-paying hospitals be opened on similar lines — mainly to absorb long-care and geriatric patients who are discharged from the overcrowded hospitals as soon as they no longer require full-time medical care, and whose care falls on their family.[66] No changes, however, followed and the present writer, in an interview with the Minister of Health in 1975, was assured that none was under consideration. No statistics relate to charges for the relatively few physicians legally in private practice, but they would not be likely to bring total direct payments for health services above 5 per cent.

Among payments not legally sanctioned, a payment of about 4 roubles to the physician who makes a house call in the course of his official duties, but not with respect to emergencies (for which payment is not expected), plus the cost of taxi in both directions, is said to be usual.[67] The informal fee of 4 roubles may be compared to that of 2 roubles an hour to school teachers for private lessons at home, for Ryan interprets evidence on comparative social status to conclude that physicians rank with teachers in the USSR, rather than above them as in most Western communities.[68]

Emergency treatment is both free and prompt. The facilities available in ambulances were the subject of special priority in the late sixties, with the provision of compact apparatus for artificial respiration and blood-transfusion and the selective supply, in high-incidence areas, of equipment to deal with traffic accidents or heart attacks.[69] The cost to the health service of each emergency call was said – to an American economist visitor to the Emergency Medical Service Centre in Kiev in 1974 – to be 7.2 roubles, of which an ordinary call costs 6 roubles and cardiac team 12 roubles:[70] these figures are in a sense in line with the private 'charge' for non-emergency calls. Visitors from abroad have remarked on lavish finance of the emergency care services. Three consultant orthopaedic surgeons on a British Council visit in 1974 'were most impressed by three unique features of the accident and emergency services . . . A service of this quality can exist only if there are enough medical personnel . . . The lack of adequate numbers of doctors precludes the establishment of services in the UK on the Russian pattern'.[71] A British general practitioner under the same auspices in 1971 concluded that 'there is no comparison between what I saw in Kiev and the majority of emergency services in the United Kingdom . . . What I saw in Kiev was the most impressive part of the Soviet Union's health service. The organization, efficiency and comprehensiveness of the services were quite fantastic.'[72] It must, however, be noted that all three visits were to the same Kiev Centre, just as there is a polyclinic on the western outskirts of the city to which English-speaking health delegations tend to be taken – in 1974 as in 1961 (including the present writer).

For gratis, non-emergency treatment the patient capable of travel goes to the local polyclinic at which he is registered, opening hours being 08.00 to 21.00 or to his appropriate 'closed-access' facility. It was only as recently as 1969 that continuous domiciliary services were experimentally introduced in large cities. Known as the 'domiciliary hospitalization method' (*metod statsionar na domu*) its introduction recognized that by 1968 in towns 19.6 per cent of physician contacts by the district doctor were at the patient's home. The method is no more than the earmarking of physicians, nurses and transport at a local hospital to be available for home visiting. As Table 2.22 summarizing the enquiry which related to visits over 40,709 days (at 29 to 30 days per patient) shows, the service is essentially for a few long-period cases, whose accommodation at home saves use of hospital beds.

Legal private practice is not very extensive because the consulting room has to be authorized as 'properly equipped' and the practitioner's income is subject to a very high rate of tax. Forms of care forbidden in private practice are treatment by hypnosis and surgery (the latter allowable in emergencies). Such practice, colloquially termed 'by advertisement' (*s ob'yavleniem*) or by sign-board (*s vyveskoi*), is chiefly confined to dentistry and to dermato-venereology.

Illegal private practice is, by contrast, much more widespread, above all because of tax evasion. The patient may call upon the physician in his own home (especially for dentistry, abortion — e.g. where there is a social case for concealment — and for consultation with a senior specialist — since private 'professorial consultancy' is not allowed in hospitals) or may have the physician come to his home (used mostly in the case of children). Although homoeopathic attention is legal if the practitioner is medically qualified, some of this care — frowned upon by the medical authorities and made more uncertain by the 1969 Law — takes place on a private, illegal basis.

The surreptitious payment of physicians and nurses in hospitals is so general as scarcely to be classified illegal, and is not surprising in a country such as the USSR where any slightly better service or access to otherwise unavailable items is invariably obtained by tips or influence. Such payment can, for example, ensure attention from a senior specialist, a bed in a particular or in a single ward, or is normal practice towards nurses who would give little attention if a person apparently able to pay did not offer something. Various charges, as covertly ruling in the late sixties, are set out below:

Radiological-oncological diagnosis by senior specialist at his home	40 roubles
Course of treatment by senior specialist for venereal disease	500 roubles
Illegal abortion at physician's home	40 roubles
Extensive dental work	150 roubles
Dental replacement (steel)	30 roubles
Homoeopathic consultation	10 roubles
Payments in hospitals	5-25 roubles

On the expenditure side, three relevant ratios are that the USSR contains one-quarter of the world's physicians, covers one-sixth of the inhabitable globe and has only one-fifteenth of mankind. Sparsity of population and the harsh conditions of winter travel between settlements have conduced to a service more highly labour-intensive than virtually anywhere else in the world. Only the Chinese 'barefoot doctors' — for whom, in late 1975, government encouragement seemed to be waning — instituted a scheme less reliant overall on physical assets.

With more than 4.5 million staff, the health service employs 4 per cent of the working, and 2 per cent of the entire, population.[73]

The generous allocation of manpower and the sparing use of capital conforms to three features of Soviet economic policy. At the outset of the industrialization drive of the First Five-Year Plan, labour was far more abundant than industrial plant: 80 per cent of the population were villagers and the urban element only exceeded 50 per cent in 1961 so that it was rational to use men to substitute as far as possible for machines. Secondly, Stalin's priority for industry lay in the manufacture of producers' goods rather than in that for consumers' goods and services, for — embracing self-sufficiency which minimized trade to the import of essential industrial equipment — such a concentration matched the forced saving on government account with physical investment goods. The health services ranked well below 'heavy industry' as recipient of home and imported equipment. Finally, health service salaries were pressed down, and kept, below the traditional 'professional' level and, scientific research excepted, the wage-differential previously accorded to university education was eliminated.

The latter issue may be developed in connection with Table 2.23. The class origins of physicians at the time of the First Five-Year Plan were still of pre-revolutionary mix — only a quarter (24.7 per cent) of serving doctors were of worker or peasant origin (according to the All-Union Health-Facilities Census of 1930),[74] and they enjoyed not far off the average wage as the Plan began. The plan period — one of rapid inflation of prices and slower rise of wages, such that living standards fell — saw a sharp erosion of the differential (by a speedier increase of industrial and building wages), from 91 in 1928 to 79 per cent of the average; and the margin was maintained and even widened under the following five-year plans, so that the ratio stood at 77 on the eve of the Second World War and 76 per cent after it.

The reaction among intending entrants to the profession should, on principles of relative salary expectancy, have been to choose other training, the more so as — the period of medical education exceeding all others — the recoupment of earnings foregone would be slower than in other professions. Rather, the First Five-Year Plan saw a record intake of medical students partly because the Soviet Government broke up the traditional training system — closing the university medical faculties and putting the facilities at the disposition of separate institutes, which shortened courses and trained for early specialization (see Section I). Other factors which enabled medicine and some other professions to continue to recruit when the lifetime earning profile deteriorated, were the shift from a predominantly male to a female composition and fostering access to higher education to those who saw education (and its place in a hitherto largely illiterate society) as desirable in itself or for the non-monetary rewards it yielded. It has been suggested that a higher wastage rate among women may somewhat affect the reduction in cost obtained under the first element in this policy.[75]

This low ranking of health staff in the earnings scale cut their real wages to 58 per cent of the 1928 level by the Second World War (in Table 2.23 the 1940 and 1950 figures happen to be the same but precision is difficult to ensure when prices in State shops and on collective-farm markets varied widely). The average real wage in the economy was almost back to its 1928 level in 1950 (93 per cent on the data in the Table) but medical personnel did not reach that stage until a decade later.

A big rise in health service pay in 1964 put the real wage well above the 1928 level, but the relativity then accorded was not maintained as other sectors achieved pay increments and even after a 20 per cent pay increase for physicians decreed in 1972, the wage in the health sector by 1973 was as low in relation to the national average as it had ever been. In the 45 years since the launching of the drive for industrialization and its associated national health service, health staff have improved their real wage by little more than half, while the national average has doubled.

Table 2.24 shows that the USSR has also managed to get the structural support for the health service most inexpensively, although, if a capital expenditure from the government budget was running in the seventies at only 5 per cent, and even if all spending by socialized enterprises were capital outlays, as most is, a combination of Tables 2.20 and 2.24 would show investment at some 9 per cent of total expenditure from all sanctioned sources. No data are published on the capital outlay of such enterprises: the relevant entry in the *Statistical Yearbook* conflates health with retail trade, municipal enterprises, forestry and agricultural procurement agencies: for what it may be worth that figure (which includes outlay by enterprises, collectives and private individuals) was exactly the same share (9.9 per cent) of national capital expenditure in 1973 as it had been in the First Five-Year Plan, 1928-32.[76] As a United States delegation in 1965 could correctly judge from the hospitals it visited, some of the economy has been derived from standardizing hospital buildings over very long periods: those built two or three years previously were, it reported, generally indistinguishable from those that were much older.[77]

Nor has much light been thrown on the recipient institutions. The latest figures, to the present writer's knowledge, are those that follow (p. 69) for 1957.[78]

Account should perhaps also be taken, in assessing the extent of private payments for health care in the USSR, of a certain amount of folk medicine. Practitioners are to be found throughout the country, even in Moscow and Leningrad where conventional medical services are at their best. All medical schools have specialists reporting on folk medical practices and in Irkutsk there is a faculty for such study.[79]

	Million roubles
Urban hospitals and dispensaries	1855
Rural hospitals and dispensaries	457
Polyclinics	15
Medical services in enterprises	29
Nursing services in enterprises	25
Feldsher and midwife posts	131
Emergency and first-aid posts	32
Blood transfusion service	19
Tuberculosis sanatoria	112
Child and adolescent sanatoria	18
Urban creches	259
Rural creches	63
Children's homes	44
Public health stations	158
Other	566
Total	3783

REFERENCES

1. *Vedomosti Verkhovnogo Soveta SSSR*, No. 52, 1969
2. For the context see M. Kaser, 'Education in Tsarist and Soviet Development', in C. Abramsky (ed.), *Essays in Honour of E. H. Carr*, London, 1974, p. 231
3. See M. Kaser, 'Entrepreneurship in Russia', *Cambridge Economic History of Europe*, Vol. VII, Cambridge, 1977
4. Quoted from Shishkov by W. H. E. Johnson, *Russia's Educational Heritage*, Pittsburgh, Pa., 1950, p. 172
5. Quoted from Versaev by G. Hyde, *The Soviet Health Service: A Historical and Comparative Study*, London, 1974, p. 18
6. Quoted from Levit by Hyde, op. cit., p. 20
7. The characterization of Russian public health pioneers is from Hyde, op. cit., Ch. 1; the essence of the pre-revolutionary history, though not the interpretation, is from Yu. P. Lisitsyn, *Sotsial'naya gigena i organizatsiya zdravookhraneniya*, Moscow, 1973, pp. 25-46, and G. A. Batkis and L. G. Lekarev, *Teoriya i organizatsiya sovetskogo zdravookhraneniya*, Moscow, 1961, Ch. III
8. S. Ya. Chikin, *KPSS i okhrana zdorovya naroda*, Moscow, 1972, p. 31: the source is particularly useful as a history since the Revolution

9.   Quoted from *Russia After Ten Years*, New York, 1927, by S. and B. Webb, *Soviet Communism: A New Civilisation*, London, 3rd edn, 1944, p. 708
10.   Intourist, *Pocket Guide to the Soviet Union*, Moscow, 1932, pp. 138, 143
11.   E. H. Carr, *The Bolshevik Revolution, 1917-1923*, Vol. 2, London, 1952, pp. 394, 397
12.   M. F. Vladimirsky (posthumous), *Voprosy sovetskogo zdravookhraneniya*, Moscow, 1960, p. 40, cited by Chikin, op. cit., p. 49
13.   Chikin, op. cit., p. 48; on the radical changes in this period see Hyde, op. cit., Ch. 6, and M. G. Field, *Soviet Socialized Medicine*, New York, 1967, pp. 66-9
14.   Chikin, op. cit., pp. 53, 106
15.   Respectively Lisitsyn (1973), op. cit., pp. 35-6 and Batkis and Lekarev, op. cit., p. 55
16.   Webb, op. cit., p. 691; Intourist, op. cit., p. 138
17.   A. Newsholme and J. A. Kingsbury, *Red Medicine*, London, 1933, p. 244, cited by Webb, op. cit., p. 690
18.   The phrase is from N. Jasny, *Soviet Industrialization 1928-1952*, Chicago, 1961, Ch. 6
19.   Quoted by Webb, op. cit., p. 679
20.   Hyde, op. cit., p. 127
21.   T. M. Ryan, *The Organization of Medical Care in the Soviet Union*, paper read to the National Association for Soviet and East European Studies Annual Conference, April 1975 (mimeograph), p. 2
22.   K. V. Maistrakh and I. G. Lavrova, *Osnovi sotsial'noi gigeni i organizatsii*, Moscow, 1969, p. 31
23.   Professor Blokhin's speech, as reported in *Soviet News*, 28 December 1969, p. 145
24.   S. V. Utechin, *Everyman's Concise Encyclopedia of Russia*, London, 1961, p. 2; the last statistical abstract on abortion appeared in 1929
25.   E. A. Sadvokasova, *Sotsial'no-gigenicheskie aspekti regulirovaviya razmerov sem'i*, Moscow, 1969, p. 117, cited Lisitsun, op. cit., p. 171. It might be noted that Lisitsyn's book for English language readers, [Y. Lisitsyn], *Health Protection in the USSR*, Moscow, 1972, does not mention termination of pregnancy in any form, although pp. 87-92 are devoted to 'Medical Care for Women and Children'. Nor does the survey of Party policy on health care in Chikin (which, op. cit., pp. 97-102, has a section 'Unremitting Care for Mothers and Children')
26.   I. Prokopets, *Zamuzhnyaya zhenshchina v sem'e i na rabote*, Moscow, 1968, p. 57, cited Lisitsyn (1973), op. cit., p. 172
27.   *Sovetskoe zdravookhranenie*, No. 5, 1973, pp. 12-13
28.   I. P. Katkova, *Rozhdaemost' v molodykh sem'yakh*, Moscow, 1971, cited Lisitsyn, loc. cit.
29.   B. V. Petrovsky, *Literaturnaya gazeta*, 11 December 1968, cited by H. P. David, *Family Planning and Abortion in the Socialist Countries of Central and Eastern Europe*, New York, 1970, p. 52
30.   C. Davis, *Report to the Master and Fellows of Clare College: A Tour of Medical Facilities in the USSR*, October 1974 (mimeograph), p. 14
31.   *Vestnik statistiki*, No. 6, 1970, pp. 91-2
32.   1968 data from ibid., p. 93
33.   The additional data for 1940, 1950 and 1966-8 are reproduced in Lisitsyn (1973, op. cit., p. 230) and in the section on 'Health' by M. G. Field, in

E. Mickiewicz (ed.), *Handbook of Soviet Social Sciences Data*, New York, 1973, p. 106

34. T. M. Ryan, 'Some Current Trends in the Soviet Health Services', *The Medical Officer*, 13 February 1970, p. 83
35. I. A. Bogatyrev (ed.), *Zabolevaemost' gorodskogo naseleniya i normativy lechebnovo-profilakticheskoi pomoshchi*, Moscow, 1967, p. 477, cited by Ryan (1970), loc. cit.
36. Personal communication by G. A. Popov, cited in J. Fry, *Medicine in Three Societies*, Aylesbury, 1969, p. 128
37. G. A. Popov, *Principles of Health Planning in the USSR*, WHO, Geneva, (Public Health Papers 43), 1971, p. 34, for Aktyubinsk survey; B. V. Petrovsky (ed.), *50 let sovetskogo zdravookhraneniya*, Moscow, 1967, p. 95 for urban hospital data
38. V. R. Ovcharov, *Vyborochny metod v sanitarnoi statistike*, Moscow, 1970, p. 16, cited by Lisitsyn (1973), op. cit., p. 229 and Davis, op. cit., p. 9 and F. A. Leedy, 'Demographic Trends in the USSR', in US Congress Joint Economic Committee, *Soviet Economic Prospects for the Seventies*, Washington, D.C., 1973, p. 462 (citing D. M. Heer, 'Abortio, Contraception and Population Policy in the Soviet Union', *Soviet Studies*, July 1965, pp. 80-1; G. Hyde, 'Abortion and the Birth Rate in the USSR', *Journal of the Biological Sciences*, No. 2, 1970; K.-H. Mehlan, 'Abortion in Eastern Europe', in R. E. Hall (ed.), *Abortion in a Changing World*, Vol. I, New York, 1970, p. 307; and E. A. Sadvokasova, op. cit., pp. 120-36)
39. D. Ferotov, *Meditsinskaya gazeta*, 25 November 1966, p. 36 (cited Hyde, loc. cit.), and Hyde, op. cit., p. 274
40. *Health Services in the USSR*, WHO, Geneva (Public Health Papers 3), 1960, p. 46
41. Lisitsyn (1973), op. cit., pp. 41, 44
42. Lisitsyn (1973), op. cit., p. 230
43. The privately circulated (*samizdat*) *Politichesky dnevnik*, No. 72, September 1970, p. 4
44. Fry, op. cit., pp. 24-5
45. Ryan (1975), op. cit., p. 14
46. Ibid., p. 5
47. *Statistical Yearbook, 1973*, p. 464
48. Ryan, op. cit., pp. 5-6
49. B. V. Petrovsky, *Meditsinskaya gazeta*, 9 January 1974, p. 1
50. N. Savchenko, ibid., 21 November 1969, p. 2
51. *Statistical Yearbook, 1973*, p. 623
52. Amnesty International, *Prisoners of Conscience in the USSR: Their Treatment and Conditions*, London, 1975, p. 141
53. *Sovetskoe ugolovnoe pravo: chast' obshchaya*, Moscow, 1972, p. 463
54. Citing another *samizdat* periodical, *Khronika tekushchikh sobitii*, No. 24, p. 146
55. Amnesty International, op. cit., p. 66
56. G. Morozov, 'Soviet Forensic Psychiatry', *Anglo-Soviet Journal*, October 1972, p. 64
57. T. M. Ryan, 'Some Aspects of the Soviet Mental Health Service', *The Medical Officer*, 6 October 1967, pp. 174-5
58. *Pravda*, 14 December 1975, pp. 1, 5
59. N. N. Rosenfeld', *Osnovy i metodika planorovaniya zdravookhraneniya*: Vol. III, *Planirovanie potrebnosti zdravookhraneniya vo vrachebnykh kadrakh*, Moscow, 1961, pp. 65-6

60.   Ibid., Vol. I, *Lechebno-profilakticheskoe obsluzhivanie sel'skogo nasele-niya*, Moscow, 1955, p. 35; O. A. Aleksandrov and Yu. P. Lisitsyn, *Sovet-skoe zdravookhranenie*, Moscow, 1972, pp. 63-4; Petrovsky (1967), op. cit., pp. 85-101

61.   B. Abel-Smith, *Paying for Health Services* (Public Health Papers 17), WHO, Geneva, 1963

62.   Cf. representations of French outlay and income in A. Maynard, *Health Care in the European Community*, London, 1975, Tables 6-8 (pp. 117-8) and E. Lévy, M. Bungener, G. Duménil and F. Fagnani, *Economie du système de santé*, Paris, 1975, Table 1.1, facing pp. 242-3

63.   *The Soviet Financial System: Structure, Operations and Statistics*, US Department of Commerce, Series P-90, No. 23, Washington, D.C., 1968

64.   A. G. Tarasova and L. M. Lemenev, *Rukovodstvo po planirovaniyu khoz-yaistvenno-finansovoi deyatel'nosti khozraschetnoi apteki*, Moscow, 1972, p. 24

65.   Cited by A. Dacquin, 'Les progrès et les coûts de la Santé Publique sovié-tique (1950 à 1965)', *Economies et sociétés*, February 1969, p. 311

66.   *Literaturnaya gazeta*, 8 December 1966

67.   R. Bernheim, *Die sozialistischen Errungenschaften der Sowjetunion*, Zurich, 1971, pp. 117-22; on influence he cites *Trud*, 28 July 1970

68.   Ryan (1970), loc. cit.

69.   L. B. Shapiro, *Organization of Emergency Medical Care*, Moscow, 1969; Novosti Agency, *USSR Health Service*, Moscow, n.d.; Lisitsyn (1972), op. cit., pp. 79-80

70.   Davis, loc. cit.

71.   J. F. Hindle, L. W. Plewes and R. G. Taylor, 'Accident and Emergency Services in Russia', *British Medical Journal*, 22 February 1975, 1, p. 447

72.   W. J. Stephen, 'Primary Medical Care in the USSR', *Update*, March 1973, p. 820; in 'Lessons from the USSR', *The Practitioner*, June 1972, p. 8, p. 831, he substituted the adjective 'staggering'

73.   Lisitsyn (1972), op. cit., pp. 5, 105

74.   *Narodnoe khozyaistvo SSSR, 1932*, Moscow, p. 566

75.   Ryan, 'A Note on the Supply of Doctors in the Soviet Union', *The Medical Officer*, 10 December 1965, p. 318

76.   *Narodnoe khozyaistvo SSSR, 1932*, p. 577

77.   United States Department of Health, Education and Welfare, *Hospital Services in the USSR*, Washington, D.C., 1966, p. 25

78.   *Raskhody na sotsial'no-kul'turnye meropriyatiya po gosudarstvennomu byudzhetu SSSR*, Moscow, 1958; in this and preceding instances it has been possible to verify that no subsequent abstract has appeared from a list of all Soviet statistical publications from 1918 to 1972, E. A. Mashi-khin and V. M. Simchera, *Statisticheskie publikatsii v SSSR*, Moscow, 1975

79.   G. St George, 'Russian Folk Medicine', *Britain-USSR*, No. 39, Spring 1973, pp. 1-3, also citing P. Kourennoff (trans. G. St George), *Russian Folk Medicine*, London, 1970

TABLES

2.1 Demographic indicators in the USSR

	Per 1000 population			Per 1000 live births
	Births	Deaths	Natural increase	Infantile mortality
1960	24.9	7.1	17.8	35.3
1965	18.4	7.3	11.1	27.2
1968	17.2	7.7	9.5	26.4
1969	17.0	8.1	8.9	25.8
1973	17.6	8.7	8.9	26.4
1974	18.2	8.7	9.5	27.8

Source: *Narodnoe khozyaistvo SSSR v 1969 godu; statistichesky sbornik* (hereafter referred to as *Statistical Yearbook*), p. 31; *1973*, p. 43; *SSSR v tsifrakh v 1974 godu* (hereafter referred to as *Concise Statistical Yearbook*), p. 18

2.2 Ethnic composition of the USSR at January 1970 census

	Millions	Per cent of total
Russians	129.0	53.4
Ukrainians	40.8	16.9
Byelorussians	9.1	3.7
Poles	1.2	0.5
Other Slavs	0.4	0.2
Sub-total Slavs	180.5	74.7
Uzbeks	9.2	3.8
Tatars	5.9	2.5
Kazakhs	5.3	2.2
Azerbaidzhanis	4.4	1.8
Armenians	3.6	1.5
Georgians	3.2	1.3
Moldavians	2.7	1.1
Lithuanians	2.7	1.1
Other non-Slavs	24.2	10.0
Sub-total non-Slavs	61.2	25.3
Total	241.7	100.0

Source: *Statistical Yearbook, 1973*, pp. 35-6

NOTE: Nationalities with fewer than 10 per cent of the population are not shown

2.3 Cities of the USSR with over one million population at 15 January 1970 (census) and 1 January 1975 (official estimates)

	Population (thousands)		Infantile mortality	Hospital beds per 10,000 population
	1970	*1975*	*1969*	*1970*
Moscow	7061	7635	22	143.3
Leningrad	3950	4311	21	136.5
Kiev	1632	1947	18	138.7
Tashkent	1385	1595	40	113.3
Baku	1265	1383	28	115.2
Kharkov	1223	1357	19	113.4
Gorky	1170	1283	20	102.7
Novosibirsk	1161	1265	23	89.3
Kuibyshev	1045	1164	28	107.7
Sverdlovsk	1025	1147	26	114.9
Minsk	(917)	1147	..	..
Tbilisi	(889)	1006	..	..

Source: *Vestnik statistiki*, No. 3, 1971, pp. 84, 86, 94; *Statistical Yearbook, 1973*, pp. 22-31; *Concise Statistical Yearbook, 1974*, p. 13

2.4 Percentage of females in Soviet population (estimates at 1 January)

	Urban	Rural	Total
1940	52.1	52.0	52.1
1959	54.8	55.1	55.0
1970	53.7	54.3	53.9
1975	..	..	53.6

Source: Census results, *Izvestia*, 19 April 1970; *Concise Statistical Yearbook, 1974*, p. 8

2.5 Projections of the Soviet population

	1970	1980	1990	2000
Births per 1000 population	17.4	18.1	16.7	15.5
Deaths per 1000 population	8.2	9.4	10.1	10.6
Increase per 1000 population	9.2	8.7	6.7	4.9
Per cent of population:				
Aged 0-15	30.9	..	..	24.6
16-39	35.6	..	..	34.4
40-59 men/54 women	18.5	..	..	21.1
60/55 and over	15.0	..	..	19.9
Total population (millions)	241.6	264.2	286.3	303.6

Source: G. Baldwin, *Projections of the Population of the USSR and Eight Sub-divisions by Age and Sex: 1973 to 2000*, International Population Reports, Series P-91, No. 24, US Department of Commerce, Bureau of the Census, Washington, D.C., June 1975, Tables E and F on series C

2.6 Soviet mortality from cardiovascular diseases in 1971-2

Deaths per 100,000 population

	MALE		FEMALE		BOTH SEXES
	Crude	Standardized	Crude	Standardized	
Arteriosclerosis and cardiosclerosis	138.8	196.0	199.5	159.0	171.5
Hypertension	68.5	92.8	93.3	75.5	81.8
— of which, lesions in central nervous system	40.0	54.9	61.5	49.9	51.6
— above, with myocardiac infarct	7.1	9.3	5.5	4.4	6.3
Vascular lesions of central nervous system	61.2	86.3	92.8	74.2	78.2
Other ischaemic diseases [a]	39.8	51.8	24.2	19.7	31.4
— of which, from myocardiac infarct	25.0	32.7	12.5	10.3	18.3
Active rheumatism, chronic rheumatic heart diseases	11.4	12.7	14.5	13.3	13.1
Other cardiovascular diseases	25.6	34.5	30.1	24.6	28.0
All cardiovascular diseases	345.3	474.1	454.4	366.3	404.0
All causes [b]	898.5	1119.7	783.4	660.6	836.6

Source: *Vestnik statistiki*, No. 12, 1973, pp. 80-1

a   Excluding hypertension
b   Disease, accident, poisoning and violence

2.7 Mortality from malignant neoplasms in 1971 and 1972

	Thousand deaths		Deaths per 100,000 population
	1971	*1972*	*1971-2*
Mouth and throat cavity	4.3	4.7	1.8
Gullet	15.5	15.4	6.3
Stomach	98.3	97.8	39.8
Intestines, excluding rectum	10.9	11.5	4.6
Rectum	9.9	10.6	4.2
Other digestive organs	27.2	27.3	11.1
Larynx, bronchi, trachea	53.7	55.3	22.1
Other respiratory organs	0.9	0.9	0.4
Mammary glands	13.0	13.8	5.4
Cervix	12.6	12.6	5.1
Other localized or unlocalized parts of the womb	7.5	7.4	3.0
Other female sex organs	9.5	9.7	3.9
Prostate glands	3.7	3.8	1.5
Other male sex organs	0.8	0.8	0.3
Urinary organs	10.3	10.3	4.2
Skin	2.1	2.3	0.9
Bones and connective tissue	3.6	3.8	1.5
Blood-creative organs and lymphatic tissue	18.5	18.6	7.5
Other localizations or localizations without indications	14.6	14.9	6.0
Total malignant neoplasms	316.9	321.5	129.6

Source: *Vestnik statistiki*, No. 12, 1973, pp. 82-3

2.8 Child mortality in the USSR by age-group

Deaths per 1000 of the corresponding ages

	1960-1	*1966-7*	*1971-2*	*1972-3*
4 years and under	9.9	6.9	6.8	7.2
5 to 9	1.0	0.8	0.7	0.7
10-14	0.7	0.6	0.5	0.5

Source: 1960-7, *Zhenshcheni i deti v SSSR*, p. 44; 1971-2, *Vestnik statistiki*, No. 12, 1973, p. 79; 1972-3, ibid., No. 12, 1974, p. 88

2.9 Adult mortality in the USSR by age-group

Deaths per 1000 of the corresponding age

	1971-2	*1972-3*
15-19	1.0	1.0
20-24	1.6	1.6
25-29	2.1	2.1
30-34	2.8	2.8
35-39	3.7	3.6
40-44	4.8	4.8
45-49	6.1	6.2
50-54	8.8	8.6
55-59	11.9	12.5
60-64	18.1	18.0
65 and over	101.6	102.7

Source: As for Table 2.8

2.10 Morbidity from communicable diseases

Per 100,000 population

	1960	*1970*	*1973*
Measles	972	194	115
Scarlet fever	313	194	128
Whooping-cough	259	16	12
Infetious hepatitis	239	167	228
Diphtheria	25	0.5	0.1
Typhoid and paratyphoid, A, B, C	22[a]	9.	8
Acute poliomyelitis	3.3	0.11	0.07
Epidemic typhus	2.9	1.2[b]	..
Tetanus	1.1	0.3	0.2
Malaria (new cases)	0.17	0.14[b]	..

Source: *Statistical Yearbook, 1969*, p. 734; *1973*, p. 759

a   Excluding paratyphoid
b   1969

2.11 Sample of reasons for care at adult polyclinics and in home visits in Leningrad

Percentages

Specialty	Polyclinics	Home visits
General medicine	41.6	87.7
Surgery	11.3	2.5
Neuropathology	5.7	2.4
Ophthalmology	8.8	0.3
ENT	8.6	0.3
Urology	2.0	0.1
Other	22.0	6.7

Source: *Sovetskoe zdravookhranenie*, No. 12, 1974, p. 52

2.12 Administrative distribution of health care facilities in the Soviet Union in 1970

	Hospitals	Number of beds in thousands	Units for ambulatory-polyclinic care	Sanitary-epidemiological stations and sanitary departments of district hospitals
Departmental services	865	107.4	2347	360
Ministry of Health	25369	2558.9	35013	4259
Total	26234	2666.3	37360	4619

Source: *Sovetskoe zdravookhranenie*, No. 2, 1972, pp. 85, 88-9

2.13 New hospital beds brought into use in the Russian Federation in 1973

	Urban areas		Rural areas	
	Number	Percentage	Number	Percentage
Beds in new units built by:				
General health service	15820	47.7	1080	26.7
Other agencies	7782	23.5	620	15.3
State farms	145	0.4	790	19.5
Beds in adapted units provided by:				
Local authorities (Executive committees)	2305	6.9	195	4.8
Industrial enterprises	1475	4.5	100	2.5
Beds in adapted and supplementary buildings of general health service organs	4881	14.7	1085	26.8
Beds added in existing hospitals (with no extra space)	772	2.3	180	4.4
Total in services controlled by Ministry of Health	33180	100	4050	100
Other government departments and cooperative organizations	299	. .	—	. .
Collective farms	—	. .	768	. .
Total all civilian hospitals	33479		4818	

Source: *Zdravookhranenie Rossiiskoi Federatsii*, No. 11, 1974, pp. 42, 43 for services controlled by the Ministry of Health, and *Statistical Yearbook, 1973*, p. 625 for total civilian additions by state and cooperative agencies whence by subtraction other governmental additions (which were assumed to be all in urban areas); the same source gave collective farm additions which would virtually all be in rural areas

2.14 Main health facilities and staff in the USSR

		1960	*1968*	*1973*	*1974*
Number of physicians (including					
dentists)	(thousands)	431.7	617.8	766.7	800
— per 10,000 population		20.0	25.8	30.6	31.6
Number of medium-qualified medical					
staff	(thousands)	1388.3	1943.6	2368.8	..
— per 10,000 population		64.2	81.2	94.4	..
Number of hospitals	(thousands)	26.7	26.4	25.1	..
Number of hospital beds	(millions)	1.74	2.49	2.87	2.94
— per 10,000 population		80.4	103.8	114.2	115.9
Number of health facilities for					
outpatient care	(thousands)	39.3	38.9 [a]	36.1 [a]	..
Number of centres for maternal					
and child care [b]	(thousands)	16.4	20.5	21.8	22
Number of maternity beds					
— in hospitals	(thousands)	175.3	193.2	206.3	210
— in maternity homes	(thousands)	38.1	30.3	18	14

Source: *Statistical Yearbook, 1969*, pp. 727-35; *1973*, pp. 751, 754, 758; *Concise Statistical Yearbook, 1974*, pp. 193-4

a   Source notes that mergers with hospitals caused the decline shown
b   Both autonomous and attached to other health facilities

2.15 Specialties of physicians and hospital beds in the USSR

Thousands

	Physicians			Hospital beds		
	1960	*1968*	*1973*	*1960*	*1968*	*1973*
General therapeutics [a]	96.2 [b]	125.6 [b]	166.2	361.7	484.5	609.5
Surgical [b]	40.5	60.2	81.4	236.7 [c]	324.6 [c]	386.0 [c]
Obstetric-gynaecological	28.7	38.5	48.1	266.6	338.1	368.9
Paediatrics	58.9	74.8	94.0	239.2	383.2	456.8
Ophthalmology	10.5	15.0	17.5	30.3	37.2	40.0
ENT	9.6	14.7	17.7	20.0	36.8	43.7
Neurology	10.5	16.5	20.6	30.5	62.1	84.7
Psychiatrics	6.4	12.5	17.5	162.5	246.5	293.0
Tuberculosis	16.5	23.1	23.6	157.2 [d]	274.7 [d]	261.0 [d]
Dermato-venereology	9.3	11.3	14.2	31.0	45.8	62.6
Radiology	15.7	23.0	27.4 }	24.2	43.2	49.5
Oncology	.. [e]	.. [e]	.. [e]			
Infectious diseases	..	..	..	91.3 [f]	102.4 [f]	114.6 [f]
Physical culture	1.6	2.6	3.8	0.2	0.3	—
Public health and epidemiology	31.5	38.7	45.4	—	—	—
Stomatology	16.2	33.7	48.8 }	.. [e]	.. [e]	.. [e]
Dentists	30.1	49.8	50.6 }			
Others	49.5	77.8	89.9	87.8	107.3	83.8
TOTAL	431.7	617.8	766.7	739.2	2486.7	2866.0

Source: *Statistical Yearbook, 1969*, pp. 729 and 733; *1973*, pp. 753 and 758

a   Including endocrinology and physiotherapy
b   Including traumatology, orthopaedics, anaesthetics and urology
c   Including specialists for infectious diseases
d   Including paediatric beds (20.9 in 1960; 28.9 in 1968; 23.9 in 1973)
e   Included with surgical
f   Excluding paediatric beds (75.3 in 1960; 84.8 in 1968; 101.9 in 1973)

2.16 Medium-level medical staff in the USSR

Thousands

	1960	1968	1973
Feldshers (medical assistants)	334.7	434.6	522.5
Midwife-feldshers	76.2	80.4	78.6
Midwives	139.3	193.2	243.0
Sanitarians	28.2	32.3	43.8
Medical nurses	623.5	944.4	1152.6
Medical laboratory staff	52.5	74.8	99.5
Radiologists	18.3	22.2	28.0
Dental technicians	13.9	23.0	29.2
Disinfectionists	52.4	68.1	84.1
Others	49.3	70.6	
TOTAL	1388.3	1943.6	2368.8

Source: *Statistical Yearbook, 1969*, p. 730; *1973*, p. 754

2.17 Soviet hospitals by type at 1 January 1968

	No. of hospitals	No. of beds (thousand)
Micro-district (*uchastkovye bol'nitsy*) [a]	11601	322.7
Central and zonal-regional (*raionnye*) [b]	3548	461.3
Town and urban district (*gorodskye-raionnye*)	4730	698.0
Provincial (*oblastnye*)	183	100.0
Specialist	1992	247.2
Inpatient dispensaries (*statsionary dispansery*) excluding psychoneurological	2663	190.2
Research institutions and teaching hospitals (*kliniki vuzov*)	154	42.0
Psychiatric and psychoneurological hospitals and psychoneurological dispensaries	565	229.2
Maternity homes (*rodil'nye doma*), excluding collective-farm maternity homes and maternity wards of general hospitals	774	79.6
Other hospitals	218	27.7
TOTAL	26428	2397.9

Source: *Zhenshchiny i deti v SSSR, 1969*, p. 161

a Hospitals serving a rural 'block'
b Hospitals in the chief town of the administrative district and those serving a group ('zone') of rural 'blocks'

2.18 Indicators of the use of hospital capacity in the Soviet Union

Days

	Annual occupancy	Mean stay
Urban hospitals in the Russian Federation, 1957		
Maternity beds	303	8.0
All other beds	325	13.5
of which: general	341	15.1
surgical	343	12.7
oncological	302	25.1
non-infectious paediatric	319	11.5
Hospitals (excluding psychiatric) of USSR Ministry of Health		
Urban 1966	320	14.1
1970	319	14.9
Rural 1966	285	11.6
1970	295	12.6
Optimal means formulated in 1967-9 for urban hospitals		
General	330	10.0
Non-infectious paediatric	335	10.5
Adult infectious	313	7.4
Infectious paediatric	304	11.0
Surgical	333	9.4
Traumatological and orthopaedic	339	8.6
Urological and nephrological	336	10.7
Stomatological	334	11.0
Oncological	347	6.8
Obstetric	291	16.9
Gynaecological	325	12.2
For abortions	326	13.5
Tuberculosis	347	11.2
Neurological	339	11.5
Ophthalmological	340	8.9
ENT	325	10.1
Dermato-venereological	338	9.7
Psychiatric	360	1.4
All beds	325	9.5

Source: 1957: G. A. Batkis and L. G. Lekarev, *Teoriya i organizatsiya sovetskogo zdravookhraneniya*, Moscow, 1961, p. 226; 1966-70 and 1967-9 study (of M. P. Roitman and L. V. Lokshina): V. V. Golovteev, P. I. Kal'yu and I. V. Pustovoi, *Osnovy ekonomiki sovetskogo zdravookhraneniya*, Moscow, 1974, pp. 88-9

2.19 Outlays in the USSR on health care and physical culture

Millions of roubles

	State budget		All indirect outlays			Social insurance outlays of a health-support type
	Total	of which physical culture	Total	excluding physical culture	other than from budget	
	(1)	(2)	(3)	(4)	(5)	(6)
1950	2140	28	2600	2572	432	185
1960	4824	64	5900	5836	1012	256
1962	4945	52	6200	6148	1203	277
1963	5257	42	6600	6558	1301	289
1964	5662	40	7200	7160	1498	300
1965	6669	38	7900	7862	1193	364
1966	7100	43	8400	8357	1257	407
1967	7451	50	9300	9250	1799	436
1968	8138	49	10200	10151	2013	490
1969	8551	41	11000	10959	2408	519
1970	9284	47	11800	11753	2469	551
1971	9623	52	12500	12448	2825	615
1972	10030	48	13000	12952	2922	645
1973	10495	56	13300	13244	2749	687

Source: *Statistical Yearbook, 1963*, pp. 656-8; *1964*, pp. 772-4; *1965*, pp. 783-6; *1967*, pp. 888-91; *1969*, pp. 771-4; *1972*, pp. 726-8; *1973*, pp. 780-2

2.20 Finance of health services in the USSR: official data and estimates for 1968

Millions of roubles

			Million roubles	Per cent
1.	**Government**			
	On health and physical culture		8138	
(a)	of which paid through:			
	1.1	All-Union and Union-Republican agencies	1069	
	1.2	Provincial (*oblastnye*) authorities	1194	
	1.3	City (*gorodskie*) authorities	3367	
	1.4	Rayon (*raionnye*) authorities	2056	
	1.5	Settlement (*poselkovye*) councils	142	
	1.6	Village (*sel'skie*) councils	310	
(b)	1.7	*less* outlay on physical culture	−49 8089	77.1
(c)	of which on health-care products			
	1.1	Supplied in hospitals	542	
	1.9	Supplied free to outpatients	385	
2.	**Social Insurance**			
	2.1	Contribution to prosthetic costs	90	
	2.2	Resort cures and dietetic needs	490 580	5.5
3.	**Other socialized enterprises**			
	3.1	State and cooperative enterprises, trade unions, collective farms	2013	
	3.2	*less* social insurance	−580 1433	13.7
4.	**Direct payment (by persons)**			
	4.1	Purchase of health-care products	288	
	4.2	Payments in polyclinics	98 386	3.7
5.	**Total of officially-sanctioned payments**		10488	100.0

Source: 1.1 to 1.6 from *Mestnye byudzhety SSSR: statistichesky sbornik*, Moscow, 1970, p. 445; 1.7, 2.2 and 3.1 from Table 2.19, cols. (2), (6), (5) respectively. 1.8 amd 1.9 from Table 2.21, rows (b) and (h); 2.1 from statement by A. Dacquin, *Economies et societés*, February 1969, p. 311 that average payment was 1.05 roubles in 1964 multiplied by total insured (85.1 million) in 1968, from *Statistical Yearbook, 1973*, p. 573; 3.2 is row 2.2 to eliminate double counting; 4.1 from Table 2.21, row (k); 4.2 130 polyclinics with payment at 1.50 roubles per visit (see text) at 0.5 million visits per year (1,600 patient visits per day in large new polyclinics) according to Yu. Lisitsyn, *Health Protection in the USSR*, Moscow, 1972, p. 75

2.21 Sales of Soviet pharmacies in 1968

Category		Million roubles	Unit	Source
(a)	Total sales	" "	1246	p. 130
(b)	of which wholesale	" "	542	p. 131
(c)	of which pharmaceuticals	" "	396	73 per cent of (b); see (r) below
(d)	retail	" "	704	p. 131
(e)	of which pharmaceuticals	" "	514	As for (c)
(f)	— on prescription	" "	154	30 per cent; (see (p)
(g)	Aggregate prescription supply	" "	550	(c) plus (f)
(h)	of which gratuitous	" "	385	70 per cent; see text
(i)	Private purchase of prescriptions	" "	165	(g) minus (h)
(j)	Private purchase of other health-care products	" "	123	(t) + (u) + (v) as per cent of (d)
(k)	Private purchase of all health-care products	" "	288	(i) plus (j)
(l)	Outpatient prescriptions per inhabitant	Number	5	p. 87
(m)	— cost per inhabitant	roubles	0.29	p. 137
(n)	*hence* cost per prescription	"	1.45	
(o)	Retail sales of medical goods per inhabitant	"	4.72	p. 106
(p)	*hence* prescriptions as per cent of pharmaceutical sales	per cent	30	
(q)	Retail sales through pharmacies per inhabitant	roubles	6.46	p. 132
(r)	*hence* pharmaceuticals as per cent of sales through pharmacies	per cent	73	
(s)	— as stated		73.1	p. 144
(t)	Retail sales of bandages	per cent	8.9	p. 145
(u)	Retail sales of medical equipment	per cent	3.6	p. 145
(v)	Retail sales of nursing products	per cent	5.0	p. 145
(w)	Retail sales of mineral water	per cent	0.8	p. 145
(x)	Retail sales of soap, cosmetics, perfume and haberdashery	per cent	8.6	p. 145

2.21 (cont)

Source: A. G. Tarasova and L. M. Lemenev, *Rukovodstvo po planirovaniyu khozyaistvenno-finansovoi deyatel'nosti khozraschëtnoi apteki*, Moscow. 1972, to which all page numbers in the final column refer

a Termed 'medical products including pharmaceuticals' on p. 131, but incorrectly called 'pharmaceuticals' on p. 106; the pharmaceutical share is shown to be 80.7 per cent thereof on p. 145. Hence sales of pharmaceuticals per inhabitant are 3.80 roubles which is also the *per capita* dividend of the sum of (c) and (d); this figure is used in Table 1.9

NOTE: Greater consistency with budget data could be achieved in valuing wholesale sales (to hospitals, polyclinics and other health care institutions) at wholesale prices instead of, as implicitly here, at retail prices. But turnover tax on pharmaceuticals is small: Tarasova and Lemenev, p. 141, shows stocks at wholesale prices at 70 per cent of total inventory and at retail prices at 74.1 per cent. Wholesale prices had been reduced by 5.32 per cent on 1 July 1967 (p. 173)

2.22 Sample data on 'domiciliary hospitalization' in Soviet cities

City	Hospital	Date service started	No. of patients served		
			1965	*1966*	*1967*
Kursk	No. 2	1960	211	194	232
Moscow	No. 40	1961	44	64	70
Izhevsk	No. 2	1962	87	71	90
Kursk	No. 1	1965	110	116	126

Source: P. P. Myacheva (Semashko Institute), *Sovetskoe zdravookhranenie*, No. 12, 1969, pp. 12-16

2.23 Wages of Soviet health service personnel

In roubles of 1961 denomination [a]

	Wages in rbls/month		Health service as per cent of average	Retail price index 1928=100	Health-service wage	
	Average	Health service			Money	Real
1928	5.85	5.32	90.9	100	100	100
1931	9.18	7.26	79.1	.. [b]	136	..
1940	33.1	25.5	77.0	821	479	58
1950	64.2	48.6	75.7	1582	914	58
1960	80.6	58.9	73.0	1182	1107	94
1970	122.0	92.0	75.4	1182	1729	146
1973	134.9	99.0	73.4	1182	1861	157

Source: Wages — 1928-31: *Statistical Yearbook, 1932*, p. 415; 1940-70: *1922-72*, pp. 351-2; 1973: *1973*, pp. 586-7; retail prices (1937 weights) — 1928-50: J. Chapman, *Real Wages in Soviet Russia since 1928*, Cambridge, Mass., 1963, p. 355. 1950 was computed as the mean of Chapman's 1948 and 1952 (1,637) and the official index excluding collective farm markets (1,527); 1960-73 official index in *Statistical Yearbook, 1922-72*, p. 409 and p. 678 on 1950 base

a A rouble from 1961 equals 10 roubles of preceding years
b Misleading to compute because of general urban rationing

2.24 Investment in the Soviet health sector

Millions of 1961 roubles

	Total expenditure	Capital outlay	Recurrent expenditure			Capital as per cent of total
			Medical	Public health	Sub-total [a]	
1940	903	15	745	79	888	2
1950	2163	19	1857	162	2144	1
1960	4841	203	3885	160	4638	4
1970	9284	499	8156	398	8785	5
1973	10495	545	9233	442	9950	5

Source: *Statistical Yearbook, 1922-72*, p. 485; *1973*, p. 781

[a] Includes small outlays on physical culture which are incorporated in the Budget for the health sector

3 BULGARIA

I. Legislation and Policy

Bulgaria has always been one of the least developed economies of Europe. Although historically Europe's first medieval state, it languished so long under Turkish occupation that its appearance as an independent country was as a collection of agrarian communities, with a pattern of ill-health typical of a poor peasantry. The expansion of administrative services and of a small industrial sector evoked the establishment of a social insurance system in 1905 for wage-earners and, later, for civil servants. This system was reinforced in 1924-5 with new laws on unemployment insurance, and in the inter-war period included a full range of health, accident disability and old-age benefits, conforming to international conventions of the International Labour Office, and compulsory for all employed persons. It was administered by the State through autonomous institutions on the basis of separate funds. By 1944 about 350,000 wage and salary earners in Bulgaria were involved in the state social insurance scheme, which officially remained in force until the creation of a national health service in 1951. Its start under the First Five-Year Plan was on a very ambitious scale, which had soon to be somewhat curtailed, but has from the beginning offered comprehensive coverage. The accompanying drive to convert Bulgaria from a predominantly agrarian economy has involved an industrialization programme including the development of a pharmaceutical industry (above all in antibiotics), whereas before the War Galanus Pharmaceuticals was the only manufacturer in the country.

A quarter-century ago Georgi Dimitrov, the hero of the Reichstag Fire trials and the postwar Communist leader of Bulgaria, took as a dictum that 'the health and fitness of the population constitute the most valuable asset of our nation',[1] – a very proper assessment of the then pattern of economic resources, characterized by a high ratio of manpower to capital.

The Bulgarian Constitution of 1971 lays down that 'The State assures all-round care of the people's health by organizing health services and institutions for treatment and prevention of disease': Article 47 goes on to state that 'Every citizen is entitled to medical care', a right implemented in detail in the Public Health Law. The State has moreover abrogated the right of health care solely to itself, Bulgaria having in 1972 (Decree 238 of the Council of Ministers) forbidden the private practice of medicine.

Bulgaria has since Classical times been renowned for its spas (those at Hissar and Kyustendil were frequented under the Romans) while the salt lagoons of the Black Sea coast yield a mud with therapeutic properties. The acquisition of the Southern Dobrudja from Romania in 1940 brought more such resorts into the national territory, notably that favoured by the Queen of Romania. The nationalization of the various establishments in 1947 was the preliminary to a great expansion, part of which has resulted in a substantial income from foreign visitors.

The transformation of health services can be partly gauged by the decline in infantile mortality. It had somewhat improved between the two World Wars, dropping from 161.1 per 1,000 live births in 1906-10 to 147.1 in 1931-5 and to 120.6 in 1944, the year of Liberation by the Soviet Army. But it has subsequently been cut to one-sixth of that level, to 25.7 in 1973.[2]

II. Demographic pattern

The census of 1 December 1965 demonstrated a remarkable feature in the precise equality of males and females (4,114,000 of each sex), although the latest official estimate, for 1973, showed 4,307,000 men and 4,314,000 women within a total of 8,621,000. Another notable parallel is the similar rate of decline from the inter-war rates in both birth rates and death rates: from a 29.3 per 1,000 average in 1931-5, births dropped to 16.0 in 1966-70 while mortality fell from 15.5 per 1,000 to 8.9.[3] In comparison with the year in which the comprehensive health service was launched, however, natality has declined much faster than mortality and stood in 1973 at 16.2 and 9.5 per 1,000 respectively.

The fall in fertility is partly due to urbanization as industrialization proceeded. The urban population rose from 25 per cent at the 1946 census to 57 per cent in 1973, a 2.8-fold increment in numbers, from 1,734,000 to 4,917,000. But it was only until the mid-sixties that a higher natality persisted in the villages, as Table 3.1 shows. The rural birthrate is now well below the urban, and migration to the towns no longer reduces the national average, although, because (due to an increase in the median age of villagers, as it is the young who migrate) the rural death rate is higher, the natural increase is smaller. Rural fertility is now so low as to be causing concern: one author, putting as factors the collectivization and mechanization of agriculture which have induced urban ways of life in the village, believes that a labour shortage is likely by 1980.[4]

The other factor in reducing fertility is abortion, policy on which is now restrictive. Bulgaria was the first country in Eastern Europe to follow the Soviet legislation of abortion: the regulation of April 1956 stated that any woman could have a pregnancy terminated on request, though after the medical staff concerned have 'done everything in their power to dissuade all women who express a wish for the interrruption of pregnancy'. Abortions had to take place in a hospital, for a flat fee of 50 leva (5 leva after the currency reform of June 1962).[5]

Registered abortions rose rapidly to 1967, when, by decree of the Party Central Committee and Council of Ministers of 28 December, a number of conditions were laid down to be fulfilled before authorization. The interruption of pregnancy, under the implementing Law of 16 February 1968, is prohibited to a woman without living children save for serious medical indications (approved by a commission of three physicians); and unmarried women may only undergo an abortion if there are 'serious social reasons', if aged under 16 or pregnant as a consequence of rape or incest. Women with three or more children, or aged over 45, may have pregnancy interrupted on request. The number of legally induced abortions dropped to 85,000 in that year. As part of first swing back to pro-natalism, family allowances were increased, with the highest allowances for the third child; only nominal payments were made for subsequent children because families of more than three children were to be discouraged (largely because housing units of sufficient size were not generally available). The same pattern was evident from the fact that the maternity grant paid for a fourth or subsequent child was one-tenth of that paid at a second birth and a mere 2.5 per cent of that at a third birth. Even so coitus interruptus remained the most widely practised birth control technique (69 per cent of respondents in a 1966 survey, 5 per cent each using condoms or the safe period, while the remaining 21 per cent took no contraceptive measures at all), for no mechanical contraceptives are manufactured in Bulgaria, condoms being imported from Czechoslovakia and some contraceptive pills (oxosiston) imported from the GDR. Trials of intrauterine devices began in 1969, when a permissive trend began to re-emerge, notably in an expansion of women's consultation centres and research and publicity conducted by the Research Institute of Gynaecology and Obstetrics, Sofia. Constraints on abortion were relaxed in 1970 when authority was given for interruption of pregnancy for all unmarried women and for married women with one child, the fee remaining at 5 leva, or about the same as a one-month purchase of imported oral contraceptives. Abortion data for that year are shown in Table 3.2, which indicates a rate of 16.8 per 1,000 population, a little above the birth rate (16.3).

A second return to a pro-natalist policy was foreshadowed in 1973 when the Party leader and President, Todor Zhivkov, called for three children per family as a 'national duty'. A third child, he declared, was necessary even if the mother was out at work because only 24 per cent of the population were under 14 (1965 census) against 40 per cent at the start of the century.[6] The number of legally registered abortions had been exceeding that of births,[7] and measures were taken in early 1974 again to reverse policy. Abortions have been restricted to unmarried women without children, to widows, to women over 40 who are either divorced or have at least one child; and on specific medical indications;[8] supplementary family allowances were introduced for certain groups (80 leva per month, valid for ten months for a first child, 12 for a second and 14 for a third);[9] and in 1975 maternity grants for all women were increased to 100 leva for the first, fourth or subsequent child, but 250 for the second and 500 for the third.[10] A proposal for a tax on childless families (currently a tax is levied on bachelors and spinsters over 30 years of age and couples without children after five years of marriage) aroused public opposition and a commentator conceded that there were 'psychological barriers' among young people to having large families.[11]

A recent Bulgarian projection of the population to the year 2000, for which a figure of 9,602,000 is given,[12] is a little below the trend to 1996 cited from the United States Bureau of the Census in Table 3.3, which assumes a constant gross reproduction rate (that shown in Table 1.1 which yields for 1996 a population of 9,600,000 and, if further projected, about 9,730,000 for 2000). At that trend, Bulgaria will have in the last decade of the century one of the highest median ages in Comecon, only the GDR and Hungary showing an older population structure.

Health care is not complicated in Bulgaria by illiteracy or by ethnic differentiation. Many Turks (a remainder from the occupation which ended a century ago) were deported in 1950-1 and at the time of the 1965 census 88 per cent declared themselves Bulgarian. There are no problems generated by large conurbations: Sofia is the only large city (946,000 population in 1973), Plovdiv and Varna being the next biggest at 288,000 and 260,000 respectively; four towns are in the 100,000 range.

III.   Health conditions

Following the VIIIth revision (1965) of the International Standard Classification of Diseases, Table 3.4 specifies all causes of death, and Table 3.5 morbidity from infectious diseases. In the conquest of the latter, Bulgaria has reached the pattern of an advanced Western society (see Table 1.4), but still experiences a two-thirds lower incidence of cancer. The general increase of the chronic and degenerative diseases to the levels found in industrial economies is making it necessary to extend services for the chronic sick and to pay particular attention to the medico-social problems associated with these diseases. The incidence of diphtheria, typhoid fever, tetanus and poliomyelitis has been gradually decreasing, but deaths from respiratory infections rank with the Romanian as the highest in all Europe. The morbidity due to infectious hepatitis is also decreasing and tuberculosis has been reduced to an incidence no higher than that of France.

Bulgaria still has a lower and, indeed, a declining impact of road-vehicle injuries than in Western Europe — though Table 1.4 puts it at that of the United Kingdom. Malaria — which was endemic before the War in the Danube borderlands and the flat coastline of the Dobrudja, affecting 500,000 people — has been all but eliminated and any cases are now imported.

Among diseases, formerly significant, of which no cases have recently occurred are poliomyelitis, typhus, Marseilles fever, relapsing fever, rabies, glanders, and tularemia, although a recurrence of the last remains a slight possibility. Measles, dysentery and hepatitis have shown an upward trend over the seventeen years covered by the table, and influenza remains a heavy epidemic element in morbidity.

The Ministry of Health places as its present priorities the improvement of occupational health and environmental health conditions related to the industrialization of the country and to the increased production of chemicals, the prevention and control of cardiovascular diseases and cancer, the combating of mental and neurological disorders, the control of communicable diseases, particularly of tuberculosis, and measures to limit the growing number of accidents and their consequences. A significant geriatric care problem has been posed by migration to the towns leading to an increase of the percentage of the solitary aged in rural areas. The very rapid growth of tourism has also required the development of health services in areas hitherto little covered.

Under plans prepared jointly by the Ministry of Health, the State Planning Committee, the Ministry of Finance and the State Committee for Science and Technical Progress, specific long-term programmes are concerned with the control of cardiovascular diseases, cancer and tuberculosis (see Table 3.6). An evaluation of the health activities over the first 25 years of the Republic carried out for the National Assembly (Parliament) by its Commission for Health and Special Welfare, stated that insufficient measures were being taken *inter alia* to prevent child mortality; among actions taken was a government decision to increase production of prepared baby-foods and powdered milk. In the field of road accidents, a cause lay in the overcrowding of roads by foreign tourists: more than 300,000 foreign vehicles entered Bulgaria in 1969 and the roads, in the main narrow and unsuitable for fast traffic, are adequate only for the relatively few Bulgarian trucks and cars and the still numerous horse, bullock and buffalo carts.

IV.   Health service administration

The responsibility for the overall organization and administration of the health service rests with the Ministry of Health. The functions of this Ministry are divided among departments of pharmacy, environmental sanitation and epidemiology, preventive and curative health services, planning and finance, medical education and research. The department of social welfare which previously was part of the Ministry of Public Health and Welfare has been transferred to the Ministry of Labour and Social Welfare. At the level of the 28 provinces, the health services are directed by the Public Health Department of the Executive Committee of the People's Council; the health officials at this level and at the lower level of the district are dually subordinate to the local People's Council and to the Ministry of Health.

At each district headquarters there is a district hospital, specialized district 'dispensaries' and a public health and epidemiology institute which is responsible for public and preventive health activities in the district, including environmental health, occupational health, nutrition, radiation protection, communicable disease control, child health including school health, health statistics and health education. There are 10 public health and epidemiology institutes, each of which covers several districts and an average population of 800,000. The administration of urban health services is, in most instances, a function of the town hospital, which controls all health establishments in the urban area concerned. The rural health service is the basic unit of the country's health organization: each rural community has a service covering environmental sanitation, personal health services and the small hospitals.

The patient's access to the health service is through three channels, of which the first is his personal physician (who keeps records of the individual) at a local polyclinic, frequently attached to a hospital. Specialized dispensaries deal with outpatients passed on by a polyclinic for specified treatment and care, e.g. of tuberculosis. A second channel is through the factory health service, all larger factories having a health centre at the service of their staff. All factories employing more than 500 females are required to maintain a gynaecological centre. All industrial workers are medically examined normally through the factory service. Factories, too, run 'night sanatoria' where workers can stay overnight and have treatment, physiotherapy and dietetic food free of charge. The third channel is the school health service.

Under a reorganization of 1968, urban maternity homes were reclassified as obstetric gynaecological hospitals and some rural maternity homes were merged with the rural health institutions while the remainder merged with the nearest urban health institutions. Rural hospitals, outpatient departments, and health centres were as far as practicable united within the rural health districts. 'Medical sanitary centres' (in the

Soviet usage) were redesignated and have been transformed into 'workers' hospitals' (*rabotnicheski bolnitsi*) and outpatient clinics.

Physicians generally work an 8-hour day divided between the hospital and the polyclinic, but while there is prohibition of private medical practice, extensive use is made of private dental services.

Three ministries other than Health operate their own health care facilities, those of Transport and Communications, of Agriculture and the Food Industry and of Defence. The last-named is outside the scope of this book and is separately administered; the Ministry of Health co-ordinates the activities of the other two and their facilities are included in Table 3.6. Social welfare institutions, such as homes for the aged, are not covered.

All medical research and training institutions were merged in 1971 into the Medical Academy: this accounts for the reduction of numbers of institutions in Table 3.7. They include four medical faculties, two stomatological faculties and one pharmacological faculty on the teaching side and eight research centres and five research institutes, some transferred from the administration of the Academy of Sciences. Total employment by the Medical Academy in 1974 was 14,500, of whom over 3,000 were professional.[13] Other institutes active in the field of research are the Army Medical Institute, the Chemo-Pharmaceutical Institute of the Ministry of Chemistry and Metallurgy and the Transport Medical Institute, and the one Institute, for Social Hygiene and Public Health Organization, which in 1971 was left under the direct authority of the Ministry of Health.

V.   Health-care facilities

Bed numbers (in thousands) were increased between 1960 and 1974 from 49.4 to 73.3 in hospitals and from 6.2 to 12.5 in sanatoria. Per 10,000 population this represented 84.2 hospital and 14.4 sanatorium beds, and the Plan for 1980 set corresponding targets of 90 and 22-23. A problem of urban concentration of facilities lay behind a decree of 10 January 1966, local authorities were required to provide free housing for medical staff working 'in villages with poor living conditions' and on industrial construction sites. But this regulation has not been wholly observed as the organ of the Communist Party reported in 1971: 'Many young doctors are not provided with living space and are compelled to live in hotels or to rent rooms at high rates. These are the reasons for the high rate of labour drift among young medical staff.'[14] From 1971 an additional salary was paid to medical graduates who undertake to work for the first five years after qualification in a rural area. Strictly, the first three years after graduation have compulsorily to be served in a rural area but in practice many evade this obligation.

Special hospitals for alcoholics and for drug addicts have recently

been established and are included among the 17 in the psychoneurological group in Table 3.7. As in all Comecon states there is one
hospital in the capital city, the Government Hospital, Sofia, which provides a high standard of care and to which access is selective by Party,
official or academic rank. On an international scale, the Pirogov Institute for Emergency Medical Assistance in Sofia ranks high for care of
accidents and burns. A Central Institute of Health was set up in Sofia
in 1968 to evaluate and provide information for planning, to train
medical and paramedical staff and to undertake research as a faculty of
the postgraduate medical school. The growth in medical staffing is
indicated in Table 3.8 and specialization in 3.9. The expansion of ancillary medical personnel is particularly notable. Feldshers are not only
widely used but their numbers more than tripled over 1956-73, while
nurse numbers have increased even faster. Recent data are as follows
for other health service workers:

	1967	1970	
Dental assistants	1048	1252	
Pharmacists	2077	2618	(1972)
Pharmaceutical assistants	2973	3399	
Physiotherapists	234	..	
Laboratory technicians	3260 ⎱	4552	
X-ray technicians	773 ⎰		
Health agents	424	..	
Medical statisticians	258	..	
Other paramedical technicians	578	..	

Doctors are trained at the medical schools in Sofia, Plovdiv and Varna,
and since 1974 also in Pleven. A postgraduate medical school was
created in 1950 in Sofia. There are also 22 training schools for nurses,
midwives, pharmaceutical assistants, laboratory technicians, etc. A
school for the training of sanitary inspectors has been established.
  Bulgaria has followed the Soviet pattern in making the most of
physician specialization. Of the 15,819 physicians in post in 1970
(18.6 per 10,000 population), just 20 per cent were 'internists' (Table
3.8); there were in addition 3,111 stomatologists (fully qualified
medical dentists).
  Data on recent use of facilities include, for 1972, 3.7 million home
visits, 48.2 million outpatient consultations and 12.3 million dental
consultations. In 1972 the emergency aid service answered 0.6 million
calls: casualty wards have been converted in the three largest cities into
'emergency treatment hospitals' and a National Consulting Service
operates from Sofia for serious emergencies.

Polyclinics are linked with hospitals, again following the Soviet system, and combine prophylactic with therapeutic measures. Within a new policy of 'the physician seeks out his patient', a prophylactic department is being established in every polyclinic for screening and other morbidity surveys. The 'dispensary method' (as defined in Chapter 2) has been adapted to Bulgarian practice and by the end of 1973 21 per cent of the population had surveillance with medical-record linkage: the aim is to bring all the population into surveillance.

The district hospitals, of which in 1973 there were 116, cater for populations between 30,000 and 100,000 and have between 250 and 400 beds: each must have a general, paediatric, surgical, maternity and isolation ward and can have a few specialized wards. But for more specialist treatment reference is to the provincial hospital, of which there are 27 (one in each provincial capital); some are classified as 'inter-provincial' for the finer specialties. At the summit of special care are the national centres and institutes within the Medical Academy.

In 1973 there were 1.32 million hospital admissions: the average stay in 1970 was 14.8 days and with beds utilized 307 days per year. There were 199,059 operations, of which the majority took place in provincial hospitals (88,921) and urban and district hospitals (70,515), with substantial numbers at the central institutes (22,675) and workers' hospitals (11,163); the hospitals of the Ministry of Transport assured 2,745. Admissions to sanatoria for tuberculosis were 10,858 and for other affections 164,497. The 'night sanatoria' (as explained above, for overnight stay where care cannot be provided at home, but the patient can go to work in the daytime) had 701 admissions, and prophylactoria 494,783.

Virtually all confinements (98.2 per cent) take place in maternity wards and there were in 1973 2,576 mother and child consultation centres. Data for sectional services, of which the latest available to the present writer are for 1967, include school health services provided at 1,890 school health centres where the whole school population was under medical and health supervision; 169 independent rehabilitation centres and 255 rehabilitation outpatient departments in hospitals. Psychiatric consultations were available in 29 clinics attached either to hospitals or to dispensaries; they were attended by 11,369 new outpatients. All industrial establishments offered medical and health services to their workers. The 45 public health laboratories carried out over 2.5 million examinations in 1967.

Measles inoculation has not been launched on a wide scale but other immunization and re-immunization procedures were carried out as shown in the table on p. 102 (data in thousands). Cervical tests are available for all women over 35, and fluoridation of drinking water is proceeding.

	1967	*1970*
Poliomyelitis	2277	629
Tetanus	1246	600
Diphtheria	1024	589
Smallpox	940	470
Whooping-cough	536	367
BCG	487	987
Typhoid and paratyphoid	121	51

Source: Direct communication for 1967; *Zdraveopazvane, 1971*, pp. 186-7 for 1970

A United Kingdom physician visiting Bulgaria under the auspices of the Royal College of General Practitioners in 1968 observed that 'throughout the country the organization was stereotyped and uniform'. He identified the basic unit of care on a territorial basis as a team of an internist and a nurse for the adult population, a paediatrician and two nurses for children up to 15, a midwife and a dentist with assistant. A gynaecologist covered two or three health teams and in some rural areas there was only one doctor, one dentist and a midwife.[15]

VI.   Finance of health care

Free non-contributory medical assistance was introduced in 1951, covering hospital, outpatient and domiciliary care. For the first five years all prescriptions were dispensed gratis, but gratuity was thenafter — and still is — restricted to the supply of pharmaceuticals in hospitals and other residential institutions. Pharmaceutical prices are fixed by the Committee on Prices and are not high in relation to other products of daily necessity; substantial price reductions were made in their retail prices in January 1968 and June 1971.

Table 3.10 reproduces the official data for the budget-financed sector, but only a very rough estimate can be made for direct expenditure by persons. Some indication can be inserted for pharmaceuticals on the assumption that, with the same regulation as in the USSR, approximately the same share of pharmaceutical consumption is paid for privately. The cost of prostheses to the Social Insurance Fund may be roughly estimated, but contributions by enterprise to industrial health services have been ignored. Capital spending has been some one-sixth of government health care outlay, but reached a peak in 1970 on the eve of the formal declaration of a fully comprehensive service. Services on gratis supply are financed wholly from taxation, expenditure being allocated as necessary between the provinces and districts by the

Ministry of Finance in conformity with a plan established with the Ministry of Health. The only in-service charge — introduced in 1968 — is for prosthetic dental work, an aggregate too small for inclusion separately in Table 3.10.

Pharmaceuticals and medical supplies (other than for inpatients) must be purchased at retail prices, but gratis certificates are issued for prescriptions of particularly expensive drugs or for chronic cases.

Prostheses are reimbursed by the Social Insurance Fund, under regulations dating from 1957 for state employees and from 1963 for cooperative-farm members. The state enterprise pays the premium for its staff and the collective farm a levy of 2 per cent of its annual revenue.

Physicians have comparatively low salaries in Bulgaria. As one consequence they readily accept service abroad, and a considerable number are working in developing countries (particularly in Algeria, Syria and the Sudan); in the fifties, when the GDR health service was being depleted by the migration of physicians to the Federal Republic of Germany (before construction of the 'Berlin Wall' in 1961), 120 Bulgarian physicians went to the GDR to fill gaps. A few Bulgarian physicians are working in Yugoslavia.

The prohibition of private medical practice in 1972 has brought a number of problems, which were summarized in a press article of November 1974.[16] Under the regulations a few 'open group practices' are allowed within the state service: they are available for any citizen who prefers to choose a specialist other than the one attached to his residential area or work-place, but the number of these group practices is 'very small' and in effect few patients can be taken. Free choice of physician among the local services has been urged in letters to the press — one woman caustically contrasted her freedom to choose a hairdresser or dressmaker with her inability to go to the gynaecologist in whom she had confidence. A certain amount of informal private practice was noted in obtaining domiciliary visits where the local practitioner was not convinced of the urgency of the case, in exchanges of services without payment (car repairs against a doctor's attention) or in the provision of care to the physician's relatives and friends. The Minister of Labour and Social Affairs was noted as having characterized as wasteful the illegality of private practice for retired physicians, and the article suggested the opening of 'paying polyclinics' or at least 'paying surgeries' in polyclinics and hospitals. In mentioning that this solution had been accepted in other socialist countries, Romania and the USSR would have been in mind.

REFERENCES

1.   Cited in H. Golemanov, *Health Services in the People's Republic of Bulgaria*, Sofia, 1974, p. 5
2.   Ibid., p. 39; for a slightly higher figure, see Table 1.2
3.   Central Statistical Office, *Zdraveopazvane, 1971*, Sofia, 1971, p. 1
4.   S. Chaparova, *Kooperativno selo*, 25 September 1974
5.   H. P. David, *Family Planning and Abortion in the Socialist Countries of Central and Eastern Europe*, New York, 1970, pp. 64, 72
6.   *Anteni*, 23 November 1973
7.   Chaparova, loc. cit.
8.   *Zemedelsko zname*, 2 May 1974
9.   *Rabotnichesko delo*, 1 March 1974
10.   Ibid., 4 April 1975
11.   T. Sharkov, *Trud*, 8 October 1974
12.   *Demografiya na Bulgariya*, Sofia, 1974
13.   Golemanov, op. cit., p. 42
14.   *Rabotnichesko delo*, 26 March 1971
15.   W. J. Stephen, 'General Practice in Eastern Europe', *The Practitioner*, July 1969, pp. 86-93
16.   D. Stefanov, *Trud*, 30 November 1974, cited in *La Documentation Française*, No. 275, 9 January 1976, pp. 29-31

TABLES

3.1 Vital statistics for urban and rural areas in Bulgaria

Five-year average rates per 1000

	Births		Deaths		Natural increment	
	Urban	Rural	Urban	Rural	Urban	Rural
1926-30	24.6	35.4	16.1	18.4	8.5	17.0
1936-40	17.4	25.0	12.4	14.0	5.0	11.0
1946-50	23.9	25.2	11.3	12.7	12.6	12.5
1956-60	16.6	19.1	6.9	9.6	9.7	9.5
1966-70	17.2	14.9	6.9	10.9	10.3	4.0

Source: Central Statistical Office, *Zdraveopazvane, 1971*, Sofia, 1971, p. 1

3.2 Registered abortions in Bulgaria in 1970

	On medical indications	Spontaneous or unspecified	Criminal	On pregnant woman's request	Total
Provincial hospitals	506	8275	73	48898	57752
District hospitals [a]	412	9743	86	50203	60444
Workers' hospitals	29	613	11	3411	4064
Research and teaching hospitals	70	754	3	3808	4635
Maternity hospitals	155	1991	3	13067	15216
Ministry of Transport hospitals	2	58	—	340	400
Total	1174	21434	176	119727	142511

Source: *Zdraveopazvane, 1971*, op. cit., p. 93

a Includes Government Hospital and Pirogov Institute

3.3 Projections of Bulgarian population

	1971	*1981*	*1996*
Percentage age-distribution			
0-14	22.6	22.0	20.5
15-39	37.1	35.4	33.7
40-64	30.4	30.7	31.1
65 and over	9.9	11.9	14.7
Median age (years)	33.4	34.4	36.8

Source: P. F. Myers, 'Population and Labor Force in Eastern Europe 1950-1996',
in US Congress Joint Economic Committee, *Reorientation and Commercial
Relations of the Economies of Eastern Europe*, Washington, D.C., 1974, p.
434

3.4 Deaths in Bulgaria by principal causes

		1968	*1973*
B2	Typhoid fever	1	—
B3	Bacillary dysentery	25	12
B4	Enteritis and other diarrhoeal	183	162
B5	Tuberculosis of respiratory system	905	589
B6	Other tuberculosis	97	58
B8	Diphtheria	1	—
B9	Whooping-cough	3	—
B10	Streptococcal sore throat and scarlet fever	1	—
B11	Meningococcal infection	7	15
B14	Measles	16	22
B17	Syphilis and sequelae	15	14
B18	Other infective and parasitic	337	346

3.4 (cont)

B19	Malignant neoplasms	11581	11941
B20	Benign and unspecified neoplasms	403	329
B21	Diabetes mellitus	682	635
B22	Avitaminoses and nutritional deficiency	18	7
B23	Anaemias	70	65
B24	Meningitis	72	101
B25	Active rheumatic fever	179	150
B26	Chronic rheumatic heart disease	1355	770
B27	Hypertension	1336	935
B28	Ischaemic heart disease	11928	17619
B29	Other heart disease	1468	2029
B30	Cerebrovascular disease	15004	16808
B31	Influenza	86	346
B32	Pneumonia	5327	4950
B33	Bronchitis, emphysema, asthma	3760	3589
B34	Peptic ulcer	453	396
B35	Appendicitis	118	74
B36	Internal obstruction and hernia	371	278
B37	Cirrhosis of liver	458	607
B38	Nephritis and nephrosis	408	385
B39	Hyperplasia of prostate	529	271
B40	Abortion	8	22
B41	Complications of pregnancy	25	26
B42	Congenital anomalies	433	516
B43	Birth injuries etc.	853	ˏ893
B44	Other perinatal mortality	149	240
B45	Symptoms and ill-defined conditions	3666	4766
B46	All other diseases	5302	4671
BE47	Motor vehicle accidents	1161	1130
BE48	Other accidents	2850	2296
BE49	Suicide	825	998
BE50	All other external causes	207	4671

Source: *Statisticheski godishnik* (hereafter *Statistical Yearbook*), *1969*, pp. 26-29; *1974*, p. 52

3.5 Registered cases of infectious diseases in Bulgaria

Number

	1956	1967	1968	1973
Diphtheria	679	12	28	—
Scarlet fever	25034	6620	5013	13351
Measles	14463	33456	32639	48556
Whooping-cough	12975	7308	1266	783
Rubella	3774	1214	1308	4913
Chickenpox	17454	26386	31146	33541
Mumps	13891	27579	45879	14899
Influenza	44997	335127	12183	28116
Epidemic cerebrospinal meningitis	442	150	156	128
Epidemic encephalitis	2	6	1	1
Acute poliomyelitis	194	42	1	—
Typhus	32	—	—	—
Marseilles fever (Boutonneuse)	11	—	—	—
Q fever	1	4	53	9
Haemorrhagic fever	28	31	21	13
Malaria	263	9	8	14
of which new cases	208	—	—	—
Papatassii fever	125	—	1	—
Typhoid fever	122	37	37	4
Paratyphoid fever	31	5	3	—
Dysentery	13358	11326	15136	17150
Toxic dyspepsia	108	145	104	118
Infectious hepatitis	12221	17541	18227	10803
Brucellosis	10	29	11	—
of which new cases	7	29	11	—
Anthrax	416	59	57	126
Rabies	1	—	—	—
Leptospirosis	448	42	10	4
Tetanus	282	83	82	56
Serous meningitis	..	57	73	105

Source: *Statistical Yearbook, 1969*, p. 253; *1973*, p. 377

3.6 Selected morbidity per 100,000 population in Bulgaria

	1968		1970	
	Total	New cases	Total	New cases
Active tuberculosis	433.5	89.9	379.2	79.9
Registered cases of venereal and infectious dermatological diseases				
Syphilis, all forms	11.0	6.1	9.7	5.3
Gonorrhoea	92.3	91.9	88.4	87.5
Soft chancre	—	—	—	—
Microsporosis	0.5	0.5	0.4	0.4
Trichophytosis	20.3	19.8	16.5	16.4
Favus	1.0	1.0	0.7	0.5
Malignant neoplasms	..	..	864.4	205.4

Source: *Zdraveopazvane, 1971*, op. cit., pp. 13-16

3.7 Number of health establishments in Bulgaria

		1956		1968		1973	
		No.	Beds	No.	Beds	No.	Beds
A.	Hospital establishments						
	Total	1143	34493	197	52729	184	62612
	Hospital	424	30893	190	51750	83	54720
	General	399	27178	153	43554	172	45091
	Orthopaedic and plastic surgery	—	—	1	100	—	—
	Infectious diseases	3	600	1	380	1	427
	Tuberculosis	4	760	12	3090	15	3546
	Paediatrics	3	260	5	490	4	501
	Psychoneurologics	11	1845	12	33067 }	17	4355
	Mental homes	4	250	3	290 }		
	Obstetrics and gynaecology	a	a	3	540	4	800
	Maternity hospitals	710	2655	a	a	a	a
	Hospital/research institutes	9	945	7	979	1 [a]	7892
B.	Outpatient clinics and departments Total	1725	3785	3423	7264	3594	6165
	Outpatient departments, health centres, etc.	1595	802	3307	4129	3437	2017
	Independent outpatient urban clinics	24	60	27	4	28	13
	Stomatological outpatient clinics	14	—	29	—	29	—
	Dispensaries	92	2923	60	3131	61	3591
	Tuberculosis	50	2068	16	1040	15	860
	Venereal	13	260	12	380	12	530
	Oncological	13	290	12	1169	12	1351
	Psychoneurological	13	305	11	542	11	856
	Curative physical medicine	3	—	9	—	11	—
C.	Children's establishments						
	Total	157	6900	468	30878	742	49490
	Permanent nurseries	141	5780	437	28560	709	46316
	Homes for mother and child	16	1120	31	2318	33	3174
D.	Resort establishments						
	Total	133	8563	166	15341	193	17202
	Sanatoria for pulmonary tuberculosis	19	2955	16	2620	12 [b]	1895
	Non-tuberculosis sanatoria	23	2940	45	10275	51	12018
	Others	91	2668	105	2446	130	3289

3.7 (cont)

	1956		1968		1973	
	No.	Beds	No.	Beds	No.	Beds
E. Other hospital establishments						
Total	138	53	35	55	52	95
First aid stations	2	—	3	—	3	—
Blood transfusion units	1	—	4	—	4	—
Isolation centres	8	53	15	55	12	55
Sanitary epidemiological centres	126	—	12	—	30	—
Institute for health education	1	—	1	—	1	—

Source: Direct communication and *Statistical Yearbook, 1969*, pp. 250-1; *1974*, pp. 374-5

a   See text for explanation of reclassification
b   Data missing for three hospitals in this group

3.8 Medical staff in Bulgaria

	1956	1960	1965	1967	1968	1970	1973
Physicians	9271	11051	13593	14475	14938	15819	17601
Dentists	2085	2393	2882	3013	3075	3111	3484
Feldshers	1560	2865	4161	4487	4697	4994	5067
Midwives	2174	3364	4529	4996	5321	5839	6435
Nurses	8574	12502	19026	21743	22950	25265	29681

Source: *Statistical Yearbook, 1969*, p. 252; *1974*, p. 376

3.9 Physician specialization in Bulgaria

	1968	*1970*
Internal	2977	3205
Surgery	1397	1459
Gynaecology	861	904
Paediatrics	1437	1559
Ophthalmology	319	358
Oto-rhinology	350	384
Neurology	471	532
Psychiatry	291	320
Tuberculosis	669	685
Dermato-venereology	284	293
Radiology	585	625
Physiotherapy	270	286
Sport medicine	102	108
Laboratory research	303	333
Public health	382	373
Epidemiology	172	187
Parasitology	39	45
Microbiology	324	374
Total	14938	15819

Source: Direct communication for 1968; *Zdraveopazvane, 1971*, op. cit., p. 99 for 1970

3.10 Finance of health care in Bulgaria

Millions of post-1962 leva

	Govern-ment	Social Insurance	Direct (on pharma-ceuticals)	Total outlay	of which	
					Capital	Per cent
1960	124.4	(0.3)	(5.8)	(130.5)	20.6	(16)
1965	162.3	(0.4)	(8.6)	(171.3)	24.4	(14)
1970	282.1	(0.5)	(12.6)	(295.2)	57.3	(19)
1972	334.1	(0.6)	(14.0)	(348.7)	57.6	(17)
1973	385.9	(0.6)	(16.0)	(402.5)	60.5	(15)

Source: *Statistical Yearbook, 1974*, pp. 71, 100 for government and capital finance; direct expenditure on pharmaceuticals 1970-3 estimated as half the total sales of Pharmakhim (*Ikonomicheski zhivot*, 20 August 1975, p. 1) with 8 per cent growth assumed back to 1960 (the rate used for a long-term projection); estimated use of prostheses assumed to be reimbursed wholly by the Social Insurance Fund

NOTE: No data are available cn outlay by enterprises

4 CZECHOSLOVAKIA

I. Legislation and Policy

The Industrial Revolution for Central-East Europe began in the Czech Lands and growth of an industrial labour force was soon followed by the creation of a compulsory social insurance scheme. Established under the Austro-Hungarian Empire (in the Czech Lands, then ruled from Vienna, in 1888 and in Slovakia, then governed from Budapest, in 1907), it provided assistance for workers and their families in old age, disability, illness, maternity and death. As wage-earning replaced peasant farming in the Czech Lands during the years of the First Republic, 1919-39, coverage by health insurance increased substantially, but not equally. The system was over-organized and had a multiplicity of insurance agencies, divided into separate branches for health, accidents and old-age pension, lacking uniformity in contribution rates, benefits and qualifications for benefits. The chief obstacles to the establishment of an integrated social security system were the vested interests in the level of benefit of individual institutions and their members. However, gradual progress towards centralization was being made after the establishment of a Central Social Insurance Institute, concentrating the major part of health contributions, and a General Pension Institute, responsible for most of the pension insurance administration. A further factor in differentiating access to health care was that the system of social insurance failed to provide compulsory insurance against unemployment. The number of persons with voluntary insurance against unemployment was 1,373,000 in November 1932, while the maximum figure of registered unemployed was 920,000 in February 1933, of which about a quarter of a million were supported by the State-subsidized 'Ghent' type of unemployment relief through the trade unions. Household income was thus severely reduced in periods of economic depression.

After September 1938 (the Munich Agreement ceding the western borderlands to Germany), Czechoslovak social security institutions lost one-third of their members and, after March 1939 (the declaration of Slovak independence and the occupation of the Czech Lands by Germany and of Ruthenia by Hungary) a further half. In the German Protectorate of Bohemia and Moravia, the various trade unions were merged into a Workers' Union Centre and the 'Ghent' system of social relief was replaced by unemployment insurance and provided, after March 1940, unemployment allowances for redundant workers.

Health services, provided on direct payment or through insurance

114

schemes, were the best in Eastern Europe. In 1937 there were already 11,851 physicians in the present territory of Czechoslovakia (i.e. excluding Ruthenia, which was incorporated in the USSR in 1945), or 1,219 inhabitants per physician. Infantile mortality, 160 per 1,000 live births in 1920-4, dropped to 111 in 1935-9 and the improvements in social services during the Second World War actually cut it further to 106 in 1940-4.

When independence was restored (Prague was the last European capital to be freed from German occupation), the number of physicians was only slightly below the pre-war level and health standards, if again gauged by infantile mortality (at a 1945-9 mean of 100), were a little better. The postwar coalition government had been forced in February 1948 to cede control to the Communist Party, whose policies favouring the workers at the expense of the middle class and peasantry were implemented in social services that same year.

The National Insurance Act of 1948 established a comprehensive social insurance scheme divided into a pension/income insurance and a sickness/maternity insurance. It eliminated the large discrepancies which had hitherto existed between the benefits of salaried employees and of workers, but restricted benefits and new advantageous rates of contribution to employees and workers of the state sector and, later, to members of 'higher-type' cooperative farms.

There was considerable discussion within the Communist Party in 1948 over the subordination of the services. Some would have preferred the health service to be administered by a Ministry of Social Services incorporating the social insurance system, others sought the creation of an operational Ministry of Health. One of the arguments against the former was that the insurance origin would be manifest in the 'economist's approach', such that services would be developed only if they were in some way economically justified. The argument for the latter was that the service would by physician-orientated if it were within a specialist Ministry of Health. The path chosen — one more readily taken because it was also the Soviet model — was that the senior administrative staff were in the main medically qualified. The Soviet administrative example was more explicitly followed in 1951 when ambulatory and public health establishments were integrated with hospitals on a territorial basis.

Transfer from an insurance to a citizen entitlement was effected under the Law on the Health Care of the People, Act No. 20 of the National Assembly of 17 March 1966. The then Minister of Health, J. Plojhar, called the measure that of 'the first country of the world' to operate a comprehensive service and to assure its implementation 'by all authorities, agencies and organizations, as well as individuals, in the development of the national economy and culture'.[1] Priority is assured in Comecon, since the relevant Soviet law was passed three years, and the Bulgarian constitutional provision five years, later.

The Law has two crucial articles in this regard. Article V of the Preamble ('Main Principles') affirms that 'health care is provided by the State free of charge to all citizens' while section I (1) of Part One ('Creation and Protection of Healthy Living and Working Conditions') specifies that 'all enterprises, cooperatives and other organizations have the duty to take within their competence all necessary measures to create and protect healthy living and working conditions and are responsible for the implementation of these duties'.

In January 1969, consequent upon the federalization of the republic under a new constitution, each of the two Republics, Czech and Slovakian, was endowed with competence in health matters, concisely in 'training, protection and promotion of healthy living and working conditions, control of communicable diseases'. Each republic has since had its own Ministry of Health, whereas before, under section 73 of the 1966 Law, virtually the only devolution was that 'the Slovak National Council participates in the implementation of the present Act'. This was much the same wording as section 10 which noted that 'The Revolutionary Trade Union Movement also participates in the control and supervision of health care of the people'.[2] Since 1948 the trade unions (ROH) have had a specific contributory function in running the unified social insurance scheme (for risks other than ill-health or disability) as well as sanatoria and rest-homes, a division of responsibilities that parallels Soviet practice.

II. Demographic pattern

At the census of March 1961 the population of Czechoslovakia was 13.75 million (of which 9.57 million were in the Czech Lands and 4.17 million in Slovakia) and by the decennial census of December 1970 it had reached 14.36 million or 133,000 short of that predicted by birth and death rates (and of which 100,000 may be accounted for by the 1968-9 emigration). The 1974 estimate is of 14.69 million.

The slow rate of demographic growth is primarily attributable to low fertility: the postwar decline in the crude birth rate from 1950 to 1968 was much faster than the average for Comecon states in Europe, though at 14.9 per 1,000 the rate in 1968 was not the lowest in the area. The birth rate in the Czech Lands was then 13.9 per 1,000, almost the same as it had been in 1960, whereas in Slovakia it was 17.0 against 22.1 in 1960. Slovakia, more rural and less industrially developed, showed the greater downward trend as it urbanized in the sixties.

Since 1968, however, the birth rate has turned markedly upward and reached 17.2 per 1,000 in 1972 and 19.8 in 1974, the second highest among the European members of Comecon (see Table 1.2). The annual rate in 1975 was estimated at some 21.6 per 1,000,[3] which would be a return to that prevailing in 1953 and well above the mean for the thirties (18.4 per 1,000). Mortality, on the other hand, is well below that of the thirties, when it was 13.5 against 11.7 in 1974, but recent levels are considerably more than the low-point of 9.2 per 1,000 reached in 1960-1. The greater ageing of the Czech population than of the Slovak has brought up the Federation's crude death rates while maintaining overall a favourable age-specific mortality.

The recovery of the birth rate can chiefly be attributed to a pronatalist government, of which a positive recent feature has been maternity allowances for the first two years of a child's life; though the decline (since 1972) in the number of women aged 15-30 is seen as an argument for more such incentives to parenthood.[4] Policy towards abortion, now again restrictive, has also been a significant factor.

Table 4.1 shows the leap in legal abortions following the enactment of a law of 19 December 1957, which greatly extended the grounds justifying an interruption of pregnancy (provided that the woman was less than three months pregnant and had not aborted within the previous six months). Since 1 August 1950 induced abortion had been a criminal offence, punishable by one-year imprisonment for the pregnant woman and up to ten years for accomplices. The 1957 law legalized abortion on medical grounds and for 'other reasons deserving special consideration', which, by amendments made between 1962 and 1966 came to include the unmarried state or advanced age of the woman, three or more living children and a difficult family situation (including death or disability of the husband). Though not explicitly stated in law, abortion was permitted for a woman prescribed a contraceptive device or pill who nevertheless conceived. In 1967 when abortions were near a peak 92 per cent of applications were approved, and abortions represented 36 per cent of completed pregnancies; the average age of the single women concerned was 22 and of married women, 30; 31 per cent of women aborting already had 2 children, 21 per cent one and 17 per cent none. The ready availability of pregnancy interruption, coupled with the relatively high cost and small extent of contraceptives, put terminations for family situations far above health indications as the stated reason. Thus 26 per cent were said to be because the mother had three living children and 19 per cent because of the financial or living conditions of the household, while 22 per cent were for considerations of health.[5] By 1970 health reasons were down to 20 per cent.[6]

Restrictive policies were introduced in 1973. The period within which a repeated abortion was forbidden was doubled (to twelve months) and permission was to be given for abortion of married women with no or one child only 'in exceptional cases'. The advantages of, and facilities for, contraception were officially promoted.[7] Already in 1973 the ratio of abortions to completed pregnancies dropped to 28.7.[8]

The Czech suction method of abortion — adapted from a Chinese technique — became widely used in the United Kingdom after the latter's liberalization of abortion. No survey seems to have been made in Czechoslovakia since 1959 of contraceptive practices, when 43 per cent declared the use of coitus interruptus and 17 per cent the condom. While there are 3 million women of child-bearing age, only 70,000 loops had been inserted by 1968 and 80,000 women were on a Czech-made pill (antigest); oral contraceptives have not been as widely requested as health authorities expected and a 1969 survey revealed that many women were anxious about side effects of the pill. On the other hand, the Government was especially concerned about the possible effects of abortion on fertility and gave that as a principal reason for tightening the abortion law in 1973.

Already nearly two-thirds urbanized, the Czechoslovak population is not concentrated in the capital city in the manner of some other Comecon states. Prague's population in 1973 was 1,091,000, three times as large as that of Brno and Bratislava, respectively the chief cities of Moravia (which with Bohemia forms the Czech Lands) and of Slovakia (the smaller of the two federated republics). Prague, the chief city of Bohemia, has in fact grown more slowly over the past half-century than the other five towns which now have over 100,000 population; the biggest expansion has been in towns of 50,000 to 100,000, reflecting the geographic dispersal of the postwar industrial growth.

Bohemia has had the longest experience of industrialization and its population corresponds in social and occupational profile to that of neighbouring Western Germany, though the standard of living — equal thereto before the Second World War — is now significantly below it. Moravia may be compared in the same senses to Austria, and the more agricultural Slovakia to Hungary.

Demographic projections, prepared by the United States Bureau of the Census, and assuming a constant gross reproduction rate at the 1973 level of 115, are shown in Table 4.2. The 1996 population would be 16.65 million with a median age 1.5 years greater than currently. No problems inhibiting access to health care arise from ethnic diversity or illiteracy. The postwar expulsion of Germans and of many Hungarians, and the severance of Ruthenia has left 5.9 per cent of the population as an ethnic minority (3.9 per cent Hungarians, and a few Poles, Germans and Ruthenes). If any illiteracy exists, it might be found in the gypsy encampments of Slovakia (*cikáni*). During the fifties over-compensatory measures were taken to assure full secondary and university education for the children of manual workers. While these have now been cut back to re-establish ability as a weightier criterion than proletarian origin for university admission, the wide availability of pre-school care and the large higher-education placement have probably evened out life chances more in Czechoslovakia than in any other Comecon nation.

III. Health conditions

The readiness of Czechoslovaks to accept what must be the world's most egalitarian health service is a consequence of a levelled-up society with remarkably uniform economic aspirations. There are virtually no pools of backwardness in which outdated attitudes to health needs survive, the use of wealth or position to obtain more medical care than the norm is the least pervasive in East Europe, and the high rate of work absences due to sickness to which attention has been drawn in Chapter 1, reflects less the standard of health than the disutility of work. Already in 1968 they represented a loss of 16.9 days per year, almost exactly the same as in the United Kingdom (15.6 days per man and 18.5 days per woman) allowing for the higher share of females in the Czechoslovak workforce, and were 17.3 days in 1972.

Per cent absence from work for ill-health			
1960	4.03	1969	4.84
1964	4.03	1970	5.13 [a]
1967	4.22	1971	4.53
1968	4.60	1972	3.96

Source: *ČSSR zdravotnictví, 1973*, Table 1.2.3 and *Mlada fronta*, 1 January 1971, p. 2

[a] Influenced by influenza epidemic

The Czechoslovak health service has had 100 per cent coverage of the population since 1966, prior to which social insurance excluded any working on their own account and farmers who were members of only a loose cooperative. The sole limitation to the free provision assured by the 1966 Law (already quoted in Section I) is that 'the Ministry of Health may specify that in exceptional cases payment may be required for the provision of certain health services which are not indispensable' (Part III, Ch. 1). Czechoslovak citizens abroad are reimbursed the entire cost of their medical treatment if they are on government service (which in an all-embracing socialist state covers, for example, most business trips) and the equivalent of what treatment in Czechoslovakia would have cost if their travel is for other purposes. Foreigners have the right to free health services in Czechoslovakia if covered under bilateral reciprocal treatment agreements (that of 23 April 1976 for the UK).

The long-term health policy of the government comprises four principal features. First, the gradual ageing of the population will require more hospitalization, for which the solution is being sought within an overall scheme of hospital consolidation and re-equipment. Secondly, the national urgency of the need for higher labour productivity requires stress on the use of advanced rehabilitation techniques after illness or accident. This policy is part of a more general trend envisaged by the Ministry of Health to update hospital practice in four areas in which deficiencies are currently felt — viz. resuscitation techniques; artificial renal equipment; neuro- and cardio-surgery; and diagnostic and examination procedures (especially biochemical, radio-isotope, ionization and electronic). Thirdly, the evolving structure of morbidity will have to be met by enlarging facilities for chronic and psychiatric diseases, and for traffic injuries while restricting those for conditions of declining incidence, exemplified in tuberculosis, poliomyelitis and streptococcicosis. Finally some expansion and realignment of the physician strength will be needed. At 26 physicians per 10,000 inhabitants the situation is broadly satisfactory, but more general practitioners are now needed (only 16 per cent in 1973), and in 1971 the government launched a long-term study on the utilization of physicians and their territorial deployment.

The Minister of Health may license in private practice outstanding specialists and retired physicians whose pension is adjudged insufficient. 'Dental surgeons' may similarly be licensed as on retirement but the lower-qualified 'dentist' — who is no longer being trained — is allowed a private surgery, though it is restricted to conservation and prosthetic operations. The Ministry of Health considers all these as of scant practical consequence. No nurses or other medical personnel work outside the health service and there are no privately-run health facilities or pharmacies. Some non-qualified practitioners still offer their services in the tradition of the so-called 'miracle doctor' (*zázračný doktor*): one in particular, Mikulášek, is a naturopathic urologist. Slovak shepherds (*bača*) have traditionally engaged in bone-setting and in naturo-manipulative therapy. Self-medication is quite usual, both in the use by popular custom of herbal infusions and in the purchase of non-prescription medicines. The latter avoids both a long wait at the physician's surgery and the queue at the pharmacy (which, where business is considerable, has separate service hatches for prescriptions and non-prescribed items).

In a review of 1970, relating to 1968-9 incidence, the Ministry of Health ranked respiratory infections (mainly influenza and acute inflammation of the upper respiratory tract) as the largest cause of work disability and as third in mortality and in morbidity. Diseases of the cardiovascular system (mainly ischaemic heart disease and affections of the cerebral vessels) were the chief cause of death and of invalidity. Accidents, poisoning and the consequences of violence were the second cause of work disability, the fourth cause of death and the fifth in morbidity. Diseases of the digestive tract were the third cause of disability as measured by occurrence and the fourth by days of absence, the fifth cause of death and the eighth of invalidity; affections of the bone and organs of movement ranked second in morbidity, third in work disability in days and fourth in disability by occurrence. Neoplasms were second in mortality and seventh in morbidity. Diseases of the nerve and sense systems constituted the fifth cause of work disability by occurrence and the sixth both by days of absence and by morbidity. Urinary and venereal diseases ranked as the eighth by days of absence. Infections and parasitic diseases — especially tuberculosis — had fallen to the ninth cause of morbidity and the tenth of mortality. Mental disturbance of all kinds was the fourth cause of morbidity, the ninth of disability by days of absence and the tenth by occurrence.

A survey among physicians suggested the following rank order of causes of consultation: pharyngitis (including that in children); heart conditions; bronchitis and complications; conditions (including gall stones) of the digestive tract, of the stomach and of the intestine; diabetes (including both registration and periodic checks); and rheumatism and arthritis (other than collagenosis, which is unimportant). Of the 160,615 deaths recorded in 1972, the main causes, as Table 4.3 (ICD 1965) shows, were ischaemic and other forms of heart diseases (79,232), malignant neoplasms (33,095), diseases of the respiratory system (12,959) and accidents (12,148). The table groups causes per 100,000 population, by those exhibiting a rising, or declining trend.

The communicable diseases most frequently notified in the sixties were: measles, scarlet fever and infectious hepatitis. By 1973, as Table 4.4 shows, inoculation had drastically cut the incidence of measles but, though the two others had declined in the previous decade, the 1970-3 trend was at a higher level. There are a few imported new cases, but malaria is entirely eradicated. The incidence of venereal disease tripled between 1960 and 1968 (from 34.7 to 109.6 per 100,000 population), mainly on account of gonorrhoea (24.8 and 104.1 respectively), which then levelled out (108.4 in 1971, 101.9 in 1974). Syphilis, too, shows a high incidence (66.7 in 1971, 68.2 in 1974), but predominantly in the Czech Lands, where venereal disease overall was 123.0 per 100,000 in 1968, against 62.6 in Slovakia. Slovakia has its own problem in the persistence of trachoma: compared to a per 100,000 incidence of 0.2 in the Czech Lands, the Slovak average was 1.7, and no less than 4.6 in Bratislava and 3.5 in the West Slovak region: it is especially prevalent among children aged from 10 to 14.

New tuberculosis cases fell from 102 per 100,000 in 1964 to 95 in 1968, those among children under 15 declining from 21 to 13 per 100,000 of that age-group, viz. by 60 per cent. The number of active tuberculosis cases declined by 40 per cent in those four years and by 66 per cent among children. A national health characteristic, though of more minor proportions, is the congenital dislocation of the hip-joint. Compulsory x-ray examination of all small children has been instituted, with low radiation-exposure equipment from the GDR.

The 1968 percentages of causes of work disability are set out in Table 4.5.

IV. Health service administration

Section 31 of the 1966 Law lays down that health care institutions be 'organized as a uniform system of health services'. The Ministry of Health must 'specify the concept and outline the main trends of the development of the health services' (section 69), and 'has the right to prohibit the establishment, construction or operation of a health institution which is contrary to (designated) principles' (section 42). Except where otherwise specified, health institutions are established by local authorities, i.e. the regional and district national committees. They run and finance the local service (available to the general public resident in a defined area), the factory service (for workers in a given state enterprise) and the school health service (in conjunction with the Ministry of Education). A few health facilities are operated and funded by the Slovak and Czech Ministries of Health but there is no federal expenditure. Separate services for their own employees are operated by the Ministries of Transport, of Defence and of the Interior and are financed from the appropriate departmental budget. The Ministry of Health 'shall exercise the supreme technical supervision and control of the health services in other branches' (section 70), and all 'Ministries and other central organs have the duty to implement . . . health measures . . . as an integral part of the control of the people's economy and culture' (section 68).

Such integration of economic and social development is a function of government planning which, partly decentralized during the four years to 1 January 1971 (when there was a Ministry of Planning on a par with other departments of state), has thenafter been exercised by the State Planning Commission. The Commission having now resumed effective supra-ministerial status formulates the main lines of Government economic policy, after deliberation by the authorities of the Communist Party. Two Federal Ministries have terms of reference affecting health products, viz. the Ministry for Technical and Investment Development and the Ministry of Foreign Trade, the former having oversight of the 'legal, technico-economic and organizational' aspects of investment policy and choice of technology 'throughout the national economy' and the latter (as previously) a monopoly of foreign trade, to be exercised in conjunction with the State Planning Commission and the appropriate supervising agency at federal or republican level. Specific intervention by the federal authorities is reserved to the People's Control Board, also a federal agency. The health service and the health products industry remain, as since 1 January 1969, under republican administration, though three ministries with peripheral interests in the field are federal, viz. the Ministry of Agriculture and Nutrition (purchase of domestic veterinary products and nutrition policy), the Ministry of Finance (subsidies to the pharmaceutical industry and turnover tax on health products) and the Ministry of Labour and Social Welfare (sickness and maternity benefits).

The Czech Lands and Slovakia have a separate Ministry of Health which operates – with the few exceptions already described – all health facilities, physician and prosthetic manufacture services and supervises the pharmaceutical and medical supplies industry (including veterinary drugs). The Ministry of Industry – until 1 January 1971 entitled the 'Board of Industry' – runs the chemical industry, supplying certain intermediate and raw materials for pharmaceuticals and the medical equipment industry. The Ministries of Health and of Industry set prices (wholesale and retail) for the products under their supervision, subject to overall directives of the Minister in charge of the Federal Price Office; each is responsible for the relevant marketing organizations, retail pharmacies thus forming an integral part of the health service.

The Planning Department of the Ministry of Health is the central policy-making unit within the ministry and formulates drafts for submission to the State Planning Commission of five-year and annual plans; it is the chief link with other government agencies in forward programmes and is in close touch (under the Minister) with the Party units of the Central Committee of the Czechoslovak Communist Party which advise that Committee and its Secretariat.

A council composed of representatives of the Czech and Slovak Ministries of Health meets every two months to coordinate laws, hospital regulations, health service salaries, etc., but each Ministry operates its health service independently.

The local-authority health service was formed in 1951 by the amalgamation of hospital, ambulatory/domiciliary and public health services. It has since been financed wholly from the budgets at the appropriate level, viz. the *Krajský Narodní Výbor* (KNV), regional national committee, and *Okresní Národní Výbor* (ONV), district national committee; the former is administered by a council of the regional national committee responsible for the *Krajský Ústav Národ-*

nlho Zdravl (KÚNZ), the regional institute of health. The Director of
KÚNZ is nominated by the KNV and effectively runs the entire health
service within the region under the authority of the executive head
of the KNV. The regional institute runs the larger hospitals, the regional
blood transfusion depot, regional sanatoria, mental hospitals, the
regional public health service ('hygiene and epidemiological stations')
and the regional health education centre. It has a Pharmaceutical
Department, a regional testing laboratory and regional stores for drugs
and medical appliances.

The regions are divided into some 10 to 12 districts (with an average
population of 12,000) in which the health service of the local authority
(ONV) is operated by the district institute of health, *Okresni Ústav
Národnlho Zdravl* (OÚNZ). Its responsibilities embrace the district
hygiene and epidemiological station, the district health education
centre, and the district blood transfusion centre, the pharmaceutical
service and all health facilities including those in the factory health
service (but not the few under the other ministries specified above).
There are generally 1 to 3 hospitals or hospital-type facilities in a district, an appropriate number of health centres and 1 or occasionally 2
polyclinics. The district is divided into 'health communities' of
approximately 4,000 inhabitants served by the local 'community
physician' and his staff. The pharmaceutical service was brought into
this comprehensive organization in 1960, since when it has operated
under the pharmaceutical service of the district institute of health.

Administratively unified, the neat hierarchy just described conceals
much unevenness. The KÚNZ has in practice a great deal of autonomy
and local politics and interests have worked against the application of
uniform policies. Seventeen large industrial concerns have their own
'factory institute of health' (Závodni ÚNZ), all − save for the uranium
mines and for corrective-education workshops − subordinate to the
local OÚNZ (or its municipal equivalent, MÚNZ).

The two Republican Ministries of Health seek to modify regional
differentials and the major programme, already referred to, which
has set up five big teaching-hospital complexes across the country
(Košice, Bratislava, Brno, Prague and Pilsen) was intended as the spearhead of the policy. The State Social Insurance Board (*Státni úřad
sociálnlho zabezpečeni*) and the Trade Union Council, *Revolučni
Odborové Hutni* (ROH) jointly run the social security system.

V.   Health-care facilities

A detailed listing of the main facilities of the Ministries of Health and
of Transport is given in Table 4.6. The pattern of change in the sixties
followed, by and large, that of health needs earlier described. The
number of general hospital beds has increased substantially but in

slightly larger hospitals; in contradistinction to the trend of need, the number of psychiatric beds has scarcely changed, though their staffing has been improved. While the number of hospitals and beds therein for respiratory complaints has expectedly diminished, that for cancer cases has increased (though with only one new specialized hospital).

Karlovy Vary in Bohemia has been a spa since 1359 and Pleštany in Slovakia had three Emperors and a Pope as patients in the sixteenth century. The analyses of Jakob Berzelius in the eighteenth century made the country's spas famous throughout Europe and 'the waters' of Carlsbad (Karlovy Vary) and Marienbad (Mariánské Lázně) became in the nineteenth century as much social as health resorts. In 1968 8 903 patients were treated from socialist countries (mostly from the GDR) and 6,592 from the rest of the world (in largest numbers from Western Germany). The Preissnítz Sanatorium at the Jeseník Spa in Moravia is widely known for the treatment of neuroses. Improvement in the health service is best reflected in the growth of the number of local health centres open to the general public, physician posts therein increasing from 10,487 in 1960 to 16,074 in 1973, while the number of health centres in industrial and similar enterprises (the 'factory health service') was 2,200 and 3,476 in the respective years. The pharmacy service was, on the other hand, consolidated into fewer establishments in the decade following its incorporation and unified financing within the district institutes of health in 1960.

Smaller specialist institutes not separately listed in Table 4.6 include two for human nutrition (95 beds), two for rheumatological research (126 beds), and one each for clinical and experimental surgery (102), for cardiovascular research (74), for the care of mother and child (146), for experimental therapy (45), for haematology and blood-transfusion (42), for traumatology (55), for physiotherapy, balneology and climatology (104), and for the application of radio-isotopes in medicine (10 beds); one for silicosis was closed in 1966.

Outpatient facilities comprised 415 polyclinics in addition to the local health centres already noted: about three-quarters were for the 'local' and the remainder for the 'factory' service. Specialized outpatient facilities operating in 1968 included 2,632 child health centres, 145 pre-natal clinics, 438 dental health units, 277 psychiatric clinics.

The 211 public health laboratories carried out 63,353 examinations in 1968, and, apart from pharmaceutical and research laboratories, there were 198 clinical laboratories (a tripling of the 1960 number of 68); in addition there were 8 haematological laboratories. The number of clinical procedures for 1968 and 1972 and immunizations (including re-immunizations) for 1967 are shown in Table 4.7.

The rapid extension of the health service to 100 per cent coverage since the Second World War involved much improvisation, many facilities being installed in buildings not intended for hospitals or poly-clinics — in some cases in large country houses and in castles. While this non-purpose accommodation was mostly required in the previously under-supplied Slovakia and Southern Moravia, the attraction of popu-lation to Prague necessitated conversion there also of blocks of flats or substantial houses. These facilities now require consolidation and housing in functional buildings, and some further equalization by region. Thus Southern Moravia still has only 7 hospital beds per 1,000 population whereas Southern and Eastern Bohemia have already reached the 'ideal norm' of 9.4 beds. A list of the best-equipped hospi-tals is set out in Table 4.8: the hospital construction programme (as distinct from reconstruction) is currently concentrated in Slovakia and Northern Moravia, but, in addition to the recent Motol Children's hospital (see Table), Prague has been afforded new hospitals at Vyso-čany and Brevnev.

The hospital programme divides establishments into three levels. At the top, and with the best possible equipment and facilities for all specializations, are teaching hospitals, of which there must be one (occasionally two) in each of the ten *kraj* (region) into which the country is divided (Prague and Bratislava rank administratively each as a *kraj*). At the second level, there should be a 'super-district' hospital serving a group of 3 to 4 districts (*okres*, the subdivision of a *kraj*), each hospital having 12 basic and certain specialist departments. At the lowest level each of the 109 *okres* would have a small 'country' hospi-tal, serving 1 to 1½ million inhabitants, those of the second 150,000 to 200,000 and of the third about 50,000 (two being established for larger districts). The implementation of this programme would reduce the number of general hospitals from the 258 of 1969 to about 160, viz.

One country hospital for each *okres* (109)	109
One general hospital for a group of 3 *okres*	36
One teaching hospital for each *kraj* (12)	12
	157

Table 4.9 states the numbers of physicians in the main specializations in 1968 and 1973, representing 22.4 and 25.5 respectively per 10,000 population, against 17.5 in 1960. In 1968 82.4 per cent worked for the local authority health service, 8.2 for the Ministry of Education (chiefly the schools health service), 2.0 for research institutes, 1.8 for 'budget financed organizations centrally administered' (viz. the Ministries of

Health, of Defence and of the Interior, which administers the police, the security services and the frontier guards), 1.7 in spas, 1.2 for the Ministry of Transport, 1.1 for social insurance, 0.9 in the Academy of Sciences, 0.3 in production enterprises run by the Ministry of Health (Spofa), 0.2 in local authority administration and 0.1 per cent for the trade unions.

Total employment in the health service in 1972 was 251,392 (including staff in spas), of which 39,591 had higher, 102,417 had middle and 11,650 lower qualifications; ancillary staff numbered 10,645, 1,715 were 'teachers' and 85,374 were classed 'workers'. A further 19,592 were employed by the Ministry in the pharmaceutical industry (mostly in Spofa).

The 'several hundreds' of physicians who left the country after the 1968 invasion were criticized for 'taking with them hundreds of millions of crowns invested in their education'.[9] As a consequence by early 1971 30 out of 2,727 local health centres in the Czech Lands were still unstaffed, a further 46 were only provisionally manned, and the number of physicians per 10,000 population remained constant in 1970 at the 1968 level of 22.4. New graduates rapidly filled the gap and the 1973 ratio cited above was already that approved by the XIVth Congress of the Czechoslovak Communist Party in April 1971 as the targets for 1975 (25.5). The Plan Directives also provided that the increment in medical personnel would be concentrated on the improvement of the outpatient service (*ambulantní služby*), so as to reduce patient waiting time.

Two economic considerations lie behind the need to accelerate the outpatient service: first, the general shortage of manpower and, second, the consequent high rate of female participation in the workforce. The improvement of ambulatory and domiciliary care can make a particular contribution in the case of short-term sickness: the sick absence rate in the first half of 1970 rose to just on 7 per cent as a result of an influenza epidemic. The effects of industrial accidents, 320,000 per annum, can also be shortened by early and more frequent attention during disability: their cost to the economy in 1970 was estimated by the trade union newspaper to be 5,000 million kčs (some $400 million).[10]

During the sixties wage employment rose by 513,000 persons but of these 490,000 were women and only 23,000 were men, by 1970 raising the proportion of women in the economically active population to 44.8 per cent (within 48.4 per cent for both sexes). This pressure on women to enter the labour force — more marked in Czechoslovakia than anywhere else in Europe — is a severe constraint upon the possibility of a patient staying at home when ill, for either the patient has no one to care for him or her or a family member must stay away from work to provide care. The availability of home calls by physicians or of home nursing would reduce both the load on hospitals and the period of work absence.

The engagement of women in industrial occupations and the great scarcity of domiciliary nurses are facets of the decline in the ratio of medical nurses to physicians, which in 1968 was 1.27 against 1.64 in 1949.

The main paramedical occupations are shown in Table 4.10. The fastest increases during 1963-72 were indicative of technological change (e.g. of x-ray assistants). The substitution of pharmacists by pharmacy assistants contrasted with the abandonment of the one grade which corresponds to the 'feldsher', viz. the lower-qualified dentist (who, as stated, is no longer being trained), there being no other medical assistants of the feldsher type in Czechoslovakia. As the lower dentists are phased out they are replaced by a combination of fully qualified practitioners and ancillary 'dental nurses', the numbers of which are expanding rapidly; increased prescription of prostheses has similarly enlarged employment as dental mechanics. The few middle-trained opticians have by now all retired, and the national eye service is now staffed by fully qualified personnel. In line with the priorities earlier noted, the various therapist grades have been particularly dynamic, a trend which will be accentuated in the future.

In 1972 physicians undertook 142.8 million consultations in the local health service and 27.2 million in the factory health service (both of which operate within the local authority service as termed above); they were so engaged for 83.9 per cent of their duty time. The number of consultations made per hour (see Table 4.11) was in 1968 the same in each service, but showed a tendency to decline in both over time. The number of gynaecological consultations in the outpatient departments of polyclinics and in women's welfare centres was 5.9 million; and of paediatric consultations in the same and in children's welfare centres was 14.8 million; physicians devoted 0.73 million hours to the school health services, to which school matrons (*školní dětské sestry*) contributed a further 1.20 million hours. There were 20.1 million dental treatments for adults and 6.5 million for children, practitioners (of both qualification levels) spending 91.8 per cent of their duty time in actual treatment. Consultations in psychiatric departments of polyclinics were 0.87 million, and 0.13 million in alcoholism treatment centres. Domiciliary visits are kept to a minimum, in 1968 0.55 million being paid to pregnant women, but no data were separately shown for all patients.

The 115,520 hospital beds available in 1972 were occupied for 84.7 per cent of the time, and provided a total of 33.29 million days hospitalization. Table 4.12 shows (for departments which nationally aggregated more than 1,000 beds) bed numbers in 1968, occupancy and average duration of stay: the occupancy of the 6,716 maternity beds (under obstetric in that Table) was 60.2 per cent for an average duration of 6.7 days.

As already indicated, the main impulse of the hospital expansion drive took place in the first decade and a half after the Second World War, as the bed numbers in Table 4.13 show. The target of the fourth Five-Year Plan, 1966-70, 177,620 by 1970, was not gained until 1974 (see Table 4.13), and the Plan for 1976-80 set a range of between 193,000 and 195,000 for 1980. The additional beds are particularly needed to relieve bottlenecks in certain areas. Although among Eastern Slovak hospitals there were occupancies of 63 per cent (1968) and 51 (1972), in others elsewhere occupancy exceeded bed capacity:[11]

	1968	*1972*
OÚNZ Prague No. 3 (Žižkov)	102.3	100.6
ÚNZ Prague 8 (Bulovka)	100.9	81.3
OÚNZ Dolný Kubín	100.6	92.9
OÚNZ Nové Zámky	93.1	101.8

VI. Finance of health care

The Law of 1966, as already noted, made the provision of health care free to all Czechoslovak citizens. The main health service under regional and district national committees is financed through those committees, and those directly under the Ministry of Health and other ministries are funded by the relevant departmental budget, all from taxation. Section 40 of the 1966 Law states that 'enterprises and other organizations must build enterprise health facilities from their own financial means as part of the uniform system of health services and according to specified types. They must also cover the costs of the maintenance and some costs associated with the operation of these facilities.'[12] A United States physician visiting Czechoslovakia in the mid-sixties found that 'in general, the material resources and standards of service in the factory units are comparable to those for the general community. However in certain of the more interested and "wealthier" industries, such as mining and steel, supplements to the public health appropriations make extra services or equipment possible.'[13]

The 1966 Law permits payment to be required for 'certain health services which are not indispensable' (section 11) and the visitor just cited was told that these included 'certain legally-required blood tests and costs of emergency treatment for inebriation'.[14]

The patient or person under prophylactic treatment is required to pay for the use of medically indicated services only under three heads. First, if he is a citizen of a country without a reciprocal health service treaty with Czechoslovakia; secondly a 1 kčs (Czechoslovak crown) 'handling charge' on purchase of every retail prescription; this charge was introduced in 1964 and relates to pharmaceuticals, materials, appliances and prostheses except that, thirdly, a higher charge is made in dental prosthetics (including gold fillings) if the patient desires a prosthesis exceeding the standard provision; a charge is made for spectacle-frames and for hearing-aids other than the standard provision (e.g. hearing aids fitted into spectacle holders, transistorized aids).

The role played by the National Insurance (*Národní Pojištění*) is restricted in the health sphere to sickness and injury benefit and retirement pensions; membership is extended to all employees of state enterprises and members of craft, consumer and farm cooperatives and of specified professions (writers, artists, scientific workers, architects, etc.). In 1968 membership was 6,962,000 while insurable employment totalled 6,672,000 (the difference arising from those on sickness absence and unemployed). National insurance membership in those employments is also valid for retirement pensions to which, following a change in regulations of 1966, a further 36,800 were insured in 1968 as members with respect to self-employment (out of a total of 170,000 self-employed, mainly very small farmers). Premia for insurable employees is paid entirely by the employing enterprise or cooperative; but has had regularly to be supplemented by subsidies from general taxation. In 1970, however, premia were sharply increased to 25 per cent of the payroll, a measure intended not only to staunch the Insurance Fund deficit but to absorb profits in what was then an inflationary situation.

An inter-agency working party (in which the present writer was a participant) convened by the WHO during 1958-61 included Czechoslovakia in a comparison of health service finance.[15] Abel-Smith, the principal consultant, compiled, with the collaboration of the officials of the countries concerned, the data shown for 1958 in Table 1.6. The classification, notably of social insurance and privately borne payments, was not the same as reported in later *Statistical Yearbooks* with respect to the former and by Penkava with respect to the latter. Abel-Smith reported payments to medical care only by Social Insurance, whereas Table 4.14 comprises all health outlay including all balneological services. Hence the increase from 7 per cent finance in 1958 to 23 per cent in 1973 (Table 1.6) is partly due to reclassification of items under 'government' in the data derived from (but not so given by) Abel-Smith. Penkava reports that in 1962 5.7 per cent of expenditure on health was paid directly by persons, rising to 6.5 per cent in 1972. He attributes the proportionate rise to the introduction of the 'handling charge' in 1964, and to higher spending on 'paid medical services of non-essential and luxury nature and the introduction of charges for medical certificates of health fitness to drive a car'.[16] He pointed out that the handling charge of 1 kčs (which can cover two medicaments on any one prescription) represented in 1972 only 2.7 per cent of the value of gratis medicaments, that the certificate of medical fitness is free for pensioners and that some of the non-essential treatment is for cosmetic surgery or costly dental plates.

The handling charge on prescriptions made up free works out proportionately at about half of that imposed by the 20p payment per prescription under the NHS in the United Kingdom; the vast bulk of direct purchases of pharmaceuticals are those bought 'over the counter' without prescription. Direct payments would cover at one extreme occasional exigencies for illegal abortions — a publicized case in Bratislava cited 1,200 kčs as paid in 1972 for the latter[17] — and at the other extreme conventional gifts in kind to country doctors, but in between there is remarkably little in the way of informal presents to secure particular services.

Expenditure by the local authority health service is shown in Table 4.15. It is entirely financed by taxation, as is that at the level of the two Republican Ministries of Health. Outlay in 1968 by organization is shown in Table 4.16, when the Ministry of Health was still a central agency and only certain outlays were effected by the Slovak National Council; from 1969, the central ministry was replaced by two Republican Ministries of Health, for the Czech Lands and for Slovakia. It will be seen from the 1972 returns below[18] that, despite devolution, Slovak spending bore a slightly lower ratio to the national total than did its population (31.8 per cent); outlay on pharmaceuticals by the health service in 1972 was 123 kčs per head in Slovakia and 136 kčs in the Czech Lands.

	Czech Lands	Slovakia	Total
Millions of kčs at current prices			
Aggregate			
Ministry	615	326	941
Local	9565	4002	13567
	10180	4328	14508
Recurrent			
Ministry	539	294	833
Local	8562	3464	12026
	9101	3758	12859

In comparing the outlays in current prices shown in Table 4.15 account should be taken of a 47 per cent rise in prices for capital goods used by the health service (in the general wholesale price reform of 1 January 1967), partly offset by a reduction of pharmaceutical prices exactly a year previously (the health service using retail prices in its accounts). Because of this cut, real outlay on pharmaceuticals rose faster in the sixties as shown in Table 4.17, and faster than equipment purchases (also in real terms), but the increment was less than might be expected from the experience of other countries with access to increasingly sophisticated medication. An estimated breakdown of health product sales is made in Table 4.18 and data derived from it and Penkava's paper, just mentioned, are put together in Table 4.14. Government Social Insurance Fund and private spending aggregated in 1973 to 21,954 kčs, of which 70 per cent was from Government. Research and development expenditure in 1968 was 50.2 million kčs, of which 36.9 million was carried out in the health service and 13.3 million in the pharmaceutical industry.

REFERENCES

1.   J. Plojhar, 'Introduction', *On Health Care of the People of the Czechoslovak Socialist Republic*, Prague, 1966, p. 5
2.   *On Health Care of the People of the Czechoslovak Republic*, pp. 71 and 25 respectively
3.   *Svĕt práce*, 22 January 1975
4.   *Hospodářské noviny*, 26 April 1974
5.   Institute of Health Statistics, *ČSSR zdravotnictví, 1969*, Prague and Bratislava, 1969, p. 26 (data for 1968)
6.   *Právny obzor*, No. 9, 1972
7.   *Tvorba*, 6 June 1973
8.   *Zdravotnicke noviny*, 3 October 1974
9.   *Tribuna*, 3 February 1971
10.   *Svĕt pracé*, 24 March 1971
11.   *ČSSR zdravotnictví, 1969* and *1973*
12.   *On Health Care*, op. cit., pp. 45 and 27 respectively
13.   E. R. Weinerman, *Social Medicine in Eastern Europe*, Cambridge, Mass., 1969, p. 53
14.   Ibid., p. 46
15.   B. Abel-Smith, *Paying for Health Services* (Public Health Papers 17), WHO, Geneva, 1963
16.   J. Penkava, 'Financing of Health Care in Eastern Europe', paper read to the International Institute for Public Finance, Nice, 1975 (mimeograph), p. 9
17.   *Novo slovo*, 26 October 1972, cited in *La Documentation Française*, No. 275, 9 January 1976, p. 17
18.   *ČSSR zdravotnictví, 1973*, Prague and Bratislava, 1973, p. 215

TABLES

4.1 Rates of births and abortions per 1,000 population in Czechoslovakia

	Abortions	Births		Abortions	Births
1953	2.4	21.2	1963	7.1	16.9
1954	2.6	20.6	1964	7.0	17.1
1955	2.7	20.3	1965	7.4	16.4
1956	2.5	19.8	1966	8.1	15.6
1957	2.8	18.9	1967	8.4	15.1
1958	6.7	17.4	1968	8.6	14.9
1959	7.7	16.0	1969	8.6	15.5
1960	8.4	15.9	1970	8.6	15.9
1961	8.7	15.8	1971	8.5	16.5
1962	8.4	15.7	1972	8.3	17.4
			1973	7.6	18.9

Source: H. P. David, *Family Planning and Abortion in the Socialist Countries of Central and Eastern Europe*, New York, 1970, p. 163 and *Statistická ročenka ČSSR* (hereafter, *Statistical Yearbook*), *1975*, pp. 109, 121

4.2 Demographic projections for Czechoslovakia

	1971	*1981*	*1996*
Total population (millions)	14.41	15.40	16.65
Per cent aged 0-14 years	23.0	24.3	23.2
15-39 years	36.8	37.5	35.3
40-64 years	28.8	26.3	29.7
65 years and over	11.5	12.0	11.8
Median age (years)	31.8	32.0	33.4
Males per 100 females	95.0	95.0	95.4

Source: P. F. Myers, 'Population and Labor Force in Eastern Europe, 1950 to 1996', in US Congress Joint Economic Committee, *Reorientation and Commercial Relations of the Economies of Eastern Europe*, Washington, D.C., 1974, pp. 434, 463 (series B projection)

4.3 Causes of death in Czechoslovakia

	Number of deaths		Rate per 100,000 population				Percentage of mortality	
	1969	1972	1960	1969	1972	1973	1969	1972
A. *Group of causes exhibiting an increase*								
VII Diseases of the circulatory system (390-458)	78231	79232	306.5	541.7	547.1	568.8	48.5	49.3
II Neoplasms (140-239)	31469	33095	184.3	217.9	228.5	228.5	19.5	20.6
VIII Diseases of the respiratory system (460-519)	15714	12959	81.5	108.3	89.5	110.9	9.7	8.1
XVII Accidents, injuries, etc. (E800-E999)	12736	12148	71.9	88.1	84.0	81.9	7.9	7.6
IX Diseases of the digestive system (520-577)	6257	6896	35.2	43.4	47.6	47.8	3.9	4.3
X Diseases of the genito-urinary system (580-629)	3795	3979	16.9	26.2	27.5	28.1	2.3	2.5
XV Diseases of early infancy (760-779)	2637	2947	17.0	18.2	20.4	22.4	1.6	1.8
B. *Group of causes exhibiting a decrease or insignificant change*								
III Allergic, endocrinal, metabolic and nutritional diseases (240-279)	2709	2574	23.1	18.7	17.8	18.9	1.7	1.6
I Infective and parasitic diseases (000-136)	2083	1474	32.6	15.0	10.2	10.1	1.3	0.9
VI Diseases of the nervous system and sensory organs (320-389)	1492	1278	104.9[a]	10.3	8.8	9.2	0.9	0.8
V Mental, psychoneurotic and personality disorders (290-315)	112	134	2.6	0.8	0.9	0.9	0.07	0.08
XIII Diseases of the bones and organs of movement (710-739)	206	181	2.4	1.4	1.2	0.8	0.1	0.1
XI Deliveries and complications of pregnancy (630-678)	46	44	0.7	0.3	0.3	0.3	0.03	0.03
XII Diseases of skin and subcutaneous tissue (680-709)	74	63	1.3	0.5	0.4	0.5	0.04	0.04
XIV Congenital malformations (740-759)	1205	1202	8.3	8.4	8.3	8.8	0.7	0.7
XVI Symptoms, senility and ill-defined conditions (780-796)	2191	2105	27.4	15.1	14.5	14.2	1.4	1.3
IV Diseases of the blood and blood-forming organs (280-289)	324	304	2.3	2.2	2.1	1.8	0.2	0.2
Total deaths	161276	160615	918.9	1118.8	1109.1		100.0	100.0

4.3 (cont)

Source: *Statistical Yearbook, 1972*, p. 119; *1975*, p. 128; *Czechoslovak Health Services, 1969*, Prague and Bratislava, 1969, p. 19 (supplement to *ČSSR zdravotnictví, 1969*)

NOTE: The 1965 International Classification (in parentheses) is used for all years except 1960, which follows the 1959 classification. These are notably incomparable for Group VI which in 1967, the last year for which the 1959 classification was used, showed 127.0, but in 1968, when the 1965 classification was introduced, showed 9.9

4.4 Morbidity from infectious diseases in Czechoslovakia

(per 100,000 population)

	1955	1960	1968	1970	1974
1. *Causes exhibiting an increase*					
Salmonella infections	16.3	32.1	44.9	37.5	76.7
Infectious dysentery	31.0	78.6	95.8	126.0	101.7
2. *Causes exhibiting a decrease*					
Measles	382.8	495.9	349.6	484.1	88.8
Typhoid fever	10.4	5.7	1.9	2.3	1.3
Paratyphoid B	7.5	1.8	0.2	0.1	0.08
Scarlet fever	306.1	268.1	118.1	144.1	144.3
Diphtheria	17.5	4.6	0.2	−	0.0
Whooping-cough	313.8	58.0	5.8	5.5	1.0
Meningitis	. .	8.8 [a]	10.4	. .	. .
Epidemic meningitis	3.4	2.7	0.5	. .	. .
Infectious hepatitis	374.7	286.2	100.9	121.0	116.1
Trachoma	4.3	2.7	0.6	0.5	0.09
3. *Causes exhibiting no change*					
Tetanus	0.7	0.8	0.7	. .	. .

Source: *Czechoslovak Health Services, 1969*, p. 21; *Statistical Yearbook, 1972*, p. 534 and *1975*, p. 551

a   1965

4.5 Causes of work disability per 100,000 insured persons in Czecho-slovakia

	1970	1973
Infections of the intestine	281	244
Tuberculosis	136	110
Other infective and parasitic diseases	996	902
Neoplasms	544	590
Diseases of the endocrine glands and of nutrition and degenerative diseases	301	318
Diseases of blood and blood-forming organs	114	124
Mental disorders	1911	1600
Diseases of the nervous system	2247	1558
Eye diseases	1474	1277
Ear conditions	1055	949
Diseases of circulatory organs	3229	3065
Diseases of the respiratory system	56231	41589
Diseases of the digestive organs	9278	8812
Diseases of the genito-urinary system	4400	4142
Complications of pregnancy, childbirth and the puerperium	2061	2047
Diseases of the skin and subcutaneous tissue	4493	3776
Diseases of the bones and organs of movement	8510	7798
Congenital malformations	29	28
Pathological symptoms and aetiologically uncertain conditions	184	211
Accidents, poisonings and violence within employment	15587	4682
Accidents, poisonings and violence outside employment		8329

Source: *Czechoslovak Health Services, 1970*, p. 9; *Statistical Yearbook, 1974*, p. 536

4.6 Health facilities in Czechoslovakia at end of year

(excluding those of the Ministries of Defence and of the Interior)

	1960	1968	1969	1973
General hospitals	243	254	258	244
Beds	102766	114119	114724	114909
Physician posts	6053	7174	7412	8177
Tuberculosis and respiratory-disease				
hospitals	53	38	38	26
Beds	11781	8681	8576	6559
Physician posts	340	255	243	222
Psychiatric hospitals	23	32	31	32
Beds	16098	16743	16596	16528
Physician posts	268	367	374	418
Oncological institutions	2	3	3	3
Beds	255	455	485	481
Physician posts	31	70	81	89
Rehabilitation institutions	2	2	2	3
Beds	296	342	342	382
Physician posts	11	8	8	12
Institute of Endocrinology	1	1	1	1
Beds	160	142	142	160
Physician posts	6	8	8	9
Paediatric hospitals	41	50	50	71
Beds	4241	5326	5268	6766
Physician posts	18	45	44	98
Night sanatoria	3	4	4	4
Beds	125	175	175	205
Physician posts	2	2	2	2
Spa sanatoria	120	112	113	122
Beds	24925	26740	26988	29066
Physician posts	382	432	459	597
Maternity homes	33	14	11	10
Beds	567	253	188	168
Physician posts	29	11	8	7
Homes for infant care	36	33	34	29
Places	2469	2310	2356	1959
Physician posts	97	76	81	69
Children's homes (under 3 years)	65	46	45	44
Places	2907	2391	2351	2472
Physician posts	21	28	26	38
Creches	1222	1643	1613	1622
Places	41307	67582	66397	67657
Research institutes with beds	12	15	15	12
Beds	1437	987	989	1032
Physician posts	302	357	367	472
Establishments with beds of the				
Railway Health Service	–	4	4	4
Beds	–	205	210	230
Physician posts	–	14	16	22
Research and other institutes managed				

4.6 (cont)

	1960	1968	1969	1973
Local health centres				
Physician posts	12687	15962	16307	19550
of which in enterprises	2200	2835	2864	3476
Joint diagnostic and medical establishments				
Physician posts	..	1486	1570	..
of which transfusion departments	..	143	147	134
physician posts therein	..	173	176	207
Ambulance service				
Vehicles	4078	5467	5680	6065
Physician posts	..	50	44	49
Persons transported (thousands)	3944	4409	4496	5403
Public health stations	136	135	137	133
Physician posts	684	821	790	922
Pharmacies	1410	1336	1334	1338
Shops for the sale of medical appliances	27 [a]	31	31	..
Shops for the sale of herbal medicines	7 [a]	6	6	..
Opticians	232 [a]	..	..	..
First-aid dispensaries	711	735	729	..
Prescription collecting centres	223 [b]	70	55	..
Pharmaceutical laboratories	..	11	11	..

Source: *Statistical Yearbook, 1963*, pp. 429-30, 434; *1969*, pp. 503-4, 512; *1970*, pp. 571-2, 520; *1974*, pp. 523-4; Comecon Secretariat, *Statistical Yearbook, 1974*, p. 444; J. Jirout *et al.*, *The Pharmaceutical Service in the CSR*, Prague, 1964, p. 17

[a]   1962; the total of the three types in 1960 was 257
[b]   1962

4.7 Immunizations and clinical procedures in Czechoslovakia

Thousands

	1968	*1972*
Biochemical qualitative examinations	21316	31731
Biochemical quantitative examinations	15875	30417
Haematological routine examinations	9895	13729
Haematological special examinations	582	911
Total clinical procedures	47688	76788
Smallpox	942	··
Poliomyelitis	868	··
Diphtheria, whooping-cough and tetanus	742	··
BCG	430	··
Typhoid and paratyphoid fevers	12	··
Cholera	10	··
Yellow fever	1	··
Plague	0.1	··

Source: Ministry of Health, direct communication for 1968 (for immunizations, 1967); *ČSSR zdravotnictví* (hereafter *Health Statistics*), *1973*, Table 5.23, for 1972

4.8 List of best-equipped hospitals in Czechoslovakia

Bed numbers in 1972

Slovakia	Nemocnice Na Kramárech, Bratislava (general hospital)	913
	Fakultiní nemocnice, Košice (teaching hospital)	1466
Moravia	Détská fakultní nemocnice, Brno (paediatric teaching hospital)	725
	Třinec ⎫ (general hospitals with	770
	Havířov ⎬ specialized divisions)	608
	Valašske Meziříčí ⎭	411
	Fakultní nemocnice, Brno (teaching hospital)	2906
Bohemia	Fakultní nemocnice, Hradec Králové (teaching hospital) Motol, Prague (paediatric hospital)	2063

Source: Selection by Ministry of Health, direct communication; beds from *Health Statistics, 1973*, pp. 325-35

4.9 Physicians by specialization in Czechoslovakia (end year)

	Number		Per cent female	
	1968	*1973*	*1968*	*1973*
General practitioners				
— in local practice	3761	4052	23.7	30.0
— in factory practice	1669	1878	35.4	42.9
total	5340	5930	. .	. .
Dentists	3531	4547	51.7	55.8
Internists	3382	3993	38.9	43.4
Paediatricians	3017	3600	68.5	72.7
Surgeons	1866	2254	19.8	17.3
Gynaecologists	1638	2061	25.2	29.8
Epidemiologists and public health officers	952	1088	41.9	51.3
Tuberculosis and respiratory specialists	847	891	35.9	40.1
Medical lecturers				
— general subjects	968	. .	71.9	. .
— theory	819	831	32.0	33.1
Health service organizers	729	648	12.2	14.4
Psychiatrists	710	893	45.6	49.6
Tribunal officers [a]	709	809	13.7	17.1
ENT specialists	662	757	30.7	36.9
Ophthalmologists	603	736	59.2	65.9
Nerve specialists	600	790	42.2	51.8
X-ray specialists	536	702	22.6	31.5
Skin specialists	502	624	52.2	61.1
Laboratory specialists	374	465	38.8	46.9
Orthopaedists	355	452	16.6	17.0
Infectious disease specialists	294	363	53.7	60.9
Pathological anatomists	273	342	23.4	28.1
Youth-care specialists	245	294	53.5	63.6
Anaesthetists	227	488	49.8	58.2
Transfusion specialists	174	212	58.6	63.2
School doctors	160	156	83.1	85.9

Source: *Statistical Yearbook, 1969*, p. 506; *1974*, p. 526

a   Assessors for degree of invalidity for pensions, accidental injuries, etc.

4.10 Staff in the Czechoslovak local authority health service, end year

(excluding pharmaceutical service)

	1963	*1968*	*1972*
Physicians	22604	26880	30635
Pharmacists	363	441	335
Other staff with senior qualifications	1114	1503	3173
Dentists [a]	2083	1773	1425
Medical nurses	34184	40964	45997
Paediatric nurses	17171	22417	22989
Dietetic nurses	691	818	957
Dental nurses	1258 [b]	2534	..
Midwives	4641	5271	6024
Rehabilitation therapists	2008	2563	3355
Assistants in public health service	1337	1708	1938
Laboratory assistants	5540	7332	8429
X-ray assistants	2279	2992	3523
Dental mechanics	3758	4817	5177
Pharmaceutical assistants	101	121	205

Source: *Health Statistics, 1969*, p. 174; *1973*, p. 265

[a] This category of lower-qualified dentists is no longer being trained
[b] 1965, no data for earlier years

4.11 Consultations per hour in 1968 by local-authority health service physicians in Czechoslovakia

Type of consultation	Local service	Factory service
Internal	3.5	3.8
Tuberculosis and respiratory	6.3	4.9
Nervous system	3.3	3.3
Psychiatric	2.5	2.3
Disabilities caused by employment	2.0	1.9
Paediatric	7.7	n/a
School health service	9.6	n/a
Gynaecological	6.3	6.6
Surgical	5.8	5.5
Orthopaedic	5.6	5.9
ENT	5.7	5.9
Urological	4.4	..
Traumatological	4.3	..
Eyes	6.3	6.7
Skin	6.9	6.8
Oncological	3.7	..
Young persons	5.7	6.9
Routine visits and referrals	8.5	7.4
Physical training	2.8	..

Source: *Health Statistics, 1969*, pp. 110-1

4.12 Hospital utilization by departments in Czechoslovakia in 1968

Department	Number of beds	Per cent occupied	Average duration of stay (days)
Internal I	23730	88.7	17.2
Internal II	4085	81.9	51.6
Surgical	20199	86.1	13.0
Gynaecological and obstetric	14732	81.6	7.9
Paediatric	11980	74.4	14.3
Infectious	7477	52.5	14.4
Tuberculosis and respiratory	6310	88.2	58.7
ENT	4289	78.9	9.1
Nervous	4149	88.0	21.1
Skin	3806	87.3	20.1
Ophthalmic	3411	82.1	16.7
Orthopaedic	3155	84.8	20.8
Psychiatric	2316	89.5	39.2
Urological	1337	91.2	15.7
Oncological	1154	86.3	29.3

Source: *Health Statistics, 1969*, pp. 118-27

4.13 Hospital beds in Czechoslovakia

		1973	*1974*
1.	Hospitals and maternity hospitals	115074	114987
2.	Specialized health institutes	31801	32062
3.	Spas	29066	29549
4.	Research institutes and other centrally-administered hospitals	1353	1328
5.	Infant and child homes	4431	4426
6.	Creches	67657	68691
7.	Total Ministry of Health excluding rows (5) and (6)	176574	177926
8.	of which: centrally-administered	33547	34233
9.	local authorities	143027	143693
10.	Railway health service	230	260
11.	Total, excluding rows (5) and (6)	176804	178186

Source: *Statistical Yearbook, 1974*, p. 522; *1975*, p. 539

4.14 Czechoslovak health expenditure

Millions of koruny (kčs)

	1960	1968	1973
Government	. .	9728	15402
of which: capital	801	1042	1952
Social Insurance Fund — health	2404	3916	4525
— spas	333	432	600
Direct purchase of pharmaceuticals	294	306	} 1427
Other direct payments	. .	. .	

Source: Tables 4.16 and 4.18; *Statistical Yearbook, 1971*, p. 211; *Dlouhodobé časové řady*, Prague, 1975, p. 64; J. Penkava, *Financing of Health Care in Europe*, IIPF, Nice, 1975 (mimeograph), pp. 9 and 16

4.15 Pattern of expenditure in Czechoslovak local authority health service

Millions of kčs at current prices

	1960	1968	1972
Capital expenditure	449.7	1039.3	1648.6
of which: buildings	319.1	730.6	. .
equipment	130.6	308.7	. .
Recurrent expenditure	5374.8	8687.6	12859.8
of which: services	. .	3848.6	. .
Pharmaceuticals	871.2	1199.4	1950.5
Blood, plasma, era	48.9	63.3	80.9
Prosthetic costs	86.7	98.2	134.5
Medical supplies	247.2	413.3	628.6
Catering supplies	. .	1398.7	. .
Other recurrent outlays	. .	1666.0	. .
Total current and capital	5824.5	9726.9	14508.5

Source: Table 4.17; *Health Statistics, 1969*, pp. 67-8 of Introduction and pp. 105, 145, 149; *Statistical Yearbook, 1969*, pp. 193-4; *Health Statistics, 1973*, pp. 215, 221

4.16 Organizational breakdown of outlays on health service in 1968

Millions of kčs

	Capital	All recurrent	Pharmaceuticals	Total
Managed centrally by Ministry of Health	57	388	11	445
Managed by Slovak National Council	29	194	8	223
Managed by National Committees (local)	954	8106	1199	9060
Total	1040 [a]	8688	1218	9728

Source: *Health Statistics, 1969*, p. 145

a 1096 million in the *Statistical Yearbook, 1974*, p. 206, which gave 1973 capital outlay as 1952 million

4.17 Expenditure on medicines and medical supplies in Czechoslovakia

Millions of kčs

	1960	*1968*	*1973*
Pharmaceuticals	871	1199	2103
— of which for outpatients	623	862	1418
Medical supplies	247	413	670
Blood, plasma and sera	49	63	79

Source: *Statistical Yearbook, 1963*, p. 438; *1970*, p. 522; *1974*, p. 533

4.18 Domestic sales of health products in Czechoslovakia

Millions of kčs at current retail prices

		1960	1968
A.	*Human use*		
1.	Pharmaceuticals	1183	1548
1.1	Over-the-counter sales	294	306
1.2	Hospital use	249	356
1.3	Free prescriptions	623	862
1.4	Other institutions	17	24
2.	Blood and sera	50	65
2.1	Hospital use	50	65
3.	Prosthetics		
3.1	Hospital use and free prescriptions	87	101
3.2	Other institutions	2	3
4.	Medical supplies		
4.1	Hospital use	110	206
4.2	Free prescriptions	137	209
4.3	Other institutions	3	6
5.	Capital equipment		
5.1	Local authority hospitals	131	309
5.2	Ministry of Health hospitals	17	27
5.3	Other institutions	3	5
B.	*Veterinary use*		
6.	Medicaments and feed additives	35	54

Source: Tables 4.15 to 4.17; some relationships for outlays other than by local authorities were estimates and further detail taken from *Health Statistics, 1969*, p. 149 and *Statistical Yearbook, 1969*, p. 52. The sum of hospital and free prescriptions in this table exceeds very slightly (by around 1 per cent) that for each entry in Table 4.15 which relates only to local authority facilities

5 THE GERMAN DEMOCRATIC REPUBLIC

I. Legislation and policy

A textbook for medical faculties in the GDR enunciates three fundamental principles as characteristic of the country's health care organization — state provision, socialist democracy and unity.[1] It traces the
origin of a State service, therefore, not to Bismarck's compulsory
health insurance of 1883, but to a scheme for a national health service
propounded by a physician, associated with the revolutionaries of
1848, Rudolf Virchow, as politically as he was professionally active in
the slums of Silesian weavers. After the First World War Alfred Grot-
jahn, the first holder of a Chair of Social Hygiene in any German
University, campaigned for a state health system, with the support of
the Union of Socialist Physicians (*Verein Sozialistischer Ärtze*) and the
Communist Party of Germany. Both organizations were proscribed
when the Nazis came to power and the right to express politically
dissident views was lost until the defeat of Germany in 1945.

When the German Democratic Republic was established in 1949
in the Soviet Zone of Occupation the opportunity to nationalize the
insurance schemes was not, however, taken and the GDR is today the
sole European member of Comecon to maintain an insurance basis
for the bulk of health care finance. Article 35 of the 1968 Constitution
states that 'every citizen of the GDR has the right to the protection of
his health and working capacity . . . Medical care, medicaments and
other medical benefits are granted free of charge . . . on the basis of a
social insurance system'. An East European economist attributes the
unique arrangements to 'the long historical tradition of social insurance'.[2]

That tradition had been established on the then united territory of
the German Reich, by Bismarck's legislation, which initially for
manual workers alone was extended within its first two decades to
transport and office workers. Between then and 1961 administration
was by numerous autonomous bodies financed by the contributions
of the employees and employers under their aegis. At that date the
agencies in the GDR were merged into a three-component system —
one for transport (where, as elsewhere in Comecon, a strong independent tradition remains), one for the self-employed and one, the largest,
for all other employees and members of cooperatives.

At the time — Maynard dates it 1958-62 — there were parallel
attempts at fundamental reform in the German Federal Republic;
they were abortive and today 'the principles enunciated in 1883 are

those which govern the present system of West German Social Health Insurance'.[3] Meanwhile, the coverage of the scheme had been gradually extended between the Wars (notably agricultural and forestry workers in 1911 and seamen in 1927), so that the arrangements inherited by the government of the GDR in 1949 were compulsory for employees. Just as the Federal Republic permits voluntary insurance, so does a second social-insurance fund in the Democratic Republic (since 1968 open to individual farmers and the free professions), such differentiation being 'motivated by social views'.[4] A continuing similarity between the insurance systems of the Democratic and the Federal Republics is that a contribution is paid by the employee whereas elsewhere in Comecon the totality is paid by the employer. In both Republics of Germany contributions are earnings related (up to an assessable maximum which is close to the average wage in the GDR but well below it in the GFR), paid in equal parts by employer and employee (save that the former bears a higher share in the GDR in mines and in cooperatives and in the GFR with respect to very low-income earners); the rate is 10 per cent of earnings in the GDR and 8½ per cent in the GFR, up to 600M and 65DM monthly.

The administrative division of the common system took place *de facto* with the separation of the Zones of Occupation in 1945, but *de jure* in 1949 with the creation of the Federal Republic on 21 September and of the Democratic Republic on 7 October. A founding department of the latter was a Ministry of Health, which, replacing a Central Health Administration, became the first Ministry of Health of a German state. That primacy remains, since the Federal Republic's agency responsible for health is that of Labour and Social Affairs. 'Social affairs' were in fact brought into the competence of the GDR Ministry of Health in 1958: the title of the Ministry was not varied, but in each region (*Bezirke*) and district (*Kreise*), its boards (*Räte*) and standing committees (*Ständigen Kommissionen*) were renamed 'for Health and Social Affairs'.[5] The Länder had already been converted (in July 1952) into 14 regions; the Länder remain the constituents of the Federal Republic and are responsible for the health services but the formal practice of each Republic converges at the level of the local Board of Health. The GDR Ministry of Health, the current Statute of which dates from October 1960, is required to execute the health objectives of the Socialist Unity Party and of the Government with regard to State and economic policy, measures of the latter figuring in the State Economic Plan.

The 'socialist democracy' of the textbook noted in the opening of this chapter is there seen as embodied in the interaction of the Ministry with the 'periphery, i.e. the local People's Managements with their Standing Commissions and functional committees (*Aktivs*), mass social organizations and regional, district and national elected assemblies.[6] A Ministerial Decree of 1964 required the Minister to have an advisory 'Kollegium'.

'Unity', the third characteristic posited by the textbook, was begun by an ordinance on the public health service of 4 December 1952, the nationalization of most hospitals be decree of 8 July 1954, and the consolidation of social insurance in 1961 into the three components described above. The contractual relationship was preserved between the insurance fund and the hospital or physician for the care of the insured person and dependants, this retaining a common practice with the past and with that prevailing in the Federal Republic.

With health conditions among the best in Europe, the improvement since the difficult forties is reflected in a decline of infantile mortality from 78.0 in 1949 to 16.0 per 1,000 live births in 1973.

II. Demographic pattern

The census of 1964 happened to be taken at the nadir of population numbers in the GDR; at 16,983,000 it compared (in mid-year terms) with a peak of 19,066,000 in 1948, when postwar resettlement had been completed but before the heavy emigration of 1949-61 to the Federal Republic; the health service incidentally suffered difficulties through such emigration which affected professionals proportionately more than the mass of workers or peasants. With the sealing of the frontier to the West in 1961 the population has been almost solely influenced by natural demographic movements, rising to 17,084,000 in 1968, slightly falling to 17,058,000 in 1970 and to 16,924,000 in 1974.

A projection of the population to 1996 (used for Table 9.1) which takes this recent drop into account and assumes an unchanged net reproduction rate at the very low level of 70 (1973) shows a 1986 total of 16.29 million and 15.88 million for 1996. The long-run decline is inevitable at the lowest reproduction and birth rates of East Europe: in 1960 the crude birth rate was 17.0 per 1,000, but had fallen to 14.3 in 1968, to 13.9 by 1970 and to 10.6 by 1974. At the same time, the crude death rate has been rising (from 13.6 per 1,000 in 1960 to 14.2 in 1968) equalling the birth rate in 1969-71 and subsequently exceeding it. With a mortality of 13.5 per 1,000 in 1974, the net natural increase was negative at 2.9 per 1,000.

As a consequence of these movements and an age-pyramid skewed in the sixties towards the upper brackets, the median age of the population has been falling (1950: 37.3; 1964: 35.0; 1971: 34.4), and with comparative stability in the proportion of children, the GDR has had a relatively favourable trend in the dependency ratio: the projection used here shows it as stable in the seventies but declining further to

30.7 in 1996 (see Table 5.1), chiefly because of the diminution of those aged 14 and under (from 3.9 million in 1972 to 2.6 million in 1986-96).

The low fertility is associated with a high rate of abortion and small family size. The 1947 repeal of the Nazi restrictions on contraception had been revoked in 1950 and until 1965 the GDR Government was strongly pro-natalist. Prohibitions on abortion during those fifteen years were the most severe in Europe. Only some 750 abortions were performed legally each year during that period (viz. less than 0.5 per 100 live births) but illegal operations terminated about one in every four pregnancies. Abortion free and in hospitals was permitted in 1965, if authorized by a district commission (normally including the local medical officer of health, a gynaecologist, two other specialists and a representative of the local women's organization): the physical and mental health of the applicant in the context of her life is taken into account. In the ensuing three years the rate of legal abortions rose to 6.1 per 100 births but began to decline in 1968, partly because, by that year, 13 per cent of all married women of reproductive age had been prescribed oral contraceptives, mainly ovosiston manufactured in the GDR (a charge is made in the case of women with less than five children). In 1972 0.5 million women were taking the pill and in 1973 1.5 million.[7] Intrauterine devices have been available since 1965 from Czechoslovakia (Dana loops), at a charge.

Abortion within the first three months of pregnancy became legal at the request of the women by a law of 10 March 1972: the pregnancy had to be terminated in a hospital and by a physician and the usual sickness and insurance benefits were applicable. Pregnancies beyond the third month could be interrupted for reasons of health.[8] The number of abortions now approximates to that of live births — quintupling within the three months after legalization, most being sought by women aged between 30 and 35 (although the maximum in East Berlin was in the 16 to 25 bracket).

Families are now typically of one or two children. A social survey of 1973 reported that a family of three or more children was 'looked down on' by neighbours, while managers were prejudiced against women workers who frequently took their entitlement of maternity leave. The decline was attributed to the higher participation rate of married women in employment, an inadequate availability of pre-school services, poor housing, the cost of child upbringing, the longer period of education (which raised the age for a first birth) and the convergence of rural living standards to those of towns.[9]

The already high level of urbanization and of concentration in larger towns is exhibited in Table 5.2; towns of 20 to 100 thousand gained relatively in the sixties but the big cities have been advancing in the seventies. Only Berlin is in excess of a million (1,094,000 in the GDR part at the end of 1974), but a further dozen cities have over 100,000 inhabitants, of which Leipzig and Dresden exceed a half-million.

Farm collectivization, completed in April 1960, and declining agricultural manpower needs strengthened already high urbanization, which, at 74 per cent in 1973, is by far the greatest in Comecon: Czechoslovakia at the same time was 64 per cent. The only national minority are the Sorbs, mainly rural and concentrated in the Cottbus Region, but social services are not affected by problems of ethnic diversity nor of illiteracy, while standards of hygiene and health education are very high. Non-professional medicine is not practiced, although there is some homoeopathy.

III. Health conditions

A change in reporting classification from a national to an ICD basis makes difficult the assessment of the trends prior to those shown in Table 5.3 for causes of death and in Table 5.4 as rates per 10,000 inhabitants. The importance of the very broad group of diseases of the circulatory system is evident: on what may not be comparable data (so large is the shift between these and 'other' causes), they accounted in 1973 for 53 per cent of all deaths, no worse in incidence than in industrialized countries of either East or West Europe (see Table 1.4). Mortality from cancer is the heaviest of any Comecon state, but the rate of deaths from violence is good in an all-European context and has been kept fairly steady. There has been no case of poliomyelitis since 1965, but, on the other hand, there were in that year 212,900 cases of diabetes, against 107,800 in 1960 and 38,200 in 1952.[10] Table 5.5 on morbidity is on comparable classification and shows from 1960 to 1972 considerable rises in dysentery (the 1973 return was 11.5) and salmonella poisoning. Scarlet fever has, surprisingly, been sharply greater in incidence, while, expectedly, tuberculosis is in recession. Venereal diseases have been greatly reduced since their peak during the Occupation: new cases of syphilis fell from 22.0 per 10,000 population in 1947 to 0.2 in 1965 while new cases of gonorrhoea dropped from 30.3 to 11.5; centres of infection are worst in Berlin, Potsdam and Halle. The two major campaigns were directed by the Soviet Army of Occupation in 1945-7 and under the ordinance on the Prevention and Combating of Venereal Diseases of February 1961: pursuant to the latter and a law of December 1965, 271 district units were established for dermatological and venereal diseases and in five regions (Berlin, Leipzig, Halle, Erfurt and Schwerin) 'restricted hospital departments' were established.[11]

The introduction of noise-abatement regulations was made part of the annual economic plan with effect from 1973: the measures of

Lärmschutz have the same force as instructions on, for example, the application of specific technologies or the production of particular goods on a subordinate enterprise. A local problem is congenital dislocation of the hip joint found especially frequently in the southern part of the country (and in neighbouring regions of Czechoslovakia): this is being combated by the compulsory radiology of all young children in the affected regions, using special low-radiation exposure equipment manufactured in the country.

IV. Health service administration

Just as the economy of the GDR was long distinguished from those of other Comecon members by a significant private sector in industry (until 1972), so its health service still comprises a substantial number of privately-owned facilities. As discussed in the following section, 82 hospitals in 1973 were in the hands of religious communities and 16 were privately owned. The contractual arrangements with the Social Insurance Funds and governmental regulations permit these to be compatible with a national health service policy.

Centrally planned since the launching of a Five-Year Plan in 1951, the GDR was 'mixed' both in economy and health system. In addition to some wholly private manufacturing, there were a few private banks and an extensive 'half-state' sector (in which government was a 50 per cent shareholder). Conversion of the majority to state enterprises in 1972 has changed the pattern of economic organization, but that of health remains.

The Ministry of Health, as already briefly mentioned, acts within the policies laid down by Party and Government and the concrete measures formulated in the Plan. It consults professional opinion through a Council for Planning and Coordinating the Medical Sciences, while its department of research and education is required to take into account the interests of the medical and scientific associations. The department of health organization oversees both inpatient and ambulatory services, with a section for mother and child care which cuts across the institutional division of those services to ensure unified prophylaxis and therapy for this group: the section is thus concerned with pre- and post-natal care, creches, kindergartens and the schools and young workers.

The same department includes the Labour Health Inspectorate and the Inspectorate of Health Conditions. Departments of hygiene and public health, of pharmacy and medical technology, of social affairs and of rehabilitation are self-explanatory; medical education is within the direct purview of one of the deputy ministers, the other having responsibility for planning and economics (including investment in health facilities).

Each of the Councils for the 14 regions and Berlin has a Department of Health and Social Affairs, the head of which is the Chief Medical Officer of the Region, and *ex officio* a member of the Council. Those which include teaching hospitals have special arrangements whereby the university clinics (Berlin, Dresden, Erfurt, Halle, Jena, Leipzig, Magdeburg and Rostock) have professional responsibility for services although administratively the entire university concerned falls under the Ministry of Higher and Specialized Education. Each regional department incorporates an Industrial Health Inspectorate, a regional pharmacist and a range of functional divisions (such as for the blood transfusion service or for combating tuberculosis and for health protection at frontiers).

Apart from the teaching hospitals (which are Grade D hospitals), all other state-owned health care facilities are managed at the district level. The district medical officer, who is also the district public health officer, has charge of a department of health and social affairs within the district council administration. The inpatient and ambulatory services are classified into medical practices, dental practices, rural health centres (*Landambulatorien*), independent polyclinics (which are the urban health centres), local hospitals with polyclinics (Grade A hospitals), district hospitals with polyclinics (Grade B) and regional hospitals (Grade C). Prophylactic, maternal and child health and pharmacy services are all administered at the district level.[12]

V.   Health-care facilities

Health planning in the GDR has been described as based on 'the envisaged development of the factors influencing health protection of the population in its biological and social environment; results expected in medical research; and the probable evolution of the state of health of the population'.[13] In the 'single process of prophylaxis, early diagnosis, treatment and convalescent care', prophylaxis and health education are seen as increasing in relative importance. Because of the high degree of industrialization, prophylaxis must and does include increasing attention to water and air purification, hygienic food-processing and handling and industrial safety and health. Mass radiology from the age of 15, introduced as elsewhere to screen tuberculosis, is now being used for the early detection of other diseases of the thorax, especially neoplastic and cardiac disease. Early diagnosis of uterine cancer has also been introduced by mass survey of women at risk and a programme of selective examination for early stages of infectious hepatitis has begun.

Compulsory examination of children (and of some adult age-groups in certain cases) is well established for smallpox, tuberculosis, poliomyelitis, tetanus, diphtheria and whooping-cough and is being introduced for measles.

Therapeutic care is being concentrated in large hospital complexes (incorporating local polyclinics), which have ten or more specialized departments. This policy would probably explain the decline in hospital bed capacity (by nearly 10,000 beds, exclusive of those for tuberculosis, in 1960-74). Highly-specialized treatment (rare diseases, use of costly equipment such as the heart-lung machine or artificial kidneys, etc.) is effected in university clinics. The hospital service in 1973 consisted of 490 in state and municipal ownership and 98 in other ownership (see Table 5.6). The GDR service is not only unusual in this respect but also in regard to trends elsewhere in Eastern Europe by a reduction in the number of beds, from 121 per 10,000 population in 1960 to 114 in 1968 and 109 in 1973. This was due to the closure of 118 tuberculosis hospitals, as occurred elsewhere, and to a running down of separate maternity homes in favour of obstetric departments in hospitals; if tuberculosis beds are ignored, there was a 4 per cent increment in general hospital capacity in 1960-73. As Table 5.7 shows, bed numbers fell in general, surgical and all specialty wards but rose in gynaecological, paediatric, cardiac, urological, ENT, radiological, stomatological, orthopaedic, neurological and psychiatric wards, in those thirteen years, and numerous intensive-care units were created. In 1969 the average days hospitalization was 23.7 in state hospitals, 20.9 in university clinics, 27.6 in hospitals of religious communities and 17.3 in private hospitals.

The number of polyclinics (*Polikliniken*) rose from 399 in 1960 to 436 in 1968, at which date 44 were independent, 210 linked with hospitals, 90 were university polyclinics and 92 in factories (*Betriebspolikliniken*). The number of outpatient centres (*Ambulatorien*) rose from 766 in 1960 to 810 in 1968, when 98 were associated with hospitals and 122 were in urban areas, 368 in rural areas and 222 in factories (*Betriebsambulatorien*). In polyclinics and outpatient centres together there were in 1968 1,245 beds of which 133 were maternity beds. Subsequent growth was directed mainly towards polyclinics: by 1973 there were 499 polyclinics against 388 rural outpatient centres. There were in the state system in 1968 100.5 million consultations, of which 43.8 million took place in polyclinics other than university polyclinics (4.4 million) and factory polyclinics (6.1 million), 26.4 million in outpatient centres and 15.6 million in state-owned general practices (*Staatliche Arztpraxen*). The number of consultations in private general practice, and the number of such practices themselves, are not published. The number of state-owned medical practices rose from 298 in 1960 to 1,072 in 1968 and state-owned dental practices from 156 to 584. Other medical institutions in the state sector for outpatient and ambulatory care (1968 numbers in parentheses) were district nurse units (4,758), tuberculosis consultation centres (281), neoplasm treatment centres (200), medical posts (1,971 staffed by a physician, 1,360 staffed by a nurse), pre-natal advisory centres (1,125) and post-natal care centres (251). The number of BCG injections could be reduced from 0.51 million in 1960 to 0.31 million in 1968.

The GDR has inherited a long-standing balneological tradition. A Committee on Cures (*Kurkomitee*) of the Trade Union Council (FDGB) and the Social Insurance Fund determines policy on curative and recuperative spas, 70 per cent of the patients to which are insured persons. The number of foreign visitors to spas such as Bad Elster and Bad Brambach is also considerable.

In Table 5.8 the traditional German distribution is drawn between the higher-qualified 'dental surgeon' (*Zahnarzt*) and the lower-qualified 'dentist' (*Dentist*); under new regulations dentists have been able to gain an official qualification (*Staatliche Anerkennerung*) and are included in the table with dental surgeons.

The emigration of physicians during the fifties virtually offset new recruitment (net of retirements) and numbers in service rose by only 580 between 1950 and 1958 (13,268 to 13,848); notable assistance was received from Bulgaria in the secondment of physicians — a loan facilitated by the tradition of Bulgarian medical training (either in Germany before the Second World War or on German lines). In the same period of the sixties, as Table 5.8 shows, the net increase exceeded 10,000, but though a further 4,700 entered service between 1968 and 1973 the 1976-80 planned increment is only 2,000.

The number of lower- and medium-qualified personnel in the state health service is not published in the *Statistical Yearbook* but is available in occasional publications. Thus in 1959, when higher-qualified staff (physicians, dental surgeons, pharmacists and graduate biologists) were 14,927, there were 62,454 medium-level medical staff, 49,093 medical ancillary staff, 85,292 lower staff and 14,411 trainees.[14]

VI. Finance of health care

A feature of the GDR health service which sets it apart from other East European systems is — as already emphasized — its continued foundation on the insurance-reimbursement principle. Health facilities do not, however, require direct payment from the insured, as they provide services for the insured under general contract with the insurance fund and may be subsidized from taxation in the case of state and municipal institutions. The insurance covers all inpatient and outpatient medical care, dental attention and prescribed pharmaceuticals, prostheses (including dental) and appliances. The existence of this system explains the availability of private physician practice and hospitals.

Under the social insurance law of 1961 there are three insurance funds, one for employees of the transport and communications services (a traditionally separate group), another for all other employees members of cooperatives, pensioners and students, and one for the self-employed. The system was reorganized in 1968 into two agencies, one remaining in the hands of the trade union central committee for employed persions and their dependants (*Sozialversicherung beim FDGB*), and the other, the State Insurance of the GDR (*Sozialversicherung bei der Staatlichen Versicherung der DDR*), covering members of farm and craft cooperatives, the self-employed and their dependants. Until 1971 those earning over 600 marks per month were excluded, but thenafter could participate in voluntary insurance. On the eve of the extension in 1967 there were 5.79 million employed workers and apprentices in the trade union insurance, out of a total gainfully occupied population of 7.71 million, of which 6.40 million were employed and 0.45 million were apprentices.[15]

Whereas elsewhere in East Europe the social insurance premium is borne entirely by the employer (except in the case of earnings-graduated pensions which are contributory) supplemented by government subsidy as necessary, the employee in the GDR contributes 10 per cent of his earnings; special rates are accorded students, members of cooperatives and family members working together; the standard rate for the self-employed is 14 per cent of personal income. The employer contributes a further 10 per cent of pay (20 per cent in the case of mines and concessional rates for cooperatives). There is a maximum pay for the calculation of contributions (as in the Federal Republic). Government finance is available to cover any deficit. It may be observed that the GDR insurance is the only one in Eastern Europe to provide unemployment benefit; like the others it provides sick pay, and retirement and industrial-injury benefit. It insures family dependants (at a flat rate per dependant), who have not invariably been covered elsewhere in East Europe.

The only persons entitled to free medical care are pregnant women and children under 3 years of age. Non-insured outside that group must bear the cost of care, but in practice these are not numerous since the scope of the insurance is virtually nationwide. Pensioners are also covered for medical benefits.

A time series of financial statistics can only be compiled on either side of a major break in classification in 1967. Table 5.9 therefore shows 1960-6 on the earlier classification and 1968-72 on the present.

The government health facilities in 1968 received the 3,162 million marks government expenditure on health institutions shown in Table 5.9 plus an estimated 2,081 million marks, which is that part of the Social Insurance Fund's 2,238 million marks spent on government and private facilities (Table 5.10) which was paid to the former (93 per cent, the share applied being that of bed capacity). Private health facilities received 157 million marks from the Insurance Fund and 13 million marks within, say, a round 200 million marks expenditure would seem reasonable. The Social Insurance Fund reimbursed prescriptions to the value of 871 million marks privately. As total pharmaceutical sales were around 1,072 million marks, the balance of some 200 million marks would have comprised a small amount of non-reimbursed prescriptions and over-the-counter purchases. The 1,072 million marks would be 42 per cent of total retail sales that year of health and cosmetic products and other consumers' goods based on chemicals. The outlays put in Table 1.6 are hence from

Government	3,162	+	13	=	3,175
Social Insurance	2,238	+	871	=	3,109
Direct payments	30	+	200	=	230
Total					6,514

REFERENCES

1. E. Paul (ed.), *Organisation des Gesundheitsschutzes in der DDR*, Berlin, 1968, p. 14
2. J. Penkava, 'Financing of Health Care in Eastern Europe', paper read to the International Institute for Public Finance, Nice, 1975 (mimeograph), p. 7
3. A. Maynard, *Health Care in the European Community*, London, 1975, p. 5
4. Penkava, op. cit. p. 8
5. Paul, op. cit., p. 20
6. Ibid., p. 21
7. K. Lungwitz, 'Economic and Social Problems of Birth Trends in the GDR', *Wirtschaftswissenschaft*, No. 11, 1974, pp. 1616-35
8. *Gesetzblatt der DDR*, Part I, No. 5, 15 March 1972 and Part II, No. 12, 20 March 1972
9. Lungwitz, loc. cit., and *Einheit*, No. 7, 1974, pp. 582-91
10. Respectively, *Bol'shaya sovetskaya entsiklopediya*, Vol. 6, 3rd edn, Moscow, 1971, p. 407; and Paul, op. cit., p. 136
11. Paul, op. cit., pp. 128-35
12. Ibid., pp. 20-9
13. M. Gehring, *GDR Health and Social System*, Dresden, 1968, p. 11
14. W. Grossmann and H. Richau, *Zür Okonomik des staatlichen Gesundheitswesens in der DDR*, Berlin, 1962, p. 80
15. *Bol'shaya sovetskaya entsiklopediya*, loc. cit.; *Statistical Yearbook, 1968*, pp. 61, 507; *DDR Wirtschaft: Eine Bestandsaufnahme*, Frankfurt am Main, 1971, p. 183; and 'Le système de santé publique en RDA', *La Documentation Française*, No. 275, 9 January 1976, pp. 18-19

TABLES

5.1 Projections of population of GDR

Percentage age distribution	*1971*	*1981*	*1996*
0-14	23.2	17.9	16.2
15-39	34.2	36.8	35.4
40-64	26.9	29.2	34.0
65 and over	15.7	16.1	14.5
Median age (years)	34.4	36.5	39.0

Source: P. F. Myers, 'Population and Labor Force in Eastern Europe, 1950-1996', in US Congress Joint Economic Committee, *Reorientation and Commercial Relations of the Economies of Eastern Europe*, Washington, D.C., 1974, p. 434

5.2 Concentration and urbanization of population in GDR

Percentage of total population

	1960	*1968*	*1973*
Rural areas			
with less than 500 inhabitants	7.8	7.6	6.9
with 500-999 inhabitants	10.2	9.7	9.2
with 1000-1999 inhabitants	10.0	9.5	9.2
Total rural population	28.0	26.8	25.3
Urban areas			
with 2000-2999 inhabitants	5.8	5.4	5.6
with 3000-4999 inhabitants	7.0	6.3	6.5
with 5000-9999 inhabitants	9.0	8.9	8.2
with 10000-19999 inhabitants	9.7	9.3	8.9
with 20000-49999 inhabitants	13.9	15.1	15.1
with 50000-99999 inhabitants	5.2	6.4	7.1
with 100000 and more inhabitants	21.4	21.9	23.3
Total urban population	72.0	73.3	74.7

Source: *Statistisches Jahrbuch der Deutschen Demokratischen Republik* (hereafter, *Statistical Yearbook*), *1971*, p. 10; *1974*, p. 10

5.3 Causes of death in the GDR

	ICD number	*1969*	*1973*
Enteritis and diarrhoea	008, 009	402	165
Tuberculosis of the respiratory organs	010-012	1472	826
Other tuberculosis	013-019	558	453
Syphilis and its sequelae	090-097	189	88
All other infections and parasitic diseases	others in 000-136	475	338
Malignant neoplasms (except 174)	140-209	35320 ⎫	37813
Malignant neoplasms of the breast	174	2319 ⎭	
Benign neoplasms and unspecified neoplasms	210-239	920	684
Diabetes mellitus	250	3563	3239
Anaemia	280-285	613	555
Meningitis	320	144	112
Rheumatic fever	390-392	139	89
Chronic rheumatic heart diseases	393-398	2089	1790
Hypertension	400-404	18557	18844
Ischaemic heart disease	410-414	25805	24766
Other diseases of the heart	420-429	21001	18028
Cerebrovascular diseases	430-438	16406	15179
Influenza	470-474	970	663
Pneumonia	480-486	4612	3481
Bronchitis, emphysema of the lung and bronchial asthma	490-493	12152	10758
Peptic and duodenal ulcers	531-533	1925	1697
Appendicitis	540-543	569	481
Intestinal obstruction and hernia	550-553, 560	1328	1063
Cirrhosis of the liver	571	2220	1924
Nephritis and nephrosis	580-584	839	585
Hyperplasia of the prostate	600	2273	1779
Abortion, other complications of childbirth and the puerperium and delivery without mention of complication	630-678	100	48
Congenital anomalies	740-759	1496	1127
Abnormal delivery and anoxic or hypoxic conditions	772-776	881	490
Other diseases of early infancy	760-763, 769-771, 773-775, 777-779	1762	1107
Senility without mention of psychosis	794	4456	3992
All accidents	N800-N999	9801	9170
All causes of death		243732	231960

Source: *Statistical Yearbook, 1971*, p. 474; *1975*, p. 426

5.4 Causes of death in the GDR per 10,000 population

	1969	1972	1973
Tuberculosis	1.2	0.9	0.7
Other infectious and parasitic diseases	0.6	0.4	0.5
Cerebrovascular diseases	9.6	9.0	9.8
Pneumonia	2.7	2.3	2.3
Diseases of the circulatory system	64.7	65.4	72.2
Peptic and duodenal ulcers	1.1	1.0	1.8
Diabetes mellitus	2.1	2.0	1.4
Malignant neoplasms	22.0	22.0	25.9
Accidents	5.7	5.5	5.9
Senility	2.6 ⎫	29.0	16.1
Other causes	30.4 ⎭		
All causes	142.7	137.5	136.6

Source: *Statistical Yearbook, 1971*, p. 478; *1974*, p. 474; *1975*, p. 430

5.5 Morbidity per 10,000 population in the GDR

	1960	1968	1972	1974
Exhibiting a decrease				
Typhoid and paratyphoid	0.7	0.2	0.1	0.1
Diphtheria	2.2	0.0	0.0	—
Poliomyelitis	0.08	—	—	—
Tuberculosis	13.6	6.9	5.0	3.9
Botulism	0.01	0.0	0.0	0.0
Epidemic meningitis	0.1	0.0	0.0	0.0
Infectious hepatitis	26.3	13.7	11.7	8.9
Rabies	4.5	4.5	3.9	2.9
Exhibiting an increase to 1972				
Scarlet fever	8.8	15.5	47.3	16.0
Dysentery	4.4	4.1	7.1	2.0
Viral meningitis and encephalitis	0.19	1.31	1.05	3.07
Salmonella poisoning	3.0	3.4	5.6	2.3

Source: *Statistical Yearbook, 1968*, p. 569; *1971*, p. 471; *1974*, p. 467; *1975*, p. 423

5.6 Hospitals and bed capacity in the GDR by ownership and type

	No. of hospitals			Bed capacity (thousand)		
	1960	*1968*	*1974*	*1960*	*1968*	*1974*
State and municipal	679	550	488	189.3	181.2	170.8
Religious communities	88	84	82	13.5	12.7	12.7
Other private owners	55	23	14	2.0	1.0	0.8
Total	822	657	584	204.8	195.0	184.2
of which						
General hospitals and separate maternity homes	522	435	393	135.9	131.6	125.8
University clinics	105	111	111	20.8	18.9	18.3
Scientific institutions	8	8	7	1.1	1.0	1.0
Tuberculosis clinics, hospitals and homes	151	60	28	21.7	11.3	6.0
Psychiatric and neurological hospitals	36	43	45	25.3	32.1	32.5

Source: *Statistical Yearbook, 1971*, p. 410; *1975*, pp. 374-5

5.7 Bed numbers by specialization in the GDR

		1960	1968	1974
General		2501	1330	792
Internal medicine		37399	38219	37438
Surgical		36335	35416	32964
of which:	neurosurgery	225	238	218
	paediatric	417	903	1033
	cardiac	39	114	191
Gynaecological		9706	10031	10565
Obstetric		7581	8023	7210
Paediatric (other than premature)		10632	12184	15740
of which:	infants	4184	5576	5446
Premature infants		1374	1430	1388
Infectious diseases		11277	12161	6618
Ophthalmological		2853	2875	2805
ENT		3865	4200	4034
Dermatological		3833	3804	3372
Venereological		848	370	232
Urological		1328	1857	2565
Radiological		1272	1636	1457
Stomatological		354	537	541
Chronic		4739	4159	4734
Orthopaedic		4956	5380	5547
of which:	tuberculosis of bone	674	234	182
Neurological		2903	3046	3055
Psychiatric		30742	33453	33826
Tuberculosis:	in hospitals	10460	3356 ⎫	
	in sanatoria	17220	9677 ⎬	6195
	in homes	2818	283 ⎭	
Convalescence		61	753	619
Intensive therapy		–	760	1524
Total		205207	194970	184214

Source: *Statistical Yearbook, 1971*, p. 411; *1975*, p. 375

NOTE: Capacity at 30 June each year

5.8 Higher-qualified health staff in the GDR

	Numbers			Per 10000 population		
	1960	*1968*	*1974*	*1960*	*1968*	*1974*
Physicians	14555	24620	30798	8.5	14.4	18.2
Dental surgeons	6361	6823	7600	3.7	3.9	4.5
Pharmacists	2240	2828	3028	1.3	1.7	1.8

Source: *Statistical Yearbook, 1971*, p. 415; *1974*, p. 403

5.9 Health and social welfare expenditure by the GDR Government

Millions of Marks

	1960	1966	
Inpatient (*stationäre*) facilities	1689	1762	
Outpatient (*ambulante*) facilities	295	601	
Facilities for mothers and children	472	1640	
Health protection and control	197	368	
Pharmacies	14	28	
Social welfare centres	159	186	
Pensions (excluding Social Insurance pensions)	242	358	
Non-pension social welfare payments	1442	262 [a]	
Labour	94	53	
Social Insurance Fund	9045	11602	
Payments to non-governmental facilities	20	25	
Total	13668	16887	

	1968	1970	1972
Inpatient facilities	1899	1991	2203
Outpatient facilities	872	1008	1184
Health protection and hygiene	132	136	
Research, training and retraining	112	118	449
Health institution supplies (*Versorgungs-einrichtungen*)	147	142	
Sub-total health outlays	3162	3395	3836
Social welfare homes	215	236	257
Creches and permanent homes	323	349	461
State support for mothers and children	1372	1566	1571
Non-pension social welfare payments	260	194	324
Payments for the performance of health care services	13	18	.. [b]
Other state institutions and mass activities	45	54	.. [b]
Pensions (excluding Social Insurance pensions)	347	334	.. [b]
Other	—	40[c]	50 [c]
Total health and social welfare	5737	6186	6499

Source: 1960 and 1966 from *Statistical Yearbook, 1968*, p. 404; 1968-72 from *Statistical Yearbook, 1971*, p. 317; *1974*, p. 311

a Change of classification (1965 outlay 1322 million)
b Classified elsewhere
c Pharmacies and workshops (*Apotheken und Werkstätte*), the latter presumably including manufacture of prostheses in 1972; unspecified in 1970

5.10 Accounts of Social Insurance Fund in the GDR

Millions of marks at current prices

	1960	1968	1973	1974
Compulsory social insurance premia	6635	7478	8711	8971
Other revenue	102	56	638	808
Total revenue	6737	7534	9349	9779
Deficit	1297	3290	6765	7097
Total expenditure	8034	10824	16114	16876
of which:				
Social insurance pensions	4436	6244	9347	9661
Sick-pay, household and personal allowances	968	962	1492	1462
Other social purposes	158	302	389	462
Prescribed pharmaceuticals and non-dental prostheses other than inpatient care	497	871	1343	1492
Medical and dental treatment, dental prostheses in government and private facilities	1699	2238	3235	3273
Balneological and recuperative services	218	129	171	175
Other outlays	58	78	77	88

Source: *Statistical Yearbook, 1971*, p. 320; *1974*, p. 312; *1975*, p. 288

6 HUNGARY

I. Legislation and policy

The assurance of free health care to every Hungarian citizen, effective in 1975 under the Health Law of 1972, came a century after an enactment which was far ahead of its time. Health Statute No. XIV of 1876 did not then achieve the far-reaching public health regulation it laid down and fifteen years later an eminent professor of medicine and health organizer, Kornél Chyser, observed: 'Our health law has remained a dead letter, which even our great-grandchildren will be unable to put into operation.'

Under the 133 days of the Hungarian Soviet Republic of Béla Kun in 1919, sickness insurance, already initiated before the First World War, was extended compulsorily to all wage and salary earners and medical care was provided free. The brief experiment was terminated with the suppression of the revolutionary government, but between the two World Wars a Hungarian townsman had one of the best health services of Europe. The country enjoyed the highest ratio of physicians to population in Central and Eastern Europe (11.7 for every 10,000 inhabitants in 1938) but their uneven distribution was such that in that year 4,668 doctors out of the 10,590 lived in Budapest. Between 1921 and 1930 the number of physicians had doubled and that of hospital beds had risen by 85 per cent to 49,000. Infant mortality had steadily fallen from an average of 192.7 per 1,000 live births in 1920-1 to 156.8 per 1,000 in 1930-1, to 123 in 1940-1 and to 92.5 in 1948-9. Although the villager had less access to therapeutic care than the city-dweller, a network of communal and district medical officers, roughly one to 4,900 persons, developed a nationwide prophylactic and public health service headed by the National Hygiene Institute. Under the Green Cross Service advice and assistance on health matters was coming to be provided in rural areas and by 1940 its 2,100 health advice centres covered 58 per cent of rural areas, all with a nurse in charge and 200 with a physician.

Social security had been relatively well developed, except for the much neglected category of agricultural labourers, under a general compulsory insurance for workers in industry and commerce. The largest insurance agency was the National Social Insurance Institute (OTI) created in 1928, which covered long-term risks (industrial accidents, invalidity, old age and death). Social insurance funds were provided by a premium of 13 per cent on all wages, paid in equal shares by the employer and the employee, with workmen's com-

166

pensation entirely financed by the employer. The State subsidized old-age pensions. Agricultural workers and domestic servants (625,000 persons) were included in the social insurance scheme as late as 1938, and given old-age pensions and funeral allowances.

In 1938 2.8 million were covered by some form of social insurance as insured or dependants, or 30.9 per cent of the population. There were 33 further insurance institutions other than OTI concerned with sickness, accident and disability until 1945, when the coalition government of democratic parties formed on Liberation promoted the absorption of all social security agencies into OTI: by 1950 only the State Railways social security fund remained autonomous. In this early postwar period, which saw the domination of the government by the Communist Party (which merged with the Social Democrats in 1948), insurance coverage rose to 47.3 per cent of the population, the number of insured increasing to 4.4 million in 1950. By contrast, with repressive policies towards trade unions (until the Liberation, when in 1947 alone membership leapt from 936.000 to 1,288,100), labour legislation, though dating back to the 1880s, did not reach the 8-hour working day, the 48-hour working week and paid holidays until 1937. Both insurance arrangements and labour legislation favoured white-collar workers, differentials which governments after 1945 eliminated.

Insurance remained the financial basis of the system until 1975, reaching 85 per cent of the population by 1960 and 97 per cent as soon as almost all country-dwellers became collective farmers or state employees in the early sixties. In 1972 coverage increased to 99 per cent and became 100 per cent in 1975 when under the law just mentioned (Act II of 1972) health care was made free also for the few non-insured: the manpower basis had greatly expanded − to more than double the ratio of physicians to population, while the improvement of health outcome may be indicated by the reduction of infantile mortality to 33.9 per 1,000 live births by 1974. Budapest still has twice as many physicians per inhabitant than the national average, but each rural area of 2,200 now has a local physician.[1]

II. Demographic pattern

Hungary did not become a country with an urban majority until 1974. In an almost stationary population (10.51 million on 1 January 1975), there were at the end of 1973 still 5.28 million villagers and 5.17 million townsmen against 5.67 and 4.34 millions respectively in 1960, and 5.36 and 4.99 millions in 1970, when the most recent census was conducted. Overall, therefore, Hungary has been predominantly rural for the period covered in this study but the overwhelming role of the capital city, with just on 20 per cent of the population, has long imparted an urbanized stamp to the Hungarian way of life. The concentration of population in the metropolis — the biggest city of Eastern Europe other than Moscow and Leningrad — is greater than in any other country of Comecon and presents its own health hazard in atmospheric pollution and inadequately purified water.

Hungary is in the middle rank of East European states as regards urbanization and population density, but has vied since the Second World War with the GDR for the lowest birth rate and the highest median age. The demographic problem affecting health care now and increasingly in the future is that of an ageing population. In economic terms, on the other hand, the numbers beyond retirement (taken as age 65) and proportionately many fewer children (under 15) make the ratio of dependants to working-age adults (15-64) lower than in any country of the group (see Table 1.1): as Table 6.1 shows, in 1971 there were 475 dependants for each 1,000 aged 15-64, on a trend which has been improving since the fifties. This trend will reverse during the seventies, though for that decade it will stay among the lowest of Eastern Europe.

In the first four years of the seventies (1971-4) the economically active population has increased by only 96,500, half that of the previous four years, although the decline in the number of children (94,000) has been smaller than was shown in the late sixties; those of retirement age have increased by 143,700.[2] These proportions underlie the pro-natalist policies of the fifties and again today. Recent maternity concessions, notably allowances — initially 600 forints (ft) a month — to employed mothers who stay at home until the child is 3 have already induced some modest improvement in the birth rate. In the first full year of operation, 1968, 92,000 women took out such allowances but after the scheme had been extended to women in cooperative farms (1969), the number rose to 178,000 by 1971. The crude birth rate was constant at 13.1 per cent for the three years 1963-5 (and at a mean of 13.2 for 1962-6) but rose to 14.6 in 1967 and 15.1 in 1968; after a temporary drop, it was back to 15.0 by 1973, and 17.8 in 1974. Since 1967 a 'layette grant' was transformed from a voucher worth 400 ft into a cash grant and raised to 2,500 ft in January 1974; from 1971, however, entitlement was restricted to a mother who had attended at least four pre-natal examinations (the first being no later than 140 days from conception).[3] In January 1974 also the maternity allowance was raised (from 600 to 800 ft per month after the first child, rising to a maximum of 1,000 ft after the third), by which date over 230,000 women were availing themselves of a scheme which remains unique in the world. Both these payments are in addition to family allowances, which are paid for a first child only to single parents but for second and subsequent children on a steeply progressive scale. 0.56 million families received an allowance in 1960 and 0.69 million in 1971. Family allowances were increased in 1975 to 850 ft for the first, 950 ft for the second and 1,050 ft for each subsequent child.[4]

Abortion policy has been a counterpoint to maternity promotion. Between 1949 and 1952 it was restricted, under severe punitive measures, to those on medical indications, but medical commissions were from 1953 enabled to authorize abortion on personal and social grounds, which were codified in a law of 3 June 1956 which 'permits a woman consciously to determine the desired family size and to interrupt an undesired pregnancy by an induced abortion'.[5] As Table 6.2 shows, the number of abortions rose rapidly in consequence and overtook the number of live births in 1959. In the sixties they ran between one-quarter and one-third above the birth rate but equality was almost regained in 1973 (when the margin fell to 8 per cent) and the ranking dramatically reversed in 1974. The changing relationship may also be perceived in rates of abortion (here, as in Table 1.2, including spontaneous) per 1,000 women of reproductive age. The rate moved from 65.1 in 1960 to 75.9 in 1968 but regained the 1960 level in 1972 (66.6) and fell below it in 1973 (63.2).

While part of the fall in abortion has not yielded higher fertility, because it is due to the much wider use of oral contraceptives (the Hungarian-made infecundin and bisecurin) available since 1967 and to the new compulsory instruction of couples prior to marriage in contraceptive techniques, some must be attributed to the restrictive legislation which came into effect on 1 January 1974. The three-member commission was reintroduced for authorization and its grounds restricted to medical indications, consequences of an illegal act, illegitimacy, or separation from the spouse, lack of separate accommodation for a married couple and cases where the expectant mother has recently given birth or is over 39 years of age. The Minister of Health, Dr Zoltán Szabó, introducing these various measures to the public in late 1973 stated that the average number of children should rise from less than two (1.87 in 1972) to nearer the 'ideal' family of three, and by mid-1975 the leading Hungarian demographer was claiming that the 1974 pro-natalist measures had gained popular support. The first stage of maternity promotion in 1966 — raising family allowances — had merely made earlier the mother's age at each birth without enlarging completed family size.[6]

Mortality has hardly altered over a quarter century: it was 11.4 per 1,000 in 1950 and 12.0 in 1974, the maximum variation being down to 9.6 in 1961 and with intermediate peaks of 11.7 in 1953 and 11.9 in 1971.

The proportion of aged (those over 60 have risen from 13.8 per cent in 1960 to 18.2 in 1974) is particularly marked among farm households, not all of whom in the past, as is noted below, have sought the requisite medical care: readiness to seek care will rise with the 1975 assurance of facilities as a civic right and with health facilities closer to isolated farmsteads. Residents of the *tanya*, or hamlet well separated from the standard Hungarian large village, did not move to farm centres as had been expected when collectivization was accomplished in the early sixties.

Virtually no illiteracy remains even among the older persons of farm households, because universal primary education has been extended to remote hamlets in the thirties. The homogeneity of the Hungarian nation (95 per cent Magyar) renders ethnic diversity no problem in health care, and non-professional medicine is no obstacle to conventional services.

III.   Health conditions

The long-term plan for health (1971-85), which indicated that three-quarters of the Hungarian population had, in a year, a condition requiring medical care was founded upon two projections. On the one hand it quantified the health needs arising from demographic change (evolution of age structure and of occupational pattern, increase in life expectation) and urbanization, from which followed the need for more hospitalization and ambulatory care as the population ages and lives closer to facilities. In this latter connection it was forecast that many of the 800,000-900,000 persons currently living in hamlets or isolated farmsteads will have either died or moved to bigger communities by 1985, not only because of the pressure of cooperative farms to concentrate the location of their membership for farm efficiency but also because younger people no longer wish to live in isolation. On the other hand, it examined the changes in treatment patterns arising from changes in public health standards, from pharmacological development, from improvements in therapeutic care and physician skills and from changes in the structure of morbidity as the environment alters. The commission also undertook economic analyses of work loss through illness and accident and of the cost of hospitalization compared with such investment in housing as would permit more home care; it pointed out, however, that home care had become rare not only because urban homes were overcrowded but because the employment rate of married women was high. As the age of the population rises, and with the unique Hungarian money incentives for mothers to stay at home while children are young, there should be more people per household available to care for a sick member.

The commission's key indicator of provision, 88 to 89 beds per 10,000 population by 1975 (and 100 to 120 beds during 1980-90), was not reached in the 1971-5 Five-Year Plan (84 in 1975), but a target of 115 has recently been confirmed for 1985. Its goals were based on studies of total morbidity in Szeged, Ballassagyarmat and Dorog.[7] The first is a major town and it was concluded that there was enough bed capacity in the city to ensure that all hospitalizable cases could obtain a bed. The second case, a district (*járás*) with agriculture as the main occupation and no hospital, was less well served. During the period of house-to-house survey (September 1963 to August 1964) 79.9 per cent of the 13,500 inhabitants had some degree of ill-health, while the remainder suffered no disease or accident; but a full medical examination of a 20 per cent sample (of which 30 per cent were aged over 60) showed that during the period there were 1.8 cases of illness per inhabitant that were not treated by the health service; these untreated cases excluded needs for dental care. While the number of consultations and treatments in the health services related to a disease was 8.7 per inhabitant, there were 3.7 visits by each inhabitant to a physician for reasons not connected with any disease. The ratio of those in need of hospital care but not hospitalized was higher in the older age-groups. The general morbidity study of Dorog (a coal-mining settlement with a hospital and a tuberculosis clinic) obtained 10,222 personal medical interview cards and revealed a relationship of 2.06 diseases per inhabitant excluding dental disorder (2.46 with dental). Again excluding dentistry, 72.6 per cent of the population appeared in health institutions during the calendar year 1964, or 77.8 per cent including dental care. Health survey is also effected through the obligatory screening system of mass radiographies for all over 15 years; these are organized annually by residential area. One-fifth of females over 30 have had a cancer test by inspection and a further (but smaller) group have undergone a cervical smear test or other check. As the network of cytodiagnostic laboratories is increased, testing will be extended. There are already some counties (the administrative division, the *megye*), where 30 per cent of females over 30 have been cancer-tested, but the tests are voluntary and — as in many other countries — some restraint has been found among women lest the condition be discovered. Every woman admitted for a disease to a hospital which has an oncological specialist is automatically checked (though not when admission is for injury resulting from an accident). Blood and urine tests are routinely made of all patients admitted to hospitals, which also serves to reveal any venereal disease. The elimination of tuberculosis — once named *morbus Hungaricus* for its prevalence — is hoped for by the end of the long-term plan.

Health planning is based on household samples and data collection on hospital inpatients, but outpatient and absence statistics are collated in certain regions. Compilation is further complicated because morbidity is recorded as the diagnosis on first physician contact, and records are not retrospectively corrected if the diagnosis is later varied. Reliance has been placed on health-facility care, because the proportion of domiciliary visits is low (about 10 per cent of all physician contacts).

The long-term plan (which is segmented to correspond to the five-year periods of the national economic plans) foresaw that between 1968, the base year, and 1980 the number of hospital discharges (including multiple discharges per person) would rise from 16 per cent (1.64 million in a population of 10.24 million) to 18 per cent. The 1980 structure of medical care would, however, significantly differ from that of the present, for more cases should be subject to treatment at an early stage and consequently generate more physician contacts and more medication, etc., per case of disease.

The disease for which discharge is made (even if multiple in the stated year) or at death is given in rank order in Table 6.3, ranked by 1965 number of cases. The classification is that of the Seventh Revision (1959) of WHO International Classification of Diseases, although the Eighth Revision (1965) has since been introduced. The first item (obstetrics) includes abortions. Coverage is not, however, complete because discharges and deaths at tuberculosis and psychiatric hospitals are excluded from the returns, nor would it necessarily coincide with the pattern shown for non-hospitalized cases.

Table 6.4 classifies diseases by direction of change between 1962 and 1973 of mortality per 100,000 population: the evolution is that familiar in Western Europe of the conquest of communicable diseases and a rise in the incidence of cancer and cardiovascular disease. Tuberculosis remains high but has fallen from 28.7 in 1962 to 16.0 in 1973. Motor vehicle accidents are among the lowest in Europe, but rising rapidly: Hungary is the only East European country which makes no motor cars of its own (a tiny vehicle for invalids' use apart) and during the sixties few cars were on the roads. 1970 data on traffic accidents were 26,464, in which 31,453 persons suffered injury (1,584 fatally). Reported occupational accidents numbered 143,951, involving 630 fatalities. Over the sixties, mortality from cirrhosis of the liver was rising almost as fast as that from motor accidents; no breakdown of road accidents caused by drunkenness has been issued, but discharges from mental-health institutions, when they were published, increased as follows (in cases per 100,000 population):

	1959	1962	1967
Alcoholic psychosis	5.3	4.0	6.8
Alcoholism	53.7	52.2	56.1
Total psychiatric discharges	319.5	338.7	421.6
Total non-psychiatric discharges	151.8	167.4	244.5

Source: *Statistical Yearbook, 1963*, p. 316; *1968*, p. 363

Under a law of 1966 an examination for alcoholism can be carried out at the request of a spouse, parent or employer and, if found to be required, a compulsory detoxication (free of charge) can be ordered. There are detoxication departments (1973) in each of the 65 mental or neurological medical centres and in ten hospitals.[8] Mortality from genito-urinary affections has moved up only slightly, a decrease in nephritis being offset by an increase in kidney infections: in turn the latter could be expected to decrease as artificial renal equipment (not produced in Hungary in the sixties) becomes available. Classified by proportion of mortality (Table 6.5), the cardiac group occupies by far the leading place, accounting for nearly one death in three.

For morbidity, three sets of measures are available, viz. reported infectious diseases (Table 6.6), samples of work-disability certificates (Table 6.7) and the special enquiries made in preparation for the long-term plan (Table 6.8).

The incidence of dysentery, though falling, remains high; due not only to deficient environmental sanitation in the rural areas but particularly to the condition of the water-supply to the capital cities, bacillary dysentery is a significant threat to health in Budapest. Of infectious diseases, measles, salmonella, enteritis, encephalitis (cerebritis) and brucellosis are the only infections to show a rise (although the number of cases of leptospirosis was as large as 179 in 1967); an anti-measles vaccination campaign was in the first phase of the long-term plan. In 1968 the number of immunizations included 0.14 million with BCG, against smallpox 0.28 million, against poliomyelitis with Sabin vaccine 0.40 million, against typhoid 0.10 million and combined inoculations against diphtheria, whooping-cough and tetanus 0.39 million. Vaccination against smallpox has of course long been standard, and the 1972 Health Law codified all the foregoing as compulsory for children at appropriate ages and added measles.

The standard of nutrition is high but in 1968 there were still 61 fatalities from thyrotoxicosis, with or without goitre, and 4 from avitaminosis, against respectively 78, 40 and 12 in 1962; there had been 166 deaths from anaemia in 1962 rising to 174 in 1968. Mortality from diabetes mellitus, however, had been sharply cut from 967 to 61.

From a start of 25 oncological clinics in 1952 to 69 in 1973, 0.5 million screenings are made annually and 22,000 malignant tumours had been revealed by the cumulative 7.5 million screenings to 1970. The number of tuberculosis clinics has begun to be reduced (to 185 in 1973 against 187 in 1960 and 190 in 1968) supplemented by 142 screening stations, but the number of tests remains high (3.99 million in 1960, 7.19 million in 1968 and 7.5 million in 1973). But whereas the number of new tuberculosis cases dropped from 28,092 to 12,413, that of neoplasm cases rose from 16,442 in 1960 to 21,000 in 1968.

The number of venereal-disease clinics was also constant (121 in 1960, 123 in 1968 and 124 in 1973) but the number of newly reported patients has been rising (in 1962-8 from 4,902 to 12,780). The movement of the pattern of morbidity towards that of an urbanized society with a highly-developed economy is reflected in the sample data of Tables 6.7 and 6.8

Between 1962 and 1968 the average duration of disability from work remained constant at 11 days but rose to nearly 13 in 1973, though the most frequent causes, influenza and other acute respiratory diseases and digestive-system afflictions, were among the briefest, showing a shorter absence (4-5 days in each of the years shown). In terms of days of work lost, the same pattern as for mortality change is reflected in the decrease of infectious diseases other than influenza, of tuberculosis (by 1973 cut to 46 days per year per 100 workers — one-third that of 1962), of pneumonia and of industrial accidents, but an increase in other accidents (including motor accidents), and in some circulatory diseases, in cancer and in mental ill-health. Duodenal ulcers and diseases of the female genitalia appear to be on a rising trend among non-fatal complaints.

The number of dental consultations rose from 7.6 million in 1964 to 9.1 million in 1968; 18.9 per cent of the consultations in 1964 involved a filling and 21.0 per cent in 1968, while the respective percentages for prostheses were 3.2 and 3.7. The rise is largely attributable to the extension of the insurance scheme to the rural population during that period and to a consequential backlog demand. It is expected that in the future dental-care needs will continue to grow faster than the average for medical care as a whole.

A second notable area of current expansion to 1980 is hearing-aids. Audiological departments are being established in polyclinics, and it is hoped that there will be eventually at least one in every county. Few hearing-aids have hitherto been either manufactured or imported, though rising demand may partially be offset by the appointment in state industrial and transport enterprises of an 'enterprise hygienist' who will monitor noise levels and require the introduction of protective measures; cases of occupational hearing afflictions should then decrease over the period to 1980.

Overall, the number of ambulatory consultations has been rising. In 1968 there were 53.05 million (each of 8.1 minutes average), and in 1972 55.87 million (each of 8.4 minutes). Thus per person there were 5.17 visits in 1968 and 5.38 in 1972.

IV.   Health service administration

Administration is currently based on the Health Law of 1972. The phrasing of the preamble is close to that in the corresponding GDR legislation cited in the previous chapter, stressing the assurance of proper conditions for health care with unified guidance, planned development and cooperation between health care institutions. The highest professional body in health affairs is the Ministry of Health, although as elsewhere in Eastern Europe it is not the sole provider of health care. Some indication of the extent of civilian service outside the Ministry's provision is that in 1972 less than 3 per cent of physicians and of hospital beds were in institutions other than those of the Ministry (see Table 6.9).

A separate health service is organized only for railway workers and for the armed forces. The former are among, as the latter are excluded from, the 'other provision' in Table 6.9. But there are two 'closed access' hospitals other than the Honvédségi (Military) Hospital — the State Central Hospital (KÁK, generally known as the 'Kutvölgyi' from the street in which it is situated) and the Otó Korvin (which is said to be run by the Ministry of the Interior). Members of the Academy of Science, University professors, directors of important factories, senior State and Party officials and holders of certain orders (e.g. the Order of the Socialist Homeland) can choose treatment at the three 'closed-access' hospitals. Ten per cent of the hospital beds within Ministry control were, in 1972, in 'clinics', viz. the teaching departments of universities (and professionally under Ministry of Health guidance). The factory health service, controlled by the Ministry in premises provided by the enterprise, is small in relation to the general provision, there being (as Table 6.10 shows) in 1968 only 105 physicians there employed, equivalent to 5 per cent of those in hospitals and to 1 per cent of general practitioners. A United States physician on a visit in 1967 observed that a 'conflicting set of lines of responsibility is represented by the factory medical unit, which must deal both directly with the district government executive and the local health director and indirectly with the plant manager, trade union, and National Institute of Industrial Health'.[9]

Health organization at the local level is controlled by the Chief County Physician (who heads the health department of the County Council) and the Municipal Chief Physician, who appoint within their respective territories the heads of county and municipal hospitals and sanatoria and manage the local prophylactic and curative services. These officers (the 'local health director' in the foregoing quotation), unlike their counterparts in, for example, the USSR, are not dually subordinate to the Ministry of Health, being solely responsible to the county or municipal authority. Local administration is of a standard two departments, medical-care services, and special medical facilities; a former third department, the public health and epidemiological inspectorate, having been separated into an independent administration 'because considerable emphasis is placed on the fact that its physician inspectors should be able to decide on public health issues without the influence of local state bodies'.[10] The head of the latter service (also organized at county and municipal level), the State Public Health and Epidemiological Chief Inspector, is a Deputy Minister of Health; previously the local inspector ranked as First Deputy to the Chief County (Municipal) Physician. Units of local government below the County and Municipal Councils (the district and village) play no part in the administration of the health service; 'health committees of these local councils do, however, maintain liaison with the district 'health staffs assigned to their area'. The micro-district, the basic unit for personal health and (separately) for maternity and child care since a recent reorganization, is normally formed for an urban or rural population of 2,500 to 2,600. Each unit has a district nurse, a health visitor and a clerk under a general practitioner.

The Ministry of Health is directly responsible for research, for postgraduate training and for highly-specialist referral, in hospitals attached to research institutes. The latter include the National Institutes for Pulmonology, Cardiology, Ophthalmology, and Dermatopathology and Sexual Pathology.

Hospitals are not, as in some other Comecon countries, differently administered by virtue of size but those having 700 to 1,000 beds normally function as county or municipal referral centres. They have only small outpatient departments, mainly for follow-up of discharged patients. Hospitals at the level of the district (*járás*) have similar outpatient functions, because the polyclinic — separate from hospitals — forms the fundamental unit for ambulatory care. The polyclinic can be very large (up to 120 physicians apiece) and, though specialists may take part-time duty in them, they do not necessarily attend those whom they may refer to their own hospital. It is a long-standing feature of Hungarian medicine that hospitals themselves are specialized by treatment.

Health care is provided by the local paediatrician to nursery-school children (6 months to 3 years) but there is a distinct school health service for kindergartens (3 to 6 years) and schools.

No separate emergency-care service is operated, hospitals and large polyclinics arranging emergency facilities in their areas among themselves.[11] Sanatoria, unlike hospitals, are run directly by the Ministry of Health; trade unions (unlike the arrangements in the USSR) have only a consultative and financial role.

V.   Health-care facilities

The Ministry of Health undertook a rationalization programme in the past decade which reduced the number of hospitals from 190 in 1964 to 176 in 1973, but bed capacity has been rapidly increased. Counting all hospitals, as in Table 6.9, their number rose from 83.6 to 91.7 under the 1971-5 Plan, raising the ratio per 10,000 population from 80.7 in 1970 to 87.0 in 1975: the Central Committee's commentary on the 1976-80 Five-Year Plan, citing the 1975 attainment, recommended an improvement in the quality of care; the Plan itself requires the addition of 9,500 to 10,500 beds by 1980. Utilization as reported by the Comecon Secretariat on an internationally-comparable basis (Table 1.5), shows a lower ratio (77.6 in 1970, 79.1 in 1974) per 10,000 population under smaller bed-capacities (80.1, 81.3 and 82.0 thousands in 1970, 1972 and 1973 respectively), fewer even than those under the Ministry (as shown in Tables 6.9 and 6.10), viz. 83.7 and 86.1 thousands in 1972 and 1973. The cause of the divergence is not readily explicable (the Comecon Secretariat states in its *Statistical Yearbook* that to qualify beds must be fully equipped and available for use, whether or not occupied). It is possible that on some other defini-tion Hungary would not rank second from the bottom (equal to Czechoslovakia with Poland lower) in Comecon (Table 1.5). The objec-tive of the long-term plan, 1965-85, is 115 beds per 11,000, which happens to be the 1973 ratio reached in the USSR.

Within an average ratio of 9 hospital physicians per 100 beds, lower rates prevailed in mental health (6) and tuberculosis (7) departments and special hospitals, whereas in teaching hospitals (university clinics), on the other hand, there were 18 physicians per 100 beds. Ratios are necessarily lower with respect to mental health and tuberculosis be-cause part of the need for hospitalization is custodial and for surveill-ance. As in most other Comecon states, intensive-care units have only recently been separately organized. The utilization of hospital beds has settled at around 90 per cent within rapidly expanding bed capacity. As data in Table 6.9 imply, the concentration of services in the capital is high, but it has been decreasing.

Since 1960 the number of physicians reported is only those on the medical register then established and is limited to those working in a medical post; others, medically qualified, could apply for registration if they were not so employed or were retired. Physician numbers in Table 6.11 comprise those persons, and the number of medical posts exceeds that number to the extent that physicians hold more than one post. Thus in 1964 there were 20,037 posts in the Ministry of Health service held among the 18,182 it employed, and in 1968, 22,986 against the 21,200 employed.

The commission on the long-term health plan found that the propor-tion of intermediate- to medically-qualified personnel was too low (see Table 6.12). The ratio of hospital physicians to their trained associate personnel had been constant at 3.9 from 1960 to 1968, but rose to 4.1

by 1973, doubtless in pursuance of the commission's proposal. Within a rather more rapid rise in the relationship of all intermediate staff to all physicians (3.1 in 1960 to 3.6 in 1973). Table 6.12 shows an 87 per cent increment in nursing staff against one of 63 per cent for physicians both overall and in hospitals separately. Medical auxiliaries (feldshers) are not employed in Hungary (as they are in some other countries of Eastern Europe); their role is partly fulfilled by qualified nurses and health-visitors. There are 99 community-nurse posts to every 100 community physicians, and outside towns the nurse usually resides in a village other than that in which the physician has his office. She gives care under his instruction throughout the community-physician's district but is on the spot for first-aid. Health visitors ('welfare workers' in Table 6.12) complement the work of the community physician (who also has a receptionist-assistant, frequently a part-time job since the consulting period is normally four hours).

The commission, finally, observed that pressure upon community physicians was, as already mentioned, a factor in overprescribing. At that time subsidies of about 3,000 million ft were being disbursed on pharmaceuticals, of which 2,000 million ft from central funds on prescriptions. Indeed, consumption of pharmaceuticals through hospital dispensaries and through retail pharmacies rose from 181 ft per inhabitant in 1960 to 360 ft in 1974.

In 1968 there were 3,668 posts in the local health-care service (providing 48.6 million consultations); 1,242 posts in the industrial health service (providing 10.2 million consultations) – some local physicians functioning also in this service; 2,125 posts in the dental service (giving 9.1 million treatments), 520 in the public health service, 2,724 in the maternity and child care service and 447 in the school health service. In the maternity service 89.9 per cent of live births had been preceded by a consultation; 89.8 per cent of the schoolchild examinations required were undertaken. Mothers make an average of 12 consultations per child in the 2.5 years (6 months to 3 years) within the maternal and child-care service. In drawing attention to the list of special health care facilities in Table 6.13 some reference must be made to the definitions used. 'Clinics' are *gondosásák*, commonly translated as 'dispensaries'; the Hungarian usage of *klinikák*, of which there were 5 in the period under review, is reserved for inpatient facilities within a medical university, used for training and research as well as for medical attention; all clinics of the same university are treated as one. An infant home is an institution for the permanent care of children under 3 years, either because the child is under state care (for lack of adequate material, moral or medical environment at home or because the parents are deceased or absent) or because the child is temporarily under care (e.g. during a parent's illness). A creche (or nursery) is also for children under 3 but of working parents, and operates mainly during the day-time, the child sleeping at home; creches are run either by factories and offices for their workers or by local authorities. Permanent creches are distinguished from 'seasonal' which are opened in villages during periods of peak farm activity. Children of 3-18 under state care are placed in 'educational homes' run by the Ministry of Education. Social institutions and homes include welfare homes run by the Social Insurance (SzTK) for the aged and those at an advanced state of reduced working activity. Six *betegotthonok*, the 'chronic sick' institutions of Table 6.10, are for the long-term care of patients not requiring active hospital treatment, and eight sanatoria, defined as providing medical care for inpatients whose illness has already been diagnosed at a hospital or clinic, are run by the Ministry of Health. Supplies of blood bank equipment are adequate and there is a blood bank in each county. Ambulance stations dealt with patients on 1.30 million occasions in 1970.

VI.   Finance of health care

The Hungarian Central Statistical Office calculated that 80 per cent of health, education and other social services in 1968 was provided free of charge.[12] Until 1963, that is before full agricultural collectivization, cover was essentially confined to state employees, viz. government officials and the staff of nationalized enterprises and services, but at that date it increased to 97 per cent of the population through the insurance of the Central Trade Union National Security Service (*Szakszervezeti Társadalom Biztositási Központ*, SzTK), which is administered by the Central Trade Union Council (*Szakszervezetek Országos Tanácsa*, SzOT). Although from 1 July 1975 free health care is a civic right, the SzTK insurance has, at least transitionally, been retained. Premia are paid exclusively by the employer, by the cooperative farm or artisan cooperative (the latter under the Mutual Insurance Institute of Craftsmen's Cooperatives), of which the insured is a member; no employee or cooperative member contribution is paid. Of the 3 per cent of the population excluded until 1971 about half were eligible for local assistance payments to meet medical costs on grounds of poverty (municipalities and rural councils have assistance funds for this purpose financed from local taxes), and various extensions in 1972 cut the proportion outside social-insurance cover to a mere 1 per cent. Expenditure of the insurance fund in 1970 (with 1968 data in brackets for cross-reference to Table 6.15) was allocated under the following heads (sums in thousands of millions of forints) in descending order of magnitude: pensions 13.00 (10.34); physician, hospital and polyclinic services net of payments made by the insured 5.53 (4.81); sick pay 3.75 (2.83); family allowances 2.85 (2.84); reimbursements on pharmaceuticals 2.55 (2.03); and maternity grants 0.67 (0.64). Other allocations included maternity allowances (i.e. those to working mothers who stay at home until the child is three), administration, contribution to holidays, reimbursement of prostheses and similar aids (0.14 in 1968), contribution to fares, funeral allowance, layette allowance, and medicinal baths (0.04 in 1968); total expenditure was 30,036 (24,752) million forints.[13] The objectives of Hungarian welfare policy for the future are further to relieve the inequalities of per-person income which result from a differing household ratio of dependants, viz. to improve family allowances and old-age pensions and to provide geriatric care for those 5,000 to 6,000 old persons on the waiting list for old-age homes; the Government is especially concerned with the widening gap between the level of living of the employed population and of the aged. This was partly due to the varying levels of retirement pensions until the Social Security Law of 11 April 1975, which introduced a uniform pension scale. After 10 years of service a pension equivalent to 33 per cent of average earnings is paid, rising by 2 points a year of service to 25 years and by 0.5 points a year to 42 years of service. All pensions are indexed to retail prices and, in addition, a further 2 per cent rise in each pension will be made annually 'to prevent living standards of pensioners falling behind an active earner'.[14]

Although social insurance cover has been virtually complete for a decade, the Ministry of Health estimated at the base year of its long-term plan that about 17 per cent of the population failed to use the rights to which it is entitled; these, as mentioned elsewhere, are to be found mainly in remote villages and homesteads to which physicians are rarely called or which they can reach only with difficulty. Only some 4,000 physicians actually practice in rural areas and in 1973 2,500 localities were without a doctor.[15] Outlays on the health service must rise as the Government extends the network of health care and as more of the households, and particularly the less-mobile (older) members thereof, use health facilities. The Ministry of Health accepts that the pattern of morbidity may change when these persons enter routine care and that some 'surprises' may be in store. Moreover, in general the rise in patient demand for medication has been increasing faster than physician-identified need and a proposal was being considered by the Government in 1970-2 to reduce the percentage of reimbursement by SzTK from 85 to 70 per cent (payment by the patient outside hospital care at 15 per cent of retail price was introduced in 1952 when free issue was abandoned). Self-medication (said to be evident in the issue of 18 prescriptions per person in Budapest in 1968)[16] will doubtless continue to rise with income, but does not involve social finance; moreover, as there are neither private insurance schemes nor an employee's contribution to social insurance, the individual was not faced with a choice between insurance premia and own purchase of medicaments. No charge is made to an insured person for a consultation whether in a domiciliary or in a health facility, the cost being reimbursed by SzTK; until 1 July 1975 payment was made by a non-insured person, and, after three months' hospitalization, with respect to a pensioner or the dependant of an insured person. Prescriptions in hospitals are free to the patient. In 1968 community physician's charges aggregated 112 million forints, of which 107 million was reimbursed by SzTK, 4 million by local assistance funds on behalf of the indigent non-insured and 1 million by other non-insured persons. For pharmaceuticals, sera and vaccines against contagious disease, diabetes and tuberculosis and for specified 'life-saving' medicaments no payment is required of the patient. The prescription form signed by the physician contains space for 100 per cent, 85 per cent, or zero reimbursement by SzTK or other agency. The pharmacy forwards the form to SzTK for reimbursement. Within the official list of specialities, *Tájékoztató a Gyogyszérkészitmenyek Rendelésére*, Hungarian products are freely prescribable, but prescriptions for 'deficit' products (mostly imports) must be countersigned by an official of the Ministry of Health. A physician may countersign himself on his own responsibility in case of emergency.

Fifty per cent of all prescribed prosthetic devices is reimbursed by SzTK, except that dental fillings are not charged for and no reimbursement is made for other dental prostheses. Medical supplies are not charged for in hospital and SzTK reimburses 75 per cent of prescriptions out of hospital. The small volume of retail sales under this head (12 and 19 million forints in 1960 and 1968 respectively) may be seen from Table 6.14, which sets out all available published pharmaceutical and prosthetic outlays, supplemented by estimates for completeness.

A physician in full-time work (which includes duty every other Saturday) for the health service can obtain permission to practice privately for one hour a day when off duty (8 hours a day is the standard). A retired physician, with permission, may practice without limit of time. Premises, usually the physician's home, must meet official standards and patients should not, legally at least, be drawn from the area in which he has public practice. The Minister of Health stated in September 1975 that between 4,000 and 5,000 physicians had a private practice and that some were still needed where the public service was insufficient.[17] Only a moderate tax is levied if the physician restricts his service to house visits, but it is high if he opens a consulting room. Most dentists work privately in addition to their work at a health service facility. Within the official health service it is standard practice for the patient to make a monetary gift to his community doctor, either per visit if the patient is reasonably well-paid or at Christmas if he is less well off. A gratuity to the nursing staff and to those serving food to the patient's bed is also usual. A substantial salary increase for nurses and paramedical personnel with effect from 1 March 1970 was intended to remedy part of the cause of the situation — the low wages of medium-trained medical staff — and to offset the adverse reaction in public opinion when something tantamount to a strike of hospital nurses took place (about 40 at one clinic left their jobs in concert). A nurse's salary of 2,500 to 3,000 forints a month plus tips is not now unreasonable, but a further pay rise was under consideration in late 1975.

The gratuities offered by patients are termed 'gratitude payments' (*hálapénz*) and are officially frowned upon. The United States visitor quoted earlier observed that 'patients frequently contribute such "tips" in the belief that this may assure more personal attention and efficient care . . . It is the strong wish of the public authorities to eliminate this activity as rapidly as possible, but again the cultural traditions of the older population and the relatively low incomes of health personnel contribute to its persistance.'[18] Some Hungarians go further and imagine that a physician who does not accept a 'tip', does so because he knows he is inefficient; attitudes of such a kind take time to obviate.

Currently the highest 'gratitude money' is paid for surgery (3,000 to 5,000 forints an operation) and some 3,000 for a normal confinement if the obstetrician is personally approached for his services. For other care a tip of about 100 forints at the start of treatment and 200 forints at its conclusion is normal, though as much as 500 forints can be paid. Physicians used not to give tips for treatment of each other or their families but the practice has now extended to them. A patient may choose his own hospital (except in urgent cases where he must accept that allocated to him) and a senior hospital physician is allowed two to three beds of his own for which he may charge. This is the nearest to a 'pay-bed' in Hungarian practice. In addition the head of a hospital department has the right to dispose of the beds in his department with the agreement of the hospital director and a few very senior specialists can allocate beds without such agreement. *Hálapénz* is usually paid for the occupation of such beds.

Until 1971 a person had to be attended by the community physician allocated to his micro-district, but wider patient choice is gradually being permitted. Thus, in any one administrative division of Budapest an individual may choose from among all the community physicians in service, though a physician in a micro-district other than that in which the patient lives can refuse to accept him. In the outlying suburbs and in rural districts, obligatory attachment to the micro-district remains, but a change is likely soon whereby a person may choose a polyclinic in the micro-district where he works (if he has no industrial health facility) rather than where he resides.

Table 6.15 compiles health outlay for all available finance, no data being published on the enterprise contribution to the industrial health service. The virtually equal shares of the Government and the Social Insurance Fund may overstate the latter because about a third of its budget is subsidized by the State, but it may reasonably be assumed that the subsidy is for other activities of the Fund, notably pensions and allowances which constituted the bulk of the Fund's 24,752 million forints budget of 1968.

The combined outlay of the Ministry and the Fund (net of transfers between them) would have been, if the estimates are correct, 12,707 million forints. The 80 per cent which was stated to be the Government's share of national outlay on health, education and other social services in 1967 could well indicate that the proportion for health alone should be lower than the 94 per cent shown in Table 6.15. Payments by enterprises are unlikely to make for much of a movement the other way, since the Ministry of Health funds all the wage and current outlays for the industrial health service and the enterprise does little more than provide the premises. The share of capital in overall expenditure by government and enterprises could be a little higher than the 14 per cent which the 1968 figures yield in Table 6.15.

REFERENCES

1. E. R. Weinerman, *Social Medicine in Eastern Europe*, Cambridge, Mass., 1969, pp. 85-7; *Hungary 74*, Budapest, 1974, pp. 147-8
2. *Statisztikai évkönyv* (hereafter, *Statistical Yearbook*), *1973*, p. 33
3. *Social Services in Hungary*, Hungarian Embassy, London, 1973
4. *Hungary 75*, Budapest, 1975, p. 150
5. Quoted in H. P. David, *Family Planning and Abortion in the Socialist Countries of Central and Eastern Europe*, New York, 1970, p. 105
6. *Társadalmi szemle*, Nos. 7-8, 1969, pp. 99-100; *Népszabadság*, 13 October and 4 December 1973; *Magyar közlöny*, 1 December 1973; *Délmagyarszág*, 21 December 1973; E. Szabady, *Magyar Nemzet*, 1 May 1975
7. Reports of the Ballassagyarmat survey by Gy. Vilman and associates and of the Dorog survey by G. Hahn and associates, *Népegészségugy*, No. 1, 1968, p. 6-19, 35-42
8. *Hungary 75*, p. 149
9. Weinerman, op. cit., p. 87
10. *Hungary 75*, p. 145
11. Weinerman, op. cit., pp. 86-95
12. A. Mód, 'Social Problems and the Standard of Living in Hungary', *Statisztikai szemle*, No. 1, 1970, p. 9
13. *Egyészégügyi helyzet (Health Statistics), 1968*, p. 140 and *Hungary 72*, Budapest, 1972, p. 19
14. Budapress, *Hungary*, No. 2, 1975, p. 30
15. *Népszabadság*, 20 November 1974
16. *Hungary 70*, Budapest, 1970, p. 76
17. *Valoság*, September 1975, cited in *La Documentation Française*, No. 275, 9 January 1976, p. 11
18. Weinerman, op. cit., pp. 95-6

TABLES

6.1 Demographic projections for Hungary

		1971	1981	1996
Total population (millions)		10.37	10.63	10.65
Per cent aged	0-14 years	20.5	20.9	18.6
	15-39	37.3	36.1	33.4
	40-64	30.5	29.9	33.7
	65 and over	11.7	13.0	14.3
Median age (years)		34.2	34.8	38.7
Males per 100 females		94.0	94.4	95.3

Source: P. F. Myers, 'Population and Labor Force in Eastern Europe, 1950 to 1996', in US Congress Joint Economic Committee, *Reorientation and Commercial Relations of the Economies of Eastern Europe*, Washington, D.C., 1974, pp. 434, 463 (series B projection); 1971 data corrected slightly from later official data

6.2 Induced abortions and live births in Hungary

Thousands

	Abortions	Births		Abortions	Births
1950	1.7	195.6	1962	163.7	130.1
1951	1.7	190.6	1963	173.8	132.3
1952	1.7	185.8	1964	184.4	132.1
1953	2.8	206.9	1965	180.3	133.0
1954	16.3	223.3	1966	186.8	138.5
1955	35.4	210.4	1967	187.5	148.9
1956	82.5	192.8	1968	201.1	154.4
1957	123.4	167.2	1969	206.8	154.3
1958	145.6	158.4	1970	192.3	151.8
1959	152.4	151.2	1971	187.4	150.6
1960	162.2	146.5	1972	179.0	153.3
1961	170.0	140.4	1973	169.7	156.2
			1974	104.0	186.0

Source: H. P. David, *Family Planning and Abortion in the Socialist Countries of Central and Eastern Europe*, New York, 1970, p. 104, supplemented by *Statistical Yearbook* and Budapress, *Hungary*, No. 2, 1975, p. 27

6.3 Ranking of diseases for which discharge is made or at death in Hungarian hospitals

		1961		1965	
		Thousand cases	Per cent	Thousand cases	Per cent
XI	Deliveries and complications of pregnancy, childbirth and the puerperium	303	23.4	320	23.5
IX	Diseases of the digestive system	186	14.4	177	13.2
VIII	Diseases of the respiratory system	168	13.0	172	12.8
X	Diseases of the genito-urinary system	109	8.5	108	8.0
VII	Diseases of the circulatory system	93	7.2	108	8.0
XVII	Accidents, poisoning and violence	88	6.8	102	7.6
II	Neoplasms	57	4.4	63	4.7
I	Infective and parasitic diseases	75	5.8	59	4.4
VI	Diseases of the nervous system and sense organs	54	4.2	59	4.4
III	Allergic, endocrine system, metabolic and nutritional diseases	39	3.1	45	3.4
XVI	Symptoms, senility and ill-defined conditions	27	2.1	36	2.7
XIII	Diseases of the bones and organs of movement	31	2.4	33	2.5
XII	Diseases of the skin and cellular tissue	26	2.0	25	1.9
XV	Certain diseases of early infancy	11	0.9	13	1.0
V	Mental, psychoneurotic and personality disorders	12	0.9	12	0.9
XIV	Congenital malformations	7	0.5	8	0.6
IV	Diseases of the blood and blood-forming organs	5	0.4	5	0.4
	Total	1292	100.0	1346	100.0

Source: *Kórhazi betegségi statisztikai fontosabb adatai 1961-65*

6.4 Mortality by group of causes in Hungary

Per 100,000 population

Group [a]		Deaths		
		1962	*1968*	*1973*
Causes exhibiting an increase				
II	Neoplasms	182.3	208.0	235.0
	of stomach (A46)	45.3	44.5	..
	of intestine (A47)	9.8	13.2	..
	of trachea, bronchus and lung (A50)	23.0	32.1	..
	of breast (A51)	9.5	11.7	..
VII	Diseases of the circulatory system	377.1	427.9	635.4
	vascular lesions of the central nervous system (A70)	150.3	164.4	..
	arteriosclerotic and degenerative heart disease (A81)	233.1	275.1	..
	other diseases of the heart (A82)	38.6	20.2	..
	hypertension (A83 + A84)	27.4	33.0	..
	diseases of arteries (A85)	66.3	84.4	..
IX	Diseases of the digestive system	42.6	42.9	47.7
	cirrhosis of the liver (A105)	8.5	12.0	..
X	Diseases of the genito-urinary system	18.3	20.3	22.3
XVII	Accidents, poisoning and violence	62.9 [b]	82.5	95.1
	motor-vehicle accidents (A138)	7.8	12.6	..
	accidental falls (A141)	11.5	16.3	..
	suicide (A148)	24.9	33.7	..
V	Mental, psychoneurotic and personality disorders	3.0	3.2	3.6
Causes exhibiting a decrease				
VI	Diseases of the nervous and sensory system	163.8	177.7	14.3 [c]
I	Infectious and parasitic diseases	38.0	25.8	21.9
VIII	Diseases of the respiratory system	75.7	56.1	49.5
	bronchitis	5.4	11.2	..
III/IV	Allergic, endocrine, metabolic and nutritional diseases and diseases of blood	30.6	23.8	10.4
XI	Complications of pregnancy, childbirth and puerperium	1.0	0.7	0.6
XII/XIII	Diseases of the skin, bones and organs of movement	5.2	3.0	2.8
XIV	Congenital malformations	9.9	10.9	9.1
XV	Certain diseases of early infancy	30.3	35.5	33.3
	birth injuries	11.1	14.8	..
XVI	Senility and ill-defined conditions	35.5	6.5	1.6
Total deaths		1076.2	1124.8	1182.6

6.4 (cont)

Source: *Statistical Yearbook, 1963*, pp. 28-33; *1968*, pp. 52-9; *1973*, p. 57

a   Any of the classes of the Seventh Revision of the International List of Causes of Death in which deaths exceeded in 1968 10 per 100,000 excepting the n.e.s. class at the bottom of each group list
b   Of the 12,018 road accidents in 1962, 3,471 were principally caused by motor cycles, 2,524 by motor cars, 2,347 by lorries, 958 by trams and trolley buses, 846 by buses, 752 by bicycles, 525 by tractors, 332 by carts and 58 by railway trains; 671 of these accidents involved a fatality and 4,398 grave injuries (*Statistical Yearbook, 1963*, pp. 329-30)
c   Major classification difference (see similarly Table 4.3)

6.5 Leading causes of death in Hungary

	Rates per 100,000 population				Per cent of cause to all causes		
	1969	*1970*	*1971*	*1974*	*1969*	*1970*	*1971*
Exhibiting an increase							
Heart disease							
B25-29	357.4	358.6	372.1	366	31.5	30.8	31.4
Malignant neoplasms							
B10	209.6	215.5	224.1	240	18.5	18.5	18.9
Accidents							
BE47-48	49.3	54.5	57.2	59 [a]	4.3	4.7	4.8
Suicide and self-inflicted injuries							
BE49	31.1	34.8	36.0	44 [b]	2.9	3.0	3.0
Influenza and pneumonia							
B31-32	26.5	27.7	27.8	3 [c]	2.3	2.4	2.3
Bronchitis, emphysema and asthma							
B33	23.9	21.8	25.0	11 [d]	2.1	1.9	2.1
Birth injuries, difficult labour, other anoxic and hypoxic conditions							
B43	19.8	20.4	23.2	..	1.7	1.8	2.0
Cirrhosis of the liver							
B37	11.9	12.9	13.8	..	1.1	1.1	1.2
Exhibiting a decrease							
Cerebrovascular diseases							
B30	169.1	169.2	170.0	166	14.9	14.5	14.3
Tuberculosis							
B5, 6	20.4	19.3	17.8	16	1.8	1.7	1.5
All other infections	..	..	7	5	..	..	..
All causes	1133.2	1163.7	1186.5	1201	100.0	100.0	100.0

Source: *World Health Statistics*, WHO, Geneva, Vol. 27, No. 9, 1974, p. 575, except 1974 from *Statisztikai havi közlemények*, No. 11, 1975, p. 12

a   18 from motor vehicles (19 in 1971)
b   Other violence (39 in 1971)
c   Influenza (15 in 1971)
d   Bronchitis (13 in 1971)

6.6 New cases of reportable infectious diseases in Hungary

Per 100,000 population

	1961	1963	1973
1. Cases exhibiting an increase			
Measles	262.2	242.1	535.7
Salmonella enteritis	9.7	15.8	46.7
Cerebritis epidemica	0.7	1.2	1.4
Brucellosis	0.4	0.8	1.3
2. Cases exhibiting a decrease			
Scarlet fever	196.8	183.2	123.9
Typhoid fever	4.8	2.4	1.0
Paratyphoid fever	0.9	0.3	0.2
Dysentery	173.2	153.1	75.4
Hepatitis epidemica	175.9	132.6	94.6
Poliomyelitis epidemica	0.1	0.1	—
Diphtheria	2.2	0.2	0.0
Whooping-cough	45.8	1.5	1.5
Epidemic meningitis	1.9	0.8	0.6
Anthrax	0.5	0.3	0.1
Serous meningitis	12.7	5.2	2.8
Tetanus	1.3	1.0	0.7
Tularemia	0.8	0.4	0.2

Source: *Statistical Yearbook, 1963*, p. 314; *1968*, p. 364; *1973*, p. 410

NOTE: The rare cases of malaria are all imported

6.7 Sample survey of diseases causing disability to work in Hungarian industry

Per 100 workers

	Cases			Days		
	1962	*1968*	*1973*	*1962*	*1968*	*1973*
Tuberculosis	0.8	0.4	0.2	136	94	46
Cancer	0.5	0.5	0.6	24	25	29
Heart disease	2.0	1.8	1.9	81	80	89
Occupational diseases	0.3	0.1	. .	6	3	. .
Duodenal ulcers	2.2	2.2	1.9	77	80	69
Diseases of the endocrine system	0.7	0.5	0.6	18	15	20
Diseases of the circulatory system n.e.s.	3.8	5.1	5.6	91	120	140
Allergies	0.6	0.6	. .	11	12	. .
Pneumonia	2.1	1.7	1.6	40	31	32
Industrial accidents	9.7	6.7	5.1	138	114	106
Psycho-neurotic diseases	6.1	6.9	8.1	98	118	149
Infectious diseases n.e.s.	1.1	1.0	5.4	19	17	40
Accidents n.e.s.	16.9	16.6	15.8	175	202	229
Diseases of the female genitalia	2.3	2.4	3.2	28	34	37
Diseases of the organs of movement	14.4	14.1	15.6	165	189	244
Abortions	1.5	0.9	2.5	13	10	84
Skin diseases	10.6	7.8	5.9	100	84	74
Diseases of the sensory organs	5.5	4.2	4.0	47	37	42
Influenza and acute respiratory diseases	75.4	68.9	66.1	361	343	381
Acute diseases of the digestive system	17.0	12.1	4.7	64	51	26
Other diseases	21.4	18.9	16.2	292	293	288
Total	194.9	173.4	165.0	1984	1953	2125

Source: *Statistical Yearbook, 1963*, p. 322; *1968*, p. 367; *1973*, p. 412

NOTE: The ranking is by average duration of disease based on reports from 214 firms

6.8 Sample survey of general morbidity in Budapest

		Per 1000 observed persons	Percentage distribution
Influenza	(480-483)	316,1	21.0
Acute upper respiratory infections	(470-475)	187.9	12.5
Diseases of teeth and supporting structures	(530-535)	167.3	11.1
Pneumonia and other diseases of the respiratory system	(490-527)	133.8	8.9
Certain symptoms referable to nervous system	(780, 781)	87.2	5.8
Diseases of the circulatory system	(400-468)	74.2	4.9
Accidents	(BE47, BE48)	61.1	4.0
Arthritis and rheumatism	(720-727)	59.6	3.9
Boil, carbuncle and other diseases of the skin	(690-716)	45.6	3.0
Mental, neurotic diseases and other diseases of the nervous system	(300-369)	37.6	2.5
Other diseases		337.1	22.4
Total		1507.5	100.0

Source: Direct communication from Ministry of Health

NOTE: Based on a sample survey of worker and employee households in Budapest. Numbering is of the International Classification of Disease

6.9 Ministry of Health and other civilian health provision in Hungary in 1972

	Ministry of Health	Other provision	Total
Number of physicians			
— in Budapest	9458	286	9744
— elsewhere	14743	447	15190
total	24201	733	24934
Hospital beds			
— in Budapest	27653	764	28417
— elsewhere	56076	1618	57694
total	83729	2382	86111

Source: *Egészségügyi helzyet* (hereafter, *Health Statistics*), *1972*, Statisztikai idöszaki közlemények No. 311, Budapest, 1973, pp. 7, 114 and 115; *Statistical Yearbook, 1973*, p. 403

NOTE: Physicians employed in pharmacology and in pharmaceutical research are not included

6.10 Hospital service of the Hungarian Ministry of Health

	No. of beds			No. of physicians	
	1968	*1972*	*1973*	*1968*	*1973*
Internal medicine	13391	14531	15287	2120	2639
Surgery	10145	19835	11428	1460	1719
Paediatrics	7231	7963	8208	1182	1357
Obstetrics-gynaecology	7877	8330	8424	1490	1822
ENT	2080	2319	..	397	477
Ophthalmology	1881	2018	..	443	506
Dermatology and venereology	1474	1539	..	376	423
Orthopaedics	1376	1338	..	112	140
Urology	1229	1360	..	179	250
Radiology	607	694	..	508	656
Stomatology	193	186	..	2125	2754
Rheumatology	667	769	..	171	240
Intensive care	—	171	..	—	— [a]
Sub-total: general departments	48151	52053	..	10563	12983
Communicable diseases	4061	3998		— [a]	— [a]
Sanatoria	2207	2461	..	— [a]	— [a]
Mental health	10220 [b]	11293	12153	548	721
Tuberculosis	..	10436	..	..	..
Tubercular osteology	..	491	..	..	..
Tubercular surgery	..	622	..	..	..
Paediatric tuberculosis	..	853	..	..	..
Sub-total: tuberculosis	13911	(12402)	..	862	906
Chronic sick	1518	1522	..	—	—
Laboratory service [c]	—	—	—	753	908
General practice	—	—	—	7339 [d]	7675
Total	80068	83729	86563	21200 [e]	24898

Source: *Statistical Report of the Ministry of Health*, 1968; *Statistical Yearbook, 1968*, p. 360; *1973*, pp. 404, 406; *Health Statistics, 1972*, p. 118

a Not separately distinguished
b 1968 data separated neurology (2,671) from mental health (7,549)
c There is a clinical laboratory in all hospitals and in the larger polyclinics
d Includes 105 physicians employed in factories and offices
e Also includes 239 prosectors and specialists in pathological histology, 465 public health specialists, 54 sports physicians, 236 experts in health organization and 141 other specialists, totalling 1,135 (corresponding total for 1973 was 1,705)

6.11 Number and activity of general health facilities run by the Ministry of Health

	1964	*1968*	*1970*	*1973*
Hospitals				
Bed capacity	74056	80068	84543	86563
Percentage of bed occupancy	91.6	90.6	89.8	89.3
Medical staff	6841	7422	7988	8710
Nursing and other intermediate staff	25444	28925	31211	35426
Number of discharges (thousands)	1502	1684	1719	1809
Mean days hospitalized	16.1	15.6	15.4	15.0
Polyclinics				
Daily number of consulting hours	24672	28675	30712	32318 [a]
Number of consultations (thousands)	48514	53046	54965	55871 [a]
of which dental (thousands)	7657	9117	. .	10164
Pharmacies				
Number	1403	1412	1406	1398
Pharmacists	3805	3946	3924	3994

Source: *Statistical Reports of the Ministry of Health, 1964* and *1968; Statistical
    Yearbooks (1973,* pp. 404-5); supplemented for polyclinics, *Hungary 75,*
    p. 147; and for pharmacies, Comecon Secretariat, *Statistical Yearbook, 1974,*
    p. 444

a   1972

6.12 Intermediate-trained medical staff in Hungary at end of year

	1960	1968	1973
Pharmacists [a]	3554	3946	3994
Nurses	16710	26110	31264
Welfare workers	3058	4026	4453
Midwives	2879	1878	2012
Children's nurses [b]	4540	7949	9874
Assistants	7015	14044	19285
Others	10488	13838	21502
Total	48244	71791	92384

Source: *Statistical Yearbook, 1968*, p. 360; *1973*, p. 404

a   Excluding those engaged in scientific research
b   Excluding nurses in factory creches

6.13 Special health-care facilities in Hungary

	1964	1968	1973
Tuberculosis clinics	195	190	185
Venereal disease clinics	123	123	124
Oncological clinics	45	60	69
Institutions and consulting rooms for physicial education and sport hygiene	169	168	..
Ambulance stations	143	150	158
— number of motor ambulances	760	920	1173
Health visitor units	2930	3497	..
Infant homes	43	44	..
Permanent creches	905	1004	1081
Social institutions and homes	218	237	..

Source: *Statistical Reports of the Ministry of Health, 1964* and *1968; Statistical Yearbook, 1973*, pp. 329, 407-14

6.14 Hungarian pharmaceutical, prosthetic and medical-supplies sales by source of finance

Millions of forints at retail prices

		1960			1965			1968		
		Private	State	Total	Private	State	Total	Private	State	Total
Pharmaceuticals										
1	Over-the-counter	331	—	331	*355*	—	*355*	434	—	434
2	Prescriptions without charge [a]	—	85	85	—	*95*	*95*	—	95	95
3	Prescriptions 15 per cent direct charge [b]	155	*880*	1035	303	*1564*	*1867*	354	*2007*	2361
4	Total retail sales	486	965	*1451*	658	1659	2317	788	2102	*2890*
5	Hospital use	—	357	357	—	496	496	—	598	598
6	Supply for human use	476	1412	*1808*	658	2155	*2813*	788	2700	*3488*
7	Supply for scientific use	—	60	60	—	100	100	—	115	115
8	Supply for veterinary use	..	..	145	..	..	236	..	..	292
9	Total domestic pharmaceutical sales	..	..	2013	..	..	3149	..	..	3895
Prostheses and medical supplies [c]										
10	Over-the-counter	*12*	—	*12*	*16*	—	*16*	*19*	—	*19*
11	Prescriptions at 50 per cent direct charge [b]	83	*83*	166	..	—	..	136	*136*	272
12	Total prosthetic and medical supplies	95	83	178	..	..	..	155	136	291

Source: Official statistics are italicised. Rows 1, 2, 3, 4, 5, 6, for 1965 were communicated in rounded form by the Ministry of Health to A. Engel and P. Siderius, WHO European Office Study on the Consumption of Drugs, 1966-7, but the stated total expenditure on drugs (2,900 million ft) was above medicament consumption (2,813 million ft) in *Statistical Yearbook, 1968*, p. 366; the difference was attributed to scientific use (row 7). Row 4 from *Statistical Reports of Ministry of Health* and *Statistical Yearbook, 1963,*

6.14 (cont)

p. 297. It was possible to extract the cost of free milk for mothers from the combined SzTK total 'reimbursement of prescriptions for pharmaceuticals and mothers' milk' (*Statistical Yearbook, 1968*, p. 347), because that for 1963, loc. cit., had given the 1960 total excluding milk; the sum of 12 million ft for milk was thus derived. Similarly the 1967 outlay on milk derived by difference with *Statisztikai évkönyv, 1967*, p. 313, was 23 million ft; as 1968 births were 4 per cent above 1967, 1968 outlay was assumed to have been 24 million ft, to deduct from the combined total of 2,031 million ft. Row 6 is from *Statistical Yearbook, 1968*, p. 366. Row 10 is from *Statistical Yearbook, 1968*, p. 218, purchases of medicinal herbs being assumed to be less than 1 million ft per year. Row 11 is from ibid., p. 347, which in that issue adopted the classification of *Health Statistics* (*1968*, p. 140), Periodical Statistical Publication, No. 25 (159), 1969

a   Paid by the Ministry of Health
b   Paid by Social Insurance
c   Excluding medical supplies purchased by health facilities

6.15 Expenditure on health in Hungary in 1968

Millions of forints

	Inpatient	Out-patient	Other	Total	Capital of which
Ministry of Health	2860	4340	13	7213	984 [a]
Social Insurance reimbursements	660	71	—	731	—
Patients' payments	13	—	—	13	—
Net outlay by Ministry	2187	4269	13	6469	984 [a]
Other Social Insurance payments					
— pharmaceuticals	—	—	—	2031	—
— prosthetic	—	—	—	136	—
— other	..	..	..	4071	—
Sub-total				6238	
Direct payments					
— to hospitals	13	—	—	13	—
— prescribed pharmaceuticals	—	354	—	354	—
— over-the-counter	—	434	—	434	—
Sub-total				801	
Total excluding enterprise funding and payments for private practice				13508	

Source: *Statistical Report of the Ministry of Health, 1968*, p. 7; Table 6.14 and data quoted in text from Social Insurance returns

a   Including 497 million forints for 'major repairs'

7 POLAND

I. Legislation and policy

At the re-establishment of a Polish state in 1918, social security provision in the areas inherited from Germany was in advance of those in the territory taken over from Austria and both were better than in the biggest constituent of the country, that which had been part of Imperial Russia. Over the two decades until it was again partitioned between its two major neighbours, the urban and industrial population benefited from the development of an insurance and social security scheme which was generally more favourable than the standards then set out in the conventions of the International Labour Office. A 46-hour working week was introduced in 1918 for all manual and salaried workers, and remained in force until 1933 when it was increased to 48 hours, while annual paid vacations were introduced by a law of 1922.

A compulsory insurance system for sickness and maternity benefits had been introduced in 1919 and, as amended in 1933, it covered all categories of salaried and manual wage-earners and members of their families; it was also extended to agricultural workers with particular benefit for the Eastern districts. By 1935, 1.79 million persons were insured under this scheme (excluding Silesia, which under the Peace Treaties enjoyed some autonomy and had its own scheme). Cash sickness benefits amounted to 60 per cent of the weekly wage averaged over the previous six months, provided that the insured had worked a minimum of four weeks. The 1933 Law also provided workmen's compensation, while retirement, disability and widow's and orphan's pensions had been introduced in 1927; all manual workers, including agricultural, were brought under it in 1934. German social legislation applied during the Occupation, but the prewar system was reintroduced on Liberation.

A unified public health inspectorate had been established in 1922, directed by the State Institute of Hygiene, with its seat in Warsaw and (by 1939) 13 branches in other towns. The number of hospital beds in 1918 was 44,205; in 1938 it had reached 75,000 in 677 hospitals. Similarly, the number of physicians rose from 6,850 in 1923 to 12,917 in 1938; dentists from 1,100 to 3,686 and midwives from 5,954 to 9,354. However, the improvements in quantity and quality of the Polish medical services were unevenly distributed between regions, Warsaw and Cracow representing an over-concentration of services.

A Ministry of Health was established by the reconstituted government in 1945 and given the administration of all health facilities (save

199

for military and for transport personnel) by decree of 28 October 1948. It set up a maternal and child health service in 1950 and nationalized pharmacies by a law of 8 January 1951. Whereas the present Constitution, adopted on 10 February 1976, can speak of 'the right to free health care for all working people and their families', that which it replaced (of 22 July 1952) limited itself to a 'right to health protection' by '(1) the development of social insurance for workers and employees against illness . . . and the expansion of various forms of social welfare; (2) the development of state organized health protection for the population (including) . . . making medical care more and more widely available'. The one obligation under that Constitution was a public health ('sanepid') service (which was transformed from a Ministry of Health department into a nation-wide inspectorate two years later). On the abolition of the Ministry of Labour and Social Welfare in 1960, the Ministry (with 'Social Welfare' added to its title) took over the rehabilitation service and orthopaedic-appliance workshops.

The peasant remained outside these schemes until 1972, for Polish agriculture is the sole among Comecon members not to have been collectivized, and cooperative farms elsewhere formed a basis for health insurance cover. The extension of social insurance and a free health service to farmers by a law of 31 December 1971 constituted one of the major reforms following the replacement of Gomulka by Gierek after the riots of December 1970. Independent farmers and their dependants were authorized to use health facilities on the same terms as employees and cover was fully provided by 1974. Thus the remaining one-third of the population was brought into gratis health-care. The gain since the national service was instituted in 1948-51 may to some degree be measured by an infantile mortality of 23.7 per 1,000 live births in 1974, against an average of 109.1 in 1945-9, but perhaps as dramatic is a comparison with 28.5 in 1972 and 29.8 in 1973 before completion of free coverage.

The number of physicians in the war-ravaged Poland as it undertook reconstruction under difficult conditions in 1947 was 7,869; by 1974 it was 72,600 and it is one of the remarkable features of the extensions of 1972-4 that medical-school graduations were, in broad measure, enough to staff the newly expanded facilities in the countryside.

II. Demographic pattern

The Polish population at the full census of 8 December 1970 was 32,642,000 and at the sample census of 30 March 1974 33,636,000. The birth rate had fallen to 16.2 per 1,000 from a postwar peak of 31.0 in 1951, but had recovered to 18.4 per 1,000 by 1974. The Roman Catholic Primate, Cardinal Wyszyński, had in March 1971 devoted a pastoral letter to the fact that 'our birth rate is the lowest in Europe and the fastest falling'. Poland's 'very existence as a nation was in danger'; he cited three factors for declining fertility, viz. a 'panic' reaction from the postwar 'baby-boom', abortion legislation and the economic conditions which militated against large families.[1] A journalist's reply to the Cardinal at the time had condemned pro-natalist views on the ground that an increased standard of living can substitute for a higher birth rate; he called for intensification of the promotion of family planning to reduce the proportion of children born in an environment 'economically and culturally deprived'.[2]

Mortality by contrast has been very stable since the creation of the national health service. In 1950 it had been 11.6 per 1,000 but it was 7.6 in both 1960 and 1968 and only began to rise as Poland began to lose its advantage of an extremely young population (see Table 7.1), being 8.7 in 1971 and 8.2 per 1,000 in 1974. The decline in infantile mortality, to which attention has already been drawn, though largely attributable to improved health conditions, and the increase in maternity-home confinements, is said to be in some part due to regulations which require special attention by physicians and hospitals to infant patients. Observers have noticed, and parents have complained, that the profusion of medical care assured under this regulation is somewhat reduced when a patient reaches the age of twelve months.

Demographic projections made in 1974 by the Polish Chief Statistical Administration, on a gross reproduction rate which declines in rural areas but is constant in towns, put the population at 35,334,500 in 1980, 37,172,400 in 1990 and 38,368,600 in 2000. Another made at the same time by the United States Bureau of the Census, assuming a constant gross reproduction rate, shows 1981 at 36,003,000, 1990 at 39,080,000 and 1996 at 40,320,000. Both imply an ageing of the population, the latter yielding by 1996 a median age of 34.1 years, against 28.4 in 1971, but, as relatively fewer children would not by then have been offset by more numerous retired persons, the dependency ratio (persons under 15 and over 64 per 1,000 persons aged 15-64) declines under both projections (see Table 7.1).

The abortion legislation, to which the Cardinal referred and which was certainly a factor in reducing fertility, is the law of 27 April 1956, not since amended, which allowed the termination of pregnancy 'on medical grounds; by reason of the difficult living conditions of the pregnant woman; where there is presumptive evidence that the pregnancy is the result of a criminal act'. Another cause of reduced fertility was the raising, shortly afterwards, of the lower limit of marriageable age from 16 to 18 for females and from 18 to 21 for males; in addition, about half of all women of reproductive age in urban areas are gainfully employed outside their homes and — in 1965 — there were places in creches for only 1 infant in 10 and in kindergartens for only 1 pre-school child in 6. No fee is charged if the abortion takes place in a health service facility (outpatient operations are permissible) and the requirement that an independent observer testify if social reasons were adduced was repealed in 1961. Any physician may sign the required form without further approval.

Registered abortions, shown in Table 7.2, rose from 5 per 100 live births in 1957 to 35 in 1960 and 42 per 100 in 1966 but have subsequently declined without any restrictive legislation (to 35 in 1973). The publicity activities of the Polish Association for Conscious Motherhood, *Towarzystwe Świadomego Macierzyństwa*, founded in 1957 to promote contraceptive education (and with a membership in 1967 of 28,000) and the introduction of new contraceptive methods were doubtless the contributory factors. Intrauterine devices were first made (by Securitas, owned by the Association for Conscious Motherhood) in 1968 and the oral contraceptive (Polish form, femigen) was put on general sale in 1969, though, like the coil, available only on prescription.[3] From a 1970 survey, it appeared that more were starting marriage by having a child. In 1956, 36 per cent of all babies had been born to newly married couples. In 1970 it was 47 per cent. However, low wages, cramped accommodation and a shortage of kindergarten places still contributed to limit the overall number of children per family,[4] and pro-natalist measures were introduced on 1 January 1976. A maternity grant then became payable on each birth equivalent to triple the monthly family allowance and not less than 500 zloty. Both grant and monthly allowance are scaled inversely to family income *per capita*, so that, for example, a third child born to a family with 1,400 zloty per month income per head occasions a grant of 1,020 zloty.

The country within its 1945 borders is nationally more homogeneous than before the Second World War; no ethnic statistics can be cited, as in other chapters, because by an exception 'rare in any country of the world', Poland collects no such data either by census or otherwise.[5]

III. Health conditions

Table 7.3 sets out the principal causes of death in 1974 and Table 7.4 provides earlier data, classifying each cause per 10,000 population by upward or downward trend.

The combating of mortality due to tuberculosis was slow in approximating to levels normal to a highly developed society, but, as Table 7.5 shows, deaths due to the disease are being restricted to older age-groups. This has been reported as due to the detection of tuberculosis cases through mass examinations, treatment of chronic tuberculosis patients in hospitals, development of microbiological research, BCG vaccination and integration of tuberculosis control into the basic medical care. Deaths due to malignant neoplasms have increased at all ages, although those attributable to non-maligant and unspecified forms have declined absolutely and particularly in the age groups to 40. Within a substantial increase in deaths due to disease of the circulatory system, the same is true up to the age of 30.

Morbidity from the main communicable diseases is set out in Table 7.6; others with smaller incidence were meningococcal infections, paratyphoid, trachoma, typhus and occasional new cases of malaria. Poliomyelitis, which had caused 2,418 cases in 1955 and was already down to 6 cases in 1967 (and between 11 and 51 cases in 1962-6) was the subject of a major recurrence in 1968 (464), but has again fallen to below 50 in 1972-3 and to 24, as shown in Table 7.6, in 1974. An improvement is also reported in urological affections, for which incidence is lower than in most industrialized countries.

As in Western Europe, venereal diseases responded initially to the introduction of antibiotics: incidence declined sharply and in the fifties a number of venereal disease clinics were closed. Antibiotic-resistant strains are now, as everywhere, appearing and, as Table 7.7 shows, there was an alarming recrudescence in the late sixties. The Ministry of Health found social causes of the rise in increased urbanization, involving the immixation of young rural workers having fewer family or social restraints than in their home village, and, to some extent, in foreign tourism. A Polish article at the time attributed the resurgence to the large, though unknown, number of prostitutes and to alcoholism; it declared that infected persons tended to be young, early school-leavers and unqualified manual labourers, and although more finance was available to confront the problem, the spreading of awareness was the crucial task.[6] Some success, particularly in sharply reducing the incidence of syphilis in Poland, which had more than doubled in the mid-sixties, can be attributed to more diffused health education and publicity and to increased detection and treatment facilities, including venereal-disease dispensaries open for 24 hours a day in districts of high prevalence. A decline of one-third in venereal disease was achieved over the six years to 1974, but alcoholism remains a problem. The average Pole in 1969 consumed 3.4 litres of distilled spirit (in 100 per cent equivalent), 5.6 litres of wine and 30.4 litres of beer, that is, 48 per cent more spirit, twice as much wine and 61 per cent more beer than 15 years previously. A 1974 study estimated the economics of alcoholism as comprising losses of 1,600 million zloty annually from accidents related to alcohol consumption, 4,000 million zloty due to absenteeism consequent upon drinking, and a reduction of 5,000 million zloty in labour productivity. Another report of the same year concluded that the state of dental care was alarming: a Pole bought a toothbrush only once every four years, while 40 per cent of work by dentists was extraction. It commented adversely on the regulation that dentures could not be fitted free unless six teeth in a row were missing, and in general upon the unsatisfactory state of dentists' equipment and the use of obsolete filling compounds.[7]

Insufficient immunization was seen as the cause of the epidemic of poliomyelitis in 1968, already mentioned, for oral vaccination against the virus 3 concerned had not been applied in Poland since 1961. On the other hand diphtheria is a rapidly declining disease, having been as high as 37,751 in 1955, but only 123 in 1968, while the recent introduction of immunization against measles has already begun to show results.

The following immunization procedures (in thousands) may be noted.

	1967	1973
Tetanus	3492.7	..
Diphtheria	2954.4	..
BCG	1795.8	4436.7
Poliomyelitis	1738.5	..
Typhoid and paratyphoid fevers	1665.4	..
Smallpox	1541.1	1683.3
Whooping-cough	1030.9	1044.7
Epidemic typhus	11.2	..
Cholera	6.6	..
Yellow fever	2.3	..
Measles	..	153.7

Because of the constant increase in the number of cancer cases (some of which may result from improved patient registration), the number of hospital beds reserved for cancer patients was increased in 1962-8 by 44 per cent and at the end of 1968 reached 0.6 beds in this category for 100,000 inhabitants. The current programme concentrates as much on early detection as on the provision of adequate treatment; oncological hospitals or wards have now been organized in all provinces, the number of health personnel in oncological polyclinics for outpatient care has been increased and the range of radiotherapeutic facilities has been extended and modernized.

An increase throughout Europe in morbidity from diseases of the circulatory system has also been observed in Poland. In 1967, the mortality caused by this group was already 33 per cent of the total number of deaths among the urban population and 31 per cent of deaths among the rural population; by 1974 the overall figure had reached 36 per cent. Provincial cardiologic polyclinics were set up and resuscitation and rehabilitation facilities were developed. It was estimated in 1970 that between 16.5 and 24 per cent of Poland's population suffer from rheumatic diseases.

In order to improve the care of rheumatic patients, provincial rheumatological polyclinics and outpatient clinics have been organized. Medical care in health resort sanatoria, rehabilitation in the inpatient and outpatient clinics and occupational rehabilitation are also being developed.

The Ministry of Health lists its major tasks for the future as the abatement of air and surface water pollution; control of diseases of the circulatory system; lowering of infant and maternal mortality; better cancer detection and treatment; prophylaxis and treatment of traumas and rehabilitation; improvement of mental health; venereal disease control; noise control, improvement of security and hygiene at work; better health protection of the rural population; prevention of dental caries; more medical care for the aged; control of food intoxications and environmental poisoning; and the limitation of doses of x-radiation. In economic terms, as indicated by length of absence from work in Table 7.8, a reduction would be desirable in losses of worktime due to diseases of the circulatory and respiratory systems and by accidents, notably at work and by poisoning in chemicals plants. Deficiency diseases are still prevalent among children and the free distribution of vitamin D_3 has been introduced to curb the incidence of rickets.

IV. Health service administration

As established by the 1948 Law, the Polish national health service does not bear the designation 'national' but 'social' (*spoteczne*) and entitlement was then not a civic right but devolved upon status as employee and dependant.[8] On the eve of its extension to self-employed farmers, 72 per cent of the population was covered; another 20 per cent used the health service on payment and the remainder did not use the service either by poverty or disinclination — e.g. elderly peasants — or by residence in regions relatively remote from a health facility. The law of 14 December 1971 required the relevant local authority to issue certificates of entitlement to persons engaged in farming and inscribe thereon the names of similarly entitled dependants.[9]

After an initial period of centralization, most health facilities were 'horizontally administered' between 1957 and 1973 by local authorities, the 'people's council' (*rada narodowa*), the health department at each territorial level being 'vertically coordinated' by the Ministry of Health and Social Welfare (hereafter, Ministry of Health). That Ministry of Health is empowered to regulate the (significant) cooperative and the (small) private medical practice. A separate health service for its employees has been, and remains, operated by the Ministry of Communications. The armed forces have their own medical services (not included in the published statistics), but army medical officers are authorized to give occasional medical assistance to the civilian population in remote (e.g. frontier) areas. Thus the 1961 regulations revising the 1956 law on abortion provided that a woman may have her pregnancy terminated by a military doctor if there is no civilian physician in her community. That military personnel are not infrequently used for obstetric attention is clear from the inclusion in returns of places of delivery (90.3 per cent in hospitals, 9.1 in maternity homes and 0.4 in other lying-in rooms in 1974[10]) not only of the Ministries of Health and of Communications, but also of Defence and of the Interior. Unless otherwise stated, statistics in this chapter include the two former, but exclude the two latter. Table 7.9 indicates the share of the railway hospitals in the total of the two Ministries as only 2 per cent in 1960-73. There were just on 1 million admissions to railway hospitals in 1973 for a mean stay of 18.3 days, against 35.9 million (and a mean stay of 15.2 days) for Ministry of Health hospitals, or 2.7 per cent.

The facilities of the national health services are divided into the 'closed' (i.e. inpatient) health service (*zamknięta opieka zdrowotna*), the 'open' (i.e. outpatient) health service (*otwarta opieka zdrowotna*), the emergency service, the public health and epidemiological service, the blood-transfusion service and the pharmacy and prosthetic service.

Before the administrative-territorial reorganizations of 1973 and 1975, most hospitals were managed by the health department of a local authority. There were in December 1972 325 micro-district and county hospitals (*rejonowe i powiatowe*), 160 town (*miejskie*) hospitals and 97 provincial voivodship (*wojewódskie*) hospitals. All but 14 of these at the two lower levels and 16 of those under a voivodship were transferred in 1973 to an Area Health Committee (*zespół opieki zdrowotnej*), there being 496 hospitals at that subordination at the end of the year. The 33 university clinics (*szpitale kliniczne*), the 10 research institutes, and the 33 (34 by the end of 1974) psychiatric hospitals were left under central direction. Of the 217,409 hospital beds in December 1973, 119,257 (55 per cent) were under Area Health Committees.[11]

The administrative-territorial changes took place in two stages. In 1973 the village district (*gromada*), of which there were then 4,315, together with a few urban-type districts ('settlements', *osiedla*) were abolished to form 1,988 'communes' (*gminna*). The latter had been the title of the unit at roughly the same level (2,997 in 1954) until their liquidation in 1955. In 1975 the 17 provinces (*województwa*) were broken down into 49 units with the same title, taking over, and hence abolishing the intermediate county (*powiat*). The hospitals that had transitionally remained under a county or a former voivodship thus fell under the Area Health Committee at the moment they fully embraced the local outpatient services.

These, since a reorganization of 31 July 1967, had been managed at three levels. The largest was the 17 voivodships and 5 towns of voivodship equivalence (Warsaw, Cracow, Łódź, Poznań and Wrocław) into 'preventive-therapeutic districts' (*obwody zapobiegawczo-lecznicze*) in turn subdivided into 'preventive therapeutic micro-districts' (*rejony*). A district normally coincided with the area of the second administrative tier, the county, of which there were 299 in 1974 (63 being urban counties), or the *dzielnica* (borough or city district), of which there were 33 in 1968. But a preventive-therapeutic district could combine a county and urban county if either was too small to justify the creation of two districts, and a county was divided if it has more than 100,000 population. The micro-district, which remains the basic unit, is required to embrace a population of 3,000 to 6,000 inhabitants and to have at least one physician and dentist in service. Until 1973 it normally coincided with the then lowest tier of administration, the village district or settlement. Entitled residents of the micro-district or those employed therein must use the outpatient facility in that district, but this is waived for emergency treatment. Under the same regulations of 1967 a request for change of doctor (from the *lekarz rejonowy*) must be 'substantiated' and be approved by the director of the outpatient service. Freedom of choice without this constraint has long been under official consideration.

Since the village district never had an administrative place in health service organization, the transfer to Area Health Committees had little practical effect at the micro-district level, but the reform was truly integrative at higher levels. A Polish speaker at the Fifth Conference on Hospital Services in Europe (1970) of the International Hospital Federation observed that

. . . inside the county area, despite the unification of management under a single centre, each institution lives its own life and enjoys quite considerable independence. This is first of all because of the great number of these institutions, and also because of the weakness of the staff of the departments of health and social welfare and the local governments. In such a situation, the coordination of the various health services fails. Each institution has its director, its own budget, its own interests and policy. As a final result, the patient suffers.[12]

The government decision to create Area Health Committees dated from 1969 and began to be experimentally implemented the following year.

Since the transitional period, 1973-5, hospitals, the emergency service, polyclinics and health centres have been administratively amalgamated at the level of the 49 voivodships.

The changes coincided with the extension of the national health service to the private farmer, fully effective in 1974, and it is relevant that on 21 July of that year the Party Leader, Edward Gierek, assured peasants that they need not be concerned about any possible collectivization, while the Chairman of the Council of Ministers, Piotr Jaroszewicz, emphasised that agriculture was 'a priority industry of national importance' and would receive 60 per cent more investment under the 1976-80 Plan. Divergent provision between rural and urban areas was noted by a United Kingdom physician, who found the local 'Pattern Centre', as he described it, staffed by a general practitioner, a dentist, a nurse and a laboratory assistant and servicing five micro-districts, whereas the 'Pattern Centre' of a town comprised an internist, a paediatrician and a gynaecologist, with support staff, and served one micro-district. Specialist outpatient services were found in polyclinics serving about a dozen micro-districts; staff specialists, moreover, did not (as elsewhere in Eastern Europe) also work in hospitals.[13]

He also visited a factory health centre, which, for 700 employees, had two internists, and a dentist, nursing, laboratory and reception staff and its own ambulance. Every employee was examined on recruitment and routinely each year.[14]

The enterprise health service (*przemysłowa słuzba zdrowia*) is partly subsidized by the enterprise to which it is attached and its quality and efficiency varies from one to another, in some measure due to the interest and pressure of the enterprise trade union committee and the director. Thus while the health centre for staff of the Ministry of Culture is of a poor standard, the clinic of the film and radio service, administered by the same Ministry, is excellent. Medical attention provided by the enterprise health service is gratis to employees.

The provision of health care through place of employment has a wider connotation in Poland than the industrial health service itself. In the first place a substantial number of senior Party and government officials are authorized to make use of the Ministry of Health Hospital in Warsaw. It has two grades of provision, one of very restricted access open to the most senior members of the Government and Party, the other more widely available under two categories, viz. for those of the rank of Head of Department and above (the Department being the main subdivision of a Ministry and an equivalence rule operating for other state and Party agencies), treatment for the official concerned and his dependants (for which there is included a special paediatric division), and, for those of Deputy Head of Department level, treatment for the official only. Certain of these senior ranks may also use the Military Hospital, the most modern in Warsaw, but this and other facilities of the Armed Forces health service are also available to civilian employees of the Ministry of Defence and their dependants (whence partly arise the numerous births in military hospitals) and to holders of Service pensions.

Parallel with the higher government health care provision is that of the Trade Union Central Committee which has its own polyclinic. When set up in 1945 it was primarily for the paid staff of the trade unions (as distinct from members and voluntary organizers), but became open to lower-level officials of ministries and of the Party Secretariat. The polyclinic has the advantage of referral for inpatient treatment to the Hospital of the Ministry of Internal Affairs, whose maternity services, already noted, arise partly through this arrangement, and which is also available to holders of special Party pensions (*renta dla zasłużonych*).

Finally, any recognized social organization (their membership is formally listed in the *Statistical Yearbook*) can organize for its members its own outpatient service. Thus the Union of Authors (ZAiKS, a pre-war body) engages its own physicians, whom a member can consult on payment of a nominal fee (5 zloty) and presentation of a chit. This provision allows for group insurance by those not entitled to free medical care, even after the 1971 Law. Full-time authors can be elected to the Writers' Union, membership of which counts as employment and hence as entitlement to social insurance.

Among special services of the national health service are the schools medical service and the emergency service. Both were semi-independent until 1973 when they came under Area Health Committees. The schools service had always been within the preventive-therapeutic district.

The emergency services, while no longer separately organized, employ their own full-time staff and ambulances for accidents and emergency and replace general practitioners for night and Sunday urgent sick calls.

Each county has a central clinical laboratory attached to the principal hospital and there is a small laboratory in almost every other hospital and outpatient facility; the dispersion, smallness of scale and housing in inappropriate premises are recognized, and a programme of centralization has begun. All new hospitals incorporate a clinical laboratory which will serve as the central laboratory for an area. Hospitals do not have significant outpatient services but at district level supervise local polyclinics. Some micro-districts are experimentally serviced by a group centre (*przychodnia rejonowa*) which has specialists in major fields assigned to it on a part-time basis.[15]

The Public Health Inspectorate has two recent and major achievements to its credit, the containment of a smallpox epidemic in Wrocław in 1963 and the sealing of the frontier with the Soviet Union when cholera threatened in 1970-1. At the local level it now functions under the Area Committee, but its tradition of autonomy remains strong and is frequently emphasised by the distance of the 'sanepid' station from the headquarters of the health department or major health facilities. The police run detoxication centres for alcoholic cases found in public places. A high charge, seen as a deterrent, is made for treatment.[16]

There were in 1973 24 blood-transfusion stations and 461 blood-transfusion posts: there were 845,780 donors (including relatives of a patient) who gave blood free and 92,864 who were paid; the proportion of the former has been significantly increasing.

University medical facilities (the Medical Academies) and their clinics are directly subordinated to the Ministry of Health, but liaison with the Ministry of Education is effected through the Standing Commission on Medical Training of the Scientific Council on Higher Education. The Ministry of Health is advised by an Expert Committee on Health Care, about one-third of whom are drawn from the provinces and the remainder from the capital. In addition to research at the Medical Academies at the State Institute of Hygiene and at 13 specialist institutes under the Ministry of Health, the Ministry of Communications runs a Central Research Institute for the Railway Health Service.

V.   Health-care facilities

Inpatient facilities are summarized in Table 7.10; the number of beds per 10,000 inhabitants rose from 55.4 in 1960 to 65.6 in 1974. The decline in tuberculosis sanatoria conforms to the decline in the incidence of that disease (see Tables 7.3 to 7.5). The closure of sick bays (*izby*, translated by the Polish Statistical Office as 'infirmaries') reflects their primitive equipment and average of only a score of beds. The lack of a substantial increase in beds for mental health patients implies tolerance by the authorities of the longest waiting lists of any specialty. Because of the shortage, it is, in general, only patients who are socially dangerous or with suicidal tendencies who are taken as inpatients; difficulties are accentuated by the inadequacy of physicians trained in this field. As is shown below, the bulk of mental health care is as outpatient and the period of hospitalization has been substantially cut (from 135 days in 1960 to 92 in 1973).

During 1969 the number of hospital beds in all specialties passed the 200,000 mark, and 220,000 in 1974, while the number of beds per hospital physician (as Tables 7.11 and 7.12 indicate) was improved — from 12 in 1960 to 9 in 1968 (no data published for 1973 or 1974). Training arrangements in the sixties were satisfactory in raising the staff physician to bed ratio during a period which saw considerable additions to bed capacity, but it is also significant that the number of graduates with other than medical qualifications and of nurses with full training increased sharply. The grade of 'assistant nurse', introduced in 1958, had brought all but 1,873 non-qualified nursing staff into a trained category by 1968 with a 'hard core' of 1,200 remaining by 1973. The discontinuance of feldsher training reduced numbers employed by 2,044 between 1960 and 1974 during which period no less than 28,241 physicians were recruited, net of retirements.

The needs for further provision were recognized at the VIIth Party Congress in December 1975, when an undertaking was given by the Prime Minister that the 1976-80 investment plan would include hospitals among priorities: 24,000 more beds would be added to general hospitals, 3,000 to psychiatric and 8,000 for long-term care. A concentration of population in towns and in large workplaces will facilitate the introduction of preventative medicine; even though the enterprise health service today could effect regular medical examination and other prophylaxis, it is, through pressure on medical-staff time and capacity, largely curative. By 1985 investment in the health service would be running at a rate triple that of 1965-70; whereas an annual increment of 4,000 hospital beds had been planned for 1965-70 (actual average 3,638), a mean of 10,000 per year was planned for 1981-85.

The Polish health service has been well ahead of other Comecon member-states in recruiting physicians, with a rise between 1960 and 1973 of 84 per cent, no less than 4.8 per cent annually. Its nearest rivals in this regard, the USSR and the GDR, showed increments over the 13 years of 78 and 76 per cent, while in Romania the increase was a mere 31 per cent. The recruitment has chiefly been of women, who constituted 63 per cent of the 1960-73 increment, bringing their proportion among physicians to just over half. As by the end of the Second World War almost half the prewar number of physicians had either died or had stayed abroad, and after medical faculties had been closed under German occupation, a crash programme had been called for. Something like the Soviet solution of 1930 had been adopted, doubling the number of medical faculties (from 5 to 10, with an eleventh for the armed forces) and making them independent of universities as separate Medical Academies under the Ministry of Health; pressure of applications remained high (3 to 4 candidates for every place). The authorities resisted the apparent attraction of cutting the period of training; courses are 5 years of study followed by one year of practical clinical training and another as houseman or intern in a hospital. Postgraduate education was founded on an organized scale in 1953 at an Institute called, since 1967, the Supplementary Training College for Physicians. More teaching hospitals were established at Bydgoszcz, Lodź, Zakopane and Wrocław.[17] The high output of medical graduates has enabled the needs of the villages, so greatly expanded since 1972, to be met almost entirely by the allocation of graduates to rural services, and from 1 January 1976 a physician who takes a post immediately after graduation in any of twenty voivodships designated as understaffed receives a grant equal to two months' salary.

The work of the hospital service is summarized in Table 7.13. The average length of stay and bed occupancy both increased over 1960-8, but declined thereafter.

The number of outpatient centres at dates between 1960 and 1974 is shown in Table 7.14, all types showing an increase save dispensaries for women; these facilities rendered redundant by the growth of the maternal and natal services of the polyclinic, such dispensaries remaining only in rural polyclinics and health centres. The total number of outpatient consultations rose from 98 million in 1960 to 148 million in 1970 and to 189 million in 1973. Per inhabitant this was an increase of from 3.3 to 5.7, but in rural areas from 35 million in 1960 to 53 million in 1973 (per inhabitant from 1.2 to 1.6 and in rural areas from 0.3 to 0.8).[18] School health services provided 6.78 million consultations (of which 80.1 per cent by physicians, the rest by feldshers) and 1.97 million dental treatments. In 1973 also 33.93 million dental treatments were given at 9,494 medical and dental clinics.

The report of the Ministry of Health for 1968 gave details of 30 independent rehabilitation centres and 16 hospital rehabilitation outpatient departments. Psychiatric consultations were given in 368 mental clinics attached to general hospitals, mental hospitals or peripheral and hospital polyclinics.[19] Inpatient and mental-health admissions rose from 11.1 million in 1960 to 13.5 million in 1973, but outpatient treatments tripled, from 0.6 million to 1.8 million.[20]

There were in 1973 2,527 clinics in industrial establishments (of which 129 were for the railways), 6,570 consultation centres, 145 'health posts' staffed by feldshers and 35 staffed by nurses only. 35.0 million workers received treatment or examination by a physician of whom 27.2 million for illness or injury and 1.6 million were seen by a feldsher, of whom 1.3 million for illness or injury; there were also 9.9 million dental treatments (of which 1.6 million were prophylactic) in the industrial health service.[21]

Over the 14 years to 1973 there has been a reduction by merger from 473 to 410 sanitary epidemiological stations, of which 8 are under the Ministry of Communications. In 1968 the Ministry's 195 public health laboratories carried out 6.75 million examinations; infractions were alleged against 31,503 state agencies or enterprises and 9,840 persons.

Table 7.14 also displays a distinctive feature of health care in Poland in two forms of health cooperative. The 318 cooperative health centres of 'Peasant Self-Help' (*Samopomoc Chlopska*) which operated in 1973 had been established as a compromise to serve private farmers and craftsmen, when they were outside the entitled population. Coopera-tors made a fixed contribution assuring 40 per cent of the costs and the local authority contributed the other 60 per cent. They had a prewar antecedent in the 'Peasant Health Cooperation' which brought a few medical services to a countryside in which only one physician resided per 14,500 rural population in 1938. The Physicians' Cooperative in urban areas, *Lekarska Spółdzielnia Pracy*, is a form of joint practice which is also traditional to Poland and was reallowed in 1960. Their number, together with a few private practices, rose from 191 in that year to 412 in 1974. Physicians working part-time in such a practice and part-time in the national health service (at a required minimum of hours) may not use the latter's equipment for their private or coopera-tive work, but in practice a hospital physician of senior status can use his influence to secure the treatment of his private patients in the service for which he is responsible, and would expect a personal pay-ment. A specialist whose work does not involve direct clinical care or requires complex or costly equipment which could not be bought by a cooperative will tend to take a second state-service post after complet-ing the minimum number of hours in his first post. For the patient, the advantage of attendance at a cooperative or a private practice is partly a saving of time in waiting. It also permits choice of physician, but this attraction may be diminished, as indicated above, if choice is allowed within the local health service.

Herbal medicine is widespread in the countryside — virtually in in-verse proportion to the ease of transport to conventional health facili-ties. There has never been any tradition of bone-setters, for surgery has always been seen as a professional task if a surgeon's services are avail-able.

VI. Finance of health care

The social health service is entirely financed from the central and local authority budgets by which the given facility is administered (Ministry of Health or of Communications), but payments are made with respect to some services by the Social Insurance Institution (*Zakłiad ubez-pieczeń Społeznych*, ZUS), and by non-entitled patients.

Each employed person, on whose behalf the employer pays a monthly premium to the ZUS, receives a social-insurance booklet which is franked on request by the employer — evidence required by the health facility that services are to be provided gratis for him or his dependants. But that frank, which is dated, is valid only three months: anyone leaving employment without immediate new employment takes the precaution of requesting a franking on his last day so that entitle-ment should run as long as possible, but those who for any reason do not resume employment within three months lose entitlement. From 1 January 1972 a 'person engaged in farming' may apply to the People's Council of the commune in which his farm is located for a certificate which entitles him and his family members listed thereon to a year's free health services. On annual reapplication he has to prove that he is still engaged in farming. Thus if the entitled person transferred his activity to handicrafts he would lose entitlement.

Inpatient and outpatient medical care and ambulance and emergency services are available without charge to all entitled persons and their dependants, to the very poor (incomes below a given sum) and to those suffering from certain diseases (contagious, tuberculosis and venereal); outpatient care is also free to expectant mothers and to all children up to 14 years of age, and inpatient care is free for mentally handicapped children and for all infants below the age of 1 year.[22] Others pay fees (which are graded according to annual income, those below a certain income limit, as just noted, paying nothing).

Medication for entitled inpatients is gratis, and outpatient or domiciliary prescriptions are free in the case of industrial diseases or injuries. The system of free prescriptions for outpatient and domiciliary care dates from the prewar system of social insurance, prescriptions being dispensed from social insurance pharmacies. These, together with ordinary retail pharmacies, were nationalized after the Second World War and gratuity was extended via all pharmacies for insured persons.

The principle of payment was introduced by a Ministry of Health regulation on 3 January 1953, which remains in force today. The entitled person pays 30 per cent of the retail price for prescriptions for himself or dependants. Payment is reduced to 10 per cent for entitled persons who are chronically sick (e.g. diabetes, diseases of the circulatory system and epilepsy) or with certain other specified diseases (tuberculosis), and to zero for those who are on retirement pension. Children of school age are accorded the 30 per cent rate and prescriptions are free for maternity and for all infants under 1 year of age. But the prescription status of children aged 1 to 7 depends on the entitlement of a parent, which until the 1971 Law left a 'gap' which required prescriptions for that age-group to be bought at the full retail price if neither parent were insured (viz. one-third of the population). As Table 7.15 shows, the proportion of sales at reduced or zero prices rose over the 13 years between 1960 and 1973 from 63 to 77 per cent. Until the 1971 Law membership of the Social Insurance Institution was the criterion for entitlement: it rose from 7.5 million in 1960 to 10.3 million in 1968, 10.9 million in 1970 and 12.7 million in 1974. Including pensioners and dependants, coverage through ZUS was 25.2 million in 1970 and 29.6 million in 1974.

Prescription forms are marked 100, 30, 10 per cent or free, as the case may be, by the physician on production of his franked insurance book or local authority certificate; in the case of an insured pensioner, a free prescription is obtained by writing the pension-entitlement number on the form. The balance of the prescription charge is reimbursed by the ZUS (or Ministry of Health in the case of the specified diseases or child care).

Prostheses are free to entitled persons save in the case of dental prostheses where only the replacement of a group of six or more teeth is gratis, and of spectacles where non-standard frames are charged for. Gold for dental fillings is available and has to be paid for, but is out of fashion both in dental practice and by consumers. The non-entitled pay for all prostheses they require. All compulsory inoculations are, of course, free.

Two health resorts at spas were built by the social-health insurance before the Second World War (at Krynica and Iwonicz), which, with the more fashionable private ones, were nationalized after the War. Some 10,000 persons (out of around 200,000 of those taking the waters) were paid for annually by social insurance before the War, and the pre-war overall level was regained in the mid-fifties. The 1973 figure was 610,320; the 385,588 in sanatoria or rest-homes stayed an average of 26 days (30,832 beds being at their disposal). This service is free to entitled persons, together with travel to the resort, on prescription.

Table 7.16 shows that outlay of the Ministry of Health rose at current prices by 2.1 times between 1960 and 1970 and tripled between 1960 and 1974. The abstract of *Health Statistics* no longer provides financial data and the latest capital figures are for 1971 when investment was below that of 1970, possibly because of a cut-back under a new five-year plan. There had been a similar nadir of capital spending in 1965, the end-year of an earlier plan period. The percentage of total outlay, which was 10.4 per cent in 1960, fell to 8.1 in 1967, and 6.7 in 1970 and with the reduction in absolute outlay reached 6.2 per cent in 1971 and 5.8 per cent in 1972.[23] Of 1972 capital spending of 1,960 million zloty, 806 million was on capital assets and 1,154 million on major repairs. The small central budget of the Ministry carried only a 3 per cent capital component while local budgets made most of the outlay, at 7 per cent. The share of local budgets in total outlay of the Ministry rose from 85 per cent in 1960 to 86 per cent in 1970 and to 87 per cent in 1974. In the latter year, 16,478 million zloty (39 per cent) of the Ministry's health outlays were spent through the Area Health Committee. An indication of the transitional nature of 1973 when the Committees were established and were taking over health facilities is that spending through them in 1973 was 11,985 million zloty. The distribution of capital and total outlay by type of service is shown in Tables 7.17 to 7.19. The sources shown are in money terms but because of slight changes in coverage and in pricing (investment is at fixed 1961 prices in *Health Statistics, 1945-64*) a percentage pattern is more meaningful for investment. The administrative reform obscures recent trends in spending, although the slow expansion of psychiatric care is evident from its increment of 45 per cent in 1970-4 when total outlay rose by 60 per cent). These outlays, mainly on sanatoria, paid vacations and rest-homes, are administered by each enterprise's 'Workers' Self-Management Conference' (*konferencia samorządu robotniczego*) or, when these are not operative, by the enterprise trade union committee (*związek zawodowy*). Trade unions rather than factories themselves own the sanatoria and rest-homes and bear capital and repair costs because they are exempt from the tax on capital assets levied on enterprises. It is for this reason that only current costs attributable to health care figure in the Ministry's budget (see note to Table 7.18).

No aggregate information is published on private expenditure on health care. Payments by non-entitled persons to hospitals and the Ministry's outpatient institutions (including prescriptions whether hospitalized or not) for medical attention must until 1972 have been a fairly large item; a similar category, being phased out after 1972, comprised the cooperator's share in capital and current costs of the rural facilities run by Peasant Self-Help. The magnitude of the change may be judged by the fact that 8.2 million rural dwellers were not insured in 1968 and that only 35 per cent of them were entitled to free medical treatment (i.e. schoolchildren and the chronic sick); on the other hand, private expenditure was far from proportionate to that with respect to entitled persons since a villager made only one-fifth the number of attendances at an outpatient facility that a town-dweller made, nearly all the latter being insured. Direct expenditure on private practice might have diminished a little since 1972, because fewer peasants would have sought private attention when free facilities became available to them, but the diversion of state resources to fill the need in the countryside may have lengthened queues in urban facilities and led more townsmen to prefer private care. As elsewhere, people turn to private practice either to jump a queue for ambulatory care or to secure a bed in a hospital of their choice, at a convenient time or under the specialist they prefer. The Ministry of Health controls the scale of fees charged in group (cooperative) practice but does not in private practice (300-500 zloty per consultation): the latter is especially relevant for gaining access to a hospital bed as desired by the patient since the fee to a senior staff-member (*ordynator*) in his private capacity can be considered a *sub rosa* payment for him to secure a bed within his allocation. A sum of 7,000-10,000 would be in order for an operation. Minor operations can be conducted in private consulting rooms (which are inspected by the Ministry) where for reasons of privacy some women prefer an abortion (a charge of 1,000 zloty is normal).

Fees in cooperative and private practice are subject to 'income tax', which is levied on income other than by employment (corresponding to Schedule D of United Kingdom income tax). The tax on earnings from employment (Schedule E in the United Kingdom system) has been abolished with effect from 1 January 1976, the Polish Government in this being the sole Comecon member to take this step, which was undertaken by Albania in 1967 and begun by the Soviet Government in 1961 (but suspended the following year). A surtax, entitled the 'equalization tax' is levied progressively on higher incomes (from 96,000 zloty per annum until 1975, 144,000 zloty from 1976).

The present minimum for such taxation, at 12,000 zloty a month, compares with average earnings in the national health service of 2,460 zloty in 1973, as Table 7.20 shows. In 1973 earnings from Ministry of Health employment were 88 per cent of the national average against 78 per cent in 1970, a significant narrowing of the differential.

The final component in private spending is on health care products, viz. either at full retail price for the non-entitled, within hospitals or in outside care, or by the entitled without prescription, or at discounted prices (30 or 10 per cent as the case may be) by the entitled on prescription. Table 7.15 sets out spending and rebates at retail pharmacies, and allowance may be made for zero and 10 per cent prescriptions by assuming that on average 25 per cent (rather than the standard 30 per cent) was paid by individuals for the reduced-charge sales. Including non-reimbursed outlay, a *per capita* expenditure of 150 zloty per year (5,013 million zloty for a 33.36 million population) is indicated for 1973. Family budget surveys showed that in that year 482 zloty was spent per person on personal hygiene and health.[24] As a rough approximation about 150 zloty could be attributed to direct payments for health care and the remainder (380 zloty) put for toiletries and cosmetics. To complete Table 7.21, therefore, an equal sum is shown for private practice fees as for pharmaceuticals.

Reimbursement of pharmaceuticals and medical supplies are shown under two heads in Table 7.21. That termed 'payment to pharmacies for prescriptions' is the sum paid by ZUS to the pharmacy (one-quarter of prescriptions issued to entitled persons). They may be compared as follows with total 'expenditure in kind' by that Fund.[25]

	1965	1973
ZUS expenditure 'in kind' (million zloty)	144020	281207
of which pharmaceuticals and medical supplies (mn zl.)	3229	6853
— percentage	2.2	2.4

The outlay termed 'prescriptions reimbursed' represents those to their members by the Social Insurance Fund for Handicrafts, *Fundusz Ubezpieczenia Spolecznego Rzemieślnikόw*, founded on 1 July 1965 and by the Social Insurance Fund for Certain Groups of the Population, *Fundusz Ubezpieczenia Spolecznego Niektόrych Grup Ludności*, founded on 1 October 1966 to cater for those working on commission in trade, oil distribution, catering and taxi-driving.[26] When these funds were starting, the former Director of the Institute of Occupational Medicine and Rural Hygiene proposed a medical insurance scheme for independent farmers whereby a compulsory premium would be added, proportionate to the land tax. An average farm household would have paid a year 160 zloty for partial and 680 zloty for comprehensive cover. In the event, the Government, of course, decided to raise the funds from general taxation.

As only a minor item (enterprise payments, which amount to only 1 per cent of aggregate outlay in 1965 and 1973) is not available for 1960 in Table 7.21 (the entry begins in the *Yearbook* for 1966), a time series can be constructed showing the substitution of government and social insurance for direct personal outlay since 1960 (in percentages)

	1960	1973
Government	67	70
Social Insurance	11	13
Enterprises	1	1
Direct personal	21	16

Some notable work has been undertaken in Poland on the programming and evaluation of the social health service.[27]

Consumption of pharmaceuticals is compiled by source of finance in Table 7.22 on the 1960 data: a direct personal payment of 1,401 million zloty on that part of prescriptions not reimbursed plus a purchase of 599 million zloty adds to exactly 2,000 million zloty, which is 2❼ per cent of the 5,990 million zloty shown as total pharmaceutical consumption in Table 7.22. A rough rounded percentage relating to a year or two later put the share at 40 per cent,[28] but this may have made allowance for the rise in entitlement in the early sixties (from 7.52 million insured, pensioners and dependants in 1960 to 8.53 million in 1963 and 9.11 million in 1965).[29] In 1968 consumption of 12,900 million zloty was 309 zloty *per capita* at retail prices. In 1969-70 the production association Polfa was using an exchange rate of 64 zloty to the US dollar for the conversion of retail pharmaceuticals.

A recent development in finance is appeal for voluntary contributions for buildings and equipment additional to that socially-funded. Enterprises, clubs and individuals are invited to support the National Health Fund (NFOZ), set up in 1972,[30] while Poles abroad and foreign firms trading with Poland (Krupp made a large donation) are helping towards the construction of a National Centre for Child Health near Warsaw.

REFERENCES

1. *The Times* (London), 23 March 1971
2. *Polityka*, 11 September 1971
3. H. P. David, *Family Planning and Abortion in the Socialist Countries of Central and Eastern Europe*, New York, 1970, pp. 81-2
4. *Głos pracy*, 25/26 November 1972
5. A. Maryański, *Problemy ludnościowe krajów socialistycznych*, Warsaw, 1974, p. 47
6. *Kultura*, 31 May 1970
7. *Trybuna Ludu*, 15 September 1974, p. 6 and 16 February 1974, p. 8
8. Article 17, para. 1, Law of 28 October 1948 on National Health Service Institutions and the Planned Economy (*Dziennik ustaw*, No. 55, 1948, item 434)
9. Articles 1 and 3, Ministerial Order of 14 December 1971 on Provision of Medical Services by National Health Service Institutions to Persons Engaged in Farming (ibid., No. 37, 1971, item 345)
10. *Statistical Yearbook, 1975*, p. 489
11. *Rocnik statystyczny – ochrony zdrowia (Health Statistics), 1974*, p. 35
12. B. Saldak, 'Integrating the Components of the Hospital and Health Services', paper read to the Fifth Conference on Hospital Services in Europe, London, 1970 (mimeograph), pp. 1-2
13. J. Stephen, 'General Practice in Eastern Europe', *The Practitioner*, July 1969, p. 88
14. Ibid., p. 89
15. E. R. Weinerman, *Social Medicine in Eastern Europe*, Cambridge, Mass., 1969, p. 132
16. Ibid., pp. 141-2
17. M. Kacprzak and B. Kożusznik, *Health Care in Poland*, Warsaw, 1963, pp. 24-31
18. *Health Statistics, 1974*, pp. 60, 62
19. *Działalność Ministerstwa Zdrowia i Opieki Spolecznej w 1968 roku*, Warsaw, 1969
20. *Health Statistics, 1974*, pp. 48, 60
21. Ibid., pp. 86-7
22. Kacprzak and Kożusznik, op. cit., p. 47 and Weinerman, op. cit., p. 122
23. Same sources as Table 7.16 and *Statistical Yearbook, 1973*, p. 589
24. *Statistical Yearbook, 1974*, p. 151
25. Ibid., p. 177, and *Health Statistics, 1974*, pp. 82, 147
26. *Statistical Yearbook, 1974*, p. 169
27. B. M. Kleczkowski, 'Planning and Evaluation of Social Health Care Programmes: Model of a General Optimizing Method', *Zdrowie publiczne*, Suppl. 2, 1968, pp. 3-41 (sections of a thesis directed by M. Kacprzak)
28. Kacprzak and Kożusznik, op. cit., p. 72
29. *Statistical Yearbook, 1966*, p. 72
30. *Polska 75*, Warsaw, 1976, p. 83

TABLES

7.1 Age-distribution in Poland

Percentage of total population

	1960	*1971*	*1981*	*1996*
0-14 years	33.8	26.2	24.4	23.2
15-39	35.8	39.1	39.5	36.1
40-64	24.4	26.2	26.3	29.3
65 and over	5.9	8.6	9.8	11.4

Source: 1960 from P. F. Myers in *Economic Developments in Countries of Eastern Europe*, 1969; and 1971-96 from same author in *Reorientation and Commercial Relations of the Economies of Eastern Europe*, 1974, both US Congress Joint Economic Committee, Washington, D.C.

NOTE: In this projection the gross reproduction rate is assumed constant at 109 (1973). In the Polish projection noted on p. 201 (from Polish Academy of Sciences, Committee for Demographic Studies, *The Population of Poland*, Warsaw, 1975, pp. 121-6), the rate is assumed to fall from 83 in 1970 to 75 in 1976 and then to be constant in urban areas, and to fall from 139 in 1970 to 100 in 1985 and then to be constant in rural areas

7.2 Abortions in Poland

	Thousands	Per 1000 population
1957	121.8	4.3
1960	233.3	7.9
1965	235.4	7.5
1970	214.0	6.6
1971	203.6	6.2
1972	204.6	6.2
1973	210.7	6.3

Source: 1957-60, H. P. David, *Family Planning and Abortion in the Socialist Countries of Central and Eastern Europe*, New York, 1970, p. 20; 1965-73, *Rocznik statystyczny ochrony zdrowia* (hereafter, *Health Statistics*), *1974*, p. 105 (Series: *Statystika Polski*, No. 45); this title was used for *Health Statistics, 1945-67* (No. 19) and *1971* (No. 51, covering up to 1970), but that covering 1971 was entitled *Ochrona zdrowia 1971* (*Statystika Polski*, No. 119)

NOTE: David, pp. 88-9, states, from a Polish informant, that abortions included a significant number of foreigners and that only Polish citizens should be counted in calculating per 1,000 of population. He quoted Polish citizens alone as 223.8 in 1960 and 223.7 in 1965; his data differ slightly from the official figures onward (his aggregate for 1965, in comparison with that given in the Table, is 234.6)

7.3 Principal causes of death in Poland in 1974

Number of cases

Diseases of the heart (total)	98562
— chronic rheumatic heart disease	2740
— ischaemic heart disease	23421
— arteriosclerosis, degenerative heart disease	39739
— other heart diseases	32662
Malignant neoplasms	50409
Symptoms, ill-defined causes, etc.	22849
Accidents, poisonings, injuries	21055
Diseases of respiratory system excluding influenza	16684
Cerebrovascular diseases	15431
Hypertension	6266
Infectious and parasitic diseases	6192
— tuberculosis	4660
Suicide	3912 [a]
Congenital malformations, birth injuries, post-natal infections	3524
Cirrhosis of liver	3277
Diabetes mellitus	3049
Nephritis and nephrosis	2541
Ulcer of stomach or duodenum	1812
Benign neoplasms	1632
Hernia or internal obstruction	1409
Influenza	441
Total deaths	277085

Source: *Rocznik statystyczny* (hereafter, *Statistical Yearbook*), *1975*, p. 45; *Health Statistics, 1974*, p. 30

a 1973

7.4 Causes of death in Poland per 10,000 population

	1960	1970	1973	1974
1. *Exhibiting a decline*				
Hypertension	0.4	2.0	1.9	1.8
Tuberculosis	3.9	2.6	1.7	1.4
Other parasitic and infectious diseases	1.3	0.5	0.5	0.4
Gastritis, colitis, enteritis	1.4	0.4	0.2	0.2
Influenza	0.2	0.4	0.3	0.1
Pneumonia	4.3	2.9	2.7	2.2
Delivery complications in childbirth, etc.	0.1	0.0	0.1	0.0
Congenital malformations	1.1	1.0	1.1	0.6
Meningitis	0.5	0.1	0.1	..
Heart diseases n.e.s.	7.9	9.1	9.8	7.1
Ill-defined causes	15.3	8.2	7.1	6.8
2. *Exhibiting an increase*				
Malignant neoplasms	8.9	13.7	14.7	15.0
Chronic rheumatic heart disease	0.2	0.7	0.8	0.8
Ischaemic heart disease	2.1	5.7	6.8	7.0
Arteriosclerosis and degenerative heart disease	1.2	9.6	11.0	11.8
Cirrhosis of the liver	0.3	0.8	1.0	1.0
Diabetes mellitus	0.3	0.9	0.9	0.9
Cerebrovascular disease	3.5	3.8	4.6	4.8
Hernia and internal obstruction	0.3	0.4	0.4	0.4
Nephritis and nephrosis	0.5	0.8	0.8	0.8
Accidents, injuries and poisonings	4.3	6.0	6.6	6.2
3. *Constant*				
Duodenal and stomach ulcers	0.5	0.6	0.5	0.5
Benign neoplasms	0.8	0.5	0.5	0.5

Source: *Mały rocznik statystyczny* (hereafter, *Concise Statistical Yearbook*), *1974*, p. 31; *1975*, p. 28

7.5 Mortality from tuberculosis in Poland

	Respiratory system			Other organs		
	1960	*1968*	*1974*	*1960*	*1968*	*1974*
Aged under 1	64	3 ⎫		55	5 ⎫	
1-4	52	5 ⎭ 1		142	7 ⎭ 4	
5-9	19	3	1	129	7	2
10-14	27	5	1	20	5	—
15-19	68	12	10	17	7	5
20-24	308	42	10	32	2	3
25-29	750	124	37	25	4	8
30-39	1716	699	197	52	20	17
40-49	1651	1073	522	62	25	37
50-59	2792	1682	573	116	36	42
60 and over	3418	5077	3043	187	111	148
	10865	8725	4394	737	229	266

Source *Statistical Yearbook, 1969*, p. 63; *1975*, p. 46

7.6 Morbidity from infectious diseases in Poland

	1960	*1968*	*1974*
Typhoid	3464	694	216
Dysentery	5970	6231	7113
Scarlet fever	50842	37383	21939
Diphtheria	6380	123	6
Whooping-cough	95968	18733	2675
Meningitis	883	1102	3849
Poliomyelitis	301	464	24
Measles	84531	112008	70857
Mumps	60301	140491	99788
Infectious hepatitis	76193	74821	75752
Influenza	230425	142811	209836
Diarrhoea of children under 2	26576	29439	29834

Source *Statistical Yearbook, 1969*, p. 491; *1975*, p. 487

7.7 Incidence of venereal disease in Poland

	Males	Females
Total: 1960	22909	11821
1968	47422	24258
1972	40050	20012
1974	33223	15311
— of which in 1974:		
Syphilis and its sequelae	4816	4376
— congenital	79	92
— acquired early	2132	1402
Gonorrhoea	28407	10935

Source: *Statistical Yearbook, 1969*, p. 490; *1973*, p. 528; *1975*, p. 487

7.8 Reasons for absence from work in Poland

Days' absence per 100 workers

		1960	1968	1972	1974
Tuberculosis	(001-019)	134.7	69.2	53.6 [a]	39.3 [a]
Diseases of the circulatory system	(400-468)	83.4	107.6	137.5	142.3
Influenza	(480-483)	52.3	35.8	36.7	49.3
Diseases of the nervous system		97.2	..	120.1	126.3
Diseases of the respiratory system	(470-475, 490-527)	100.8	129.5	231.2 [b]	227.0 [b]
Gastric and peptic ulcers	(540-541)	31.0	36.7	34.6	35.7
Diseases of the female genitalia, complications of pregnancy and childbirth	(620-637, 640-652, 670-689)	49.3	60.0	76.6	82.4
Accidents, poisoning, occupational and non-occupational injuries	(N800-N999)	187.9	253.3 [c]	257.4	274.3
Total all causes		1059.4	1160.1	1381.1	1421.5

Source: *Statistical Yearbook, 1969*, p. 495; *1973*, p. 532; *1975*, p. 491

a   Excludes 'silicosis' type
b   Includes 'silicosis' type
c   In 1969 32,000 work accidents were caused by people under the influence of alcohol, costing the economy 1,600 million zloty (*Polityka*, 9 September 1970, p. 2)

NOTE: Changes signified in footnotes a and b are due to the adoption from 1 January 1970 of the 1965 revision of the International Classification; data for 1960 and 1968 and the codes in parentheses are of the 1955 Revision, except for diseases of the nervous system, a series unpublished when the 1955 Classification was in use

7.9 Administrative subordination of Polish hospitals

	1960	1973
Ministry of Health	642	668
Ministry of Communications	11	14

Source: *Health Statistics, 1974*, pp. 34-5

7.10 Inpatient facilities in Poland

	No. of facilities			No. of beds thousands			Beds per 10,000 inhabitants		
	1960	1968	1974	1960	1968	1974	1960	1968	1974
Hospitals	653	675	677	165.0	199.2	221.9	55.4	61.4	65.6
of which mental	27	30	34	30.0	34.5	37.7	10.1	10.6	11.2
Sick bays (*izby*)	170	80	28	2.7	1.6	0.6	0.9	0.5	—
Maternity homes	812	636	410	6.2	5.1	3.6	2.1	1.6	1.1
Tuberculosis sanatoria	86	69	52	23.8	20.4	15.9	8.0	6.3	4.7
Semi-sanatoria	15	14	11	1.4	1.2	0.9	0.5	0.4	0.3
Preventoria	59	34	20	7.5	4.6	2.8	2.5	1.4	0.8
Sanatoria for nervous diseases	3	3	3	1.1	1.5	0.6	0.4	0.5	0.2
Sanatoria for neuro-psychiatric children	3	6	4	0.8	1.9	1.9	0.3	0.6	0.6
Alcoholic clinics	2	6	8	0.1	0.5	0.7	—	—	—
Hospitals for seriously retarded children under 3 years	2	2	2	0.2	0.1	0.1	—	—	—
Rehabilitation sanatoria	22	30	39	2.0	3.5	5.0	0.7	1.1	1.5

Source: *Statistical Yearbook, 1969*, p. 482; *1975*, p. 481

NOTE: Facilities of the Ministry of Communications are included

7.11 Hospital beds by specialization in Poland at the end of year

Thousands

	1960	1968	1973
Internal	27.6	32.6	35.5
Surgical	31.9	37.6	40.6
Paediatric	12.9	17.0	18.5
Gynaecological-obstetric	20.4	23.6	25.4
Infectious	13.7	12.9	13.0
Tuberculosis	11.7	15.4	14.3
Skin and venereal diseases	3.6	4.0	4.3
Psychiatric	30.8	35.7	39.6
Neurological	2.1	3.5	4.2
Laryngological	3.4	4.7	5.3
Ophthalmic	2.8	3.5	3.9
Total	165.0	199.2	217.4

Source: *Statistical Yearbook, 1969*, p. 484; *1974*, p. 563

7.12 Medical staff employed in Poland at end of year

	In hospitals		Total			
	1960	*1968*	*1960*	*1968*	*1972*	*1974*
Physicians	13760	21400	28708	44827	53040	56949
Qualified dentists	..	..	9316	12632	14614	15656
Pharmacists	..	..	7924	11396	13367	14398
Feldshers (medical assistants)	..	..	6650	5328	4687	4606
Fully trained nurses	17165	28265	39635	69295	93003	106236
Assistant nurses	} 11661	11442	3517	21015	18396	17240
Other nursing staff			18755	1873	1876	1173
Midwives	3337	5238	9199	11456	12911	13813

Source: *Health Statistics, 1945-64*, p. 485; *Statistical Yearbook, 1969*, p. 485; *1973*, p. 518; *1975*, p. 479

NOTE: Employment by the Ministry of Communications included

7.13 Hospitalization data for Poland

		1960	*1968*	*1972*	*1974*
Admissions	thousands	2470.7	3004.7	3359.3	3588.2
Treated	"	2564.9	3123.8	3487.1	3714.4
Discharged	"	2424.9	2928.8	3274.3	3490.4
Died	"	53.6	71.8	87.0	96.8
Patients per bed		19	19	20.0	20.4
Average length of stay	days	15	16	15.0	14.9
Days of bed occupation		296	310	311	304

Source *Statistical Yearbook, 1969*, p. 485; *1972*, p. 522; *1975*, p. 482

7.14 Outpatient health centres in Poland at end of year

No. of centres	1960	1968	1972	1974
Urban polyclinics	4255	4973	5819	4317
of which for				
enterprises	2168	2287	2463	2590
cooperatives or private service	191	363	425	412
Health centres	1764	2688	..	..
of which in				
rural areas	1394	2307	2775	3037
state	1318	2022	2457	..
cooperative	76	285	318	318 [a]
Dispensaries	2378	1675	1625	899
Women's consultation centres	2880	2091	2221	2193

Source: *Statistical Yearbook, 1969*, p. 488; *1973*, p. 525; *1975*, p. 485

a   1973

7.15 Rebates for pharmaceuticals in Poland

Thousand millions of zloty

	1960	1970	1973
Sold at a reduced price	2.40	7.38	9.13
Sold at full price	1.40	2.47	2.73
Total	3.80	9.85	11.87
Per inhabitant (zloty)	128	300	356
Percentage at reduced price	63	75	77

Source: *Health Statistics, 1974*, p. 82

NOTE: Prices are current, including subsidies from the state budget paid for pharmaceuticals covered by insurance. Pharmaceuticals dispensed in Ministry of Health and Ministry of Communications pharmacies and pharmacy posts (that is, virtually all inpatient prescriptions) are excluded

7.16 Central and local outlays of the Polish Ministry of Health

Millions of zloty at current prices

	Central budget	Local budget	Total
Investment			
1960	405	940	1345
1967	201	1580	1781
1970	131	1658	1788
Total			
1960	2468	10433	12901
1967	3291	18785	22076
1970	3738	23144	26881
1974	5531	37388	42919

Source: *Statistical Yearbook, 1972*, p. 524; *1975*, p. 505; *Health Statistics, 1945-64*, p. 527; *1971*, pp. 460-1

7.17 Percentage distribution of capital outlay by Polish Ministry of Health

	1960	*1967*	*1970*
Inpatient service	51.9	55.9	54.8
Outpatient service	20.3	27.5	25.6
Maternal and child care	1.9	2.5 ⎫	19.6
Other health services	25.9	14.1 ⎭	

Source: *Health Statistics, 1945-64*, p. 532; *1971*, p. 467

7.18 Distribution of total outlay by Polish Ministry of Health

Millions of zloty

	1970 Total	1974 Total	1974 Central budget
Hospitals, sick bays and maternity homes	8167	4872 [a]	2198
Institutions for neurological and psychiatric diseases	1165	1688	45
Inpatient facilities for tuberculosis	888	904	89
Sanatoria	382	659 [b]	655
Outpatient institutions	5004	2415 [a]	561
Pharmaceuticals and prostheses to entitled persons	6723	9202	532
Emergency units	541	331 [a]	48
Transport	729	1320	—
Blood-transfusion service	317	435	—
Public health service	512	918	—
Creches	655	1215	13
Area Health Committees	. .	16478	—
Total	26881	42919	5531

Source: *Statistical Yearbook, 1975*, p. 505

a   Substantial share transferred to Area Health Committees
b   Current outlays only

NOTE: Outlay excludes that on clinics of research institutes directly run by the Ministry

7.19 Outlays on health by state enterprises and administrations

Millions of zloty

	1967	1968	1969	1970	1974
Wages	56	65	75	86	196
Amortization	48	54	61	68	65
Materials	82	91	104	112	150
Total	383	440	482	527	793

Source: *Statistical Yearbook, 1968*, p. 578; *1969*, p. 568; *1970*, p. 551; *1975*, p. 519; *Health Statistics, 1971*, p. 466

7.20 Average earnings of full-time staff in the Polish Health Service

zloty per month

	1970	1972	1973
Physicians	3466	3700	4954 [a]
Medically qualified dentists	2787	3075	3872
Medium-qualified medical staff	1629	1815	2314
Lower-qualified medical staff	1095	1236	1618
Technicians, accountancy and administrative staff	1967	2136	2627
Manual and service staff	1409	1590	1942
All staff of Ministry of Health	1753	1953	2460
National average for all employment [b]	2235	2509	2798
of which industry	2389	2634	3283

Source: *Health Statistics, 1974*, p. 140; *Statistical Yearbook, 1975*, p. 116

a   Coverage of probationers changed in 1973 data
b   Converting part-time employees to full-time equivalent

7.21 Expenditure on health care in Poland

Millions of zloty

	1960	1965	1973
Ministry of Health	12901	18009	42919
Social Insurance			
— hospitals and sanatoria	243	356	1014
payment to pharmacies for prescriptions	1796	3229	6853
— prescriptions reimbursed	—	46 [a]	195
Enterprises			
— from basic funds	..	7	22 [b]
— from social funds	..	222	694
Direct payments wholly non-reimbursed			
— pharmaceuticals	1401	1761	2733
non-reimbursed part of prescriptions	599 [c]	1080 [c]	2280 [c]
— other health care	2000 [d]	2800 [d]	5000 [d]
Total	..	27510	61710

Source: Tables 7.15 and 7.16; *Statistical Yearbook, 1966*, pp. 540, 541; *1974*, pp. 589, 605; *1975*, pp. 122, 125; *Health Statistics, 1974*, pp. 55, 57, 82

a Not separately distinguished, but shown by difference between total outlays and pensions (with allowance made for minor other expenditure) of the Social Insurance Fund for Handicrafts (*Statistical Yearbook, 1974*, p. 172)

b Not separately distinguished but included in 'other expenditure' (ibid., p. 607) which was 3 per cent of expenditure from basic funds, an entry which accounted for 2.4 per cent in 1965 (*Statistical Yearbook, 1966*, p. 541): this small sum was hence estimated pro rata to social-fund expenditure

c Assumed to be 25 per cent of reduced-charge sales (Table 7.15) and rounded

d Estimated (see p. 217)

NOTE: Pharmaceuticals include medical supplies

7.22 Domestic sales of pharmaceuticals in Poland

Millions of zloty

	1960	1965	1967
Index of retail prices of pharmaceuticals and medical supplies 1960 = 100	100.0	102.0	109.8
A. At retail prices			
Retail sales to			
insured persons	2394	4309	53G6
other persons	1401	1762	2077
total	3795	6071	7443
Institutional purchases for prescription through government services	2194	3682	4833
of which			
through local authorities	2031	3400	4479
Total for human consumption	5989	9753	12276
Estimated other consumption	479	780	982
Total	6468	10533	13258
Taxes, transport and mark-up net of subsidies (by difference)	3804	..	3460
B. At manufacturers' prices			
Production at 1960 prices	2751	6717	8658
Production at current prices	2751	6851	9506
Global output of pharmaceutical industry at 1960 prices	3244	..	9188
Exports	220	..	3400
Imports	133	..	459
Domestic consumption at current prices	2664	..	6565

Source: Consumption data from *Health Statistics, 1945-64*, pp. 478, 528, 530; *Statistical Yearbook, 1969*, production from pp. 129 and 159 and price index p. 351

8 ROMANIA

I. Legislation and policy

No country in Europe between the two World Wars had conditions of health that were worse than the Romanian. The expectation of life and birth in 1932 was a mere 42 years, fully eight years shorter than in any other of the score of states for which data were compiled. In the difficult Soviet conditions of the twenties the life expectation was around 45 years and Albania and Yugoslavia (on which data was wholly lacking) probably had about the same experience on this measure as Romania. Infantile mortality was well above that of those two states (179 deaths per 1,000 live births, against 133 in Yugoslavia and 100 in Albania in 1938-9) and was the highest in Europe. In 1938 only Spain, in the throes of civil war, exhibited a higher mortality rate than the Romanian, and that only marginally. About one-tenth of the total deaths in 1938 were from tuberculosis, and the percentage of deaths from the deficiency disease, pellagra, was the highest in Europe. Epidemic diseases such as typhoid, typhus and malaria were no more than kept under control. There was an acute shortage of physicians, particularly in the countryside. Many districts in Romania had but a single pharmacy for 30,000 inhabitants. For a population on the prewar territory very close to twenty million there were in 1938 only 5.5 million medical consultations, and 480,000 cases treated in hospitals, which disposed a total of 40,242 beds. If the services had been evenly spread, 1 inhabitant would have gone the doctor every 4 years and would have been hospitalized just once in his lifetime. But the services were not so distributed: 1 hospital bed in 6 was in Bucharest and another 1 in 6 were in rural areas. Yet 3 per cent of the population lived in the capital city and 80 per cent lived in the countryside. There was 1 physician for every 515 townsmen within an average of 8,160 for the nation as a whole.

The government was by no means idle. Three Institutes of Hygiene and National Health were established in 1933 (Bucharest, Iaşi and Cluj), and the Institute of Statistics, under a medical director, Dr Sabin Manuilă, paid special attention to public health data and made evident what a vast improvement was needed.

A law on social insurance of 1912 introduced three categories of employee insurance (sickness, accident and retirement and invalidity). They 'functioned in a bureaucratic manner and with extremely high premia'.[1] A contemporary calculation put the cost of a medical consultation for a food industry worker at three to four days' pay. An

235

occupational disease did not qualify for employers' liability unless the insured was two-thirds disabled. The Law of 8 April 1933 unified the schemes into a government-controlled Central Social Insurance Fund (*Casa centrală a asigurărilor sociale*), with a compulsory flat-rate premium of 6 per cent of wages, assimilated occupational disease fully with industrial injuries under employers' liability and increased the period of free hospitalization. The bureaucratic manner of administration, a recent Romanian study observes, remained. An extension of 22 December 1938 added free dental prostheses and balneological cures to the Fund's provision, but raised the premium to 8 per cent of salary. Compulsory cover under the 1933 law was restricted to employees in public and private industrial and commercial enterprises and institutions with a salary not exceeding 6,000 lei per month; government employees were covered by a scheme introduced in 1925. The wide unprotected groups included those in agriculture, a majority of the population, and out-workers and domestic staff. The number insured (including dependants) reached 0.85 in 1936/7 and 0.93 million in 1937/8, which may be compared with the number of employed workers outside agriculture and public enterprise of 0.50 million in 1937.[2]

The huge territorial changes of the Second World War broke up what little had been done. Southern Dobrudja was made over to Bulgaria, Bessarabia and the Northern Bukovina to the USSR and Northern Transylvania to Hungary. The Nazi invasion of the USSR not only temporarily regained the ceded territories but added the former Soviet Autonomous Republic of Moldavia and beyond; Transylvania was reunited in 1945. But more serious was the application of some of the Nazi anti-semitic legislation, which after 1940 forced Jewish physicians out of practice. By 1941, on a reduced territory and with many Romanian physicians conscripted for the armed forces, there were just 5,671 ethnic Romanian, 490 German and 71 Hungarian physicians. There was a corresponding disruption of pharmaceutical supply, for, of 1,451 pharmacies in Romania in 1940 (before any territorial changes and the expropriation of the Jews took place) 606 were owned by Romanians, 438 by Jews, 220 by Hungarians and 187 by Germans. This was all the more serious because the bulk of prescriptions were magistral, prepared or branded pharmaceuticals being imported from Germany and Italy at very inflated prices.[3]

Medical education was not, however, interrupted and by 1948 there were already 12,650 physicians where, on comparable territory, there had been 8,234 in 1938 (data of the medical register, those in retirement were included in the published statistics until 1968). The number of hospital beds, also adjusted to postwar territory, had risen from 33,763 in 1938 to 47,758 in 1948.

The nationalization law of 1948 brought only larger institutions into state management and medical education was radically re-shaped in the same year. The three university medical faculties were replaced by five medico-pharmaceutical institutes, each with five departments (general medicine, public health, paediatrics, dentistry and pharmacology). Private practice (except for dentistry) was officially disapproved and eventually forbidden, and the fact that the 1948 census recorded 10,821 physicians, whereas later *Statistical Yearbooks* (which did not resume publication until 1956) put the number at 12,650 (against 8,234 on comparable territory in 1938) could have been due to concealment from the official enumerator.

The nationalization of 1948 opened the way for a national health service in 1951. The Constitution of 1952 (superseded in 1965) laid down that health care was to be provided by a state-supported system of social insurance, which must include free medical attention and the provision of convalescent and health resort facilities (Article 79). Under the 1951 organization, which lasted until 1969, inpatient and outpatient facilities were separately administered but a major reform of the latter year put the entirety of facilities under new Country Health Boards. The prewar division of the country (*judeţ*) into counties, liquidated in favour of larger 'regions' (*regiune*) in 1952, had been resumed in 1966 and the health service reform was part of a general scheme of decentralization which in 1969 devolved the operational management of industry from ministries to 'central offices' (*centralele*) and in 1973 vested the direction of state and cooperative farming into county agricultural directorates (*direcţii agricole judeţene*). The completion of farm collectivization in the early sixties had brought virtually all the peasantry under social insurance cover and a standardization of farmers' renumeration (through state-supported prices related to per hectare yields) was accompanied by an extension of the rural health care service in 1973.[4] Individual farmers (whose cultivated areas have remained at a steady 4½ per cent for the past decade) and craftsmen remain outside social insurance and the only service to which every citizen is entitled remains inoculation and emergency treatment; natal and child care services are also gratis. Cover by the Social Insurance Board increased from 88.1 per cent of the gainfully occupied population in 1960 to 93.8 per cent in 1968, when the inclusion of artisans outside cooperatives and of a much wider range of dependants substantially increased the availability of free care.

The 1969 reorganization had also instituted a Higher Health Council (*Consiliul sanitar superior*), not as an administrative agency supplanting the Minister of Health, but as a governmental locus of discussion and policy-making. In October 1975 the Council was subordinated to the Supreme Council of Social and Economic Development, but specifically empowered, as the agent of the Supreme Council in health affairs, to draw up long-term programmes for the development of health care and to supervise the Ministry of Health in the discharge of its functions. The Minister of Health is only one of the Vice-Chairmen of the Council whose chairman is a Deputy Prime Minister, at that time being the Minister of Education.[5]

President Ceauşescu took the occasion of the inaugural session of the reorganized Council to criticize the uneven distribution of medical personnel, who were still concentrated in large cities and insufficiently available in small towns and villages, the over-narrow specialization of medical education, over-prescribing, and the poor progress in eradicating tuberculosis and some communicable diseases which had been almost eliminated but were now recurrent.[6] He had only a few months earlier (in July 1975) spelled out a more stringent labour policy in stating that 'we must tell the workers that the factory is not an institution for providing social assistance',[7] though with 'featherbedding' rather than the industrial health service in mind; some years before (in October 1968) he had castigated the Romanian pharmaceutical industry as 'second-rate'.[8] Romania shows the lowest consumption of pharmaceuticals per head in Europe (Albania possibly excepted). It has the lowest ratio of physicians to population (15.9 per 10,000 in 1974) among the European members of Comecon (although this group shows much higher ratios than prevail in Western Europe) and the highest infantile mortality below Yugoslavia and, probably, Albania. At 38.2 per 1,000 live births in 1974, however, this measure of health conditions was a great improvement on the postwar peak of 198.8 in 1947 and the 74.6 at which it was running in 1960.

II. Demographic pattern

In 1970 Romania had the highest rate of population growth in Europe (Albania alone excepted) and in 30 years had made up its population by the 5 million by which the 1940 cession of territory (and the relatively few war losses) had reduced it. The rate was already slackening, from a peak of 18.1 per 1,000 in 1968 to 8.4 in 1973, but rose to 11.2 in 1974, so that the census of 1 July 1974 showed a population of 21.03 million, of which 43 per cent were urban and 57 per cent rural.

A previous decline in fertility, from a postwar record of 27.6 per 1,000 in 1949, had brought the introduction of modest family allowances and state orders and decorations for mothers of four children and over in 1952. On 25 September, however, the world's most permissive abortion legislation was enacted, whereby abortion was provided on request regardless of any therapeutic or social indication. Centres for the interruption of pregnancy (at a fee of 30 lei) were established in large and medium-sized hospitals, but abortion undertaken outside such a designated centre was a punishable offence. Pregnancy over 3 months, however, might be interrupted only on medical indication. The birth rate dropped precipitately and went below 15 per 1,000 in 1965 and 1966. In 1965 there were nearly 4 abortions for every live birth, that is, 1.12 million abortions. At 59 per 1,000 of population, the rate was around 2½ times that of the other two East European states with almost as open legislation, the USSR and Hungary, at the time (see Table 1.2); a survey showed that only 4 per cent of women were using contraceptives.[9]

The law was abruptly reversed after the Central Committee of the Romanian Communist Party had called for a report from the Ministry of Health. A decree of 29 September 1966 restricted abortion to women who were over 45 or already had four children, after rape or for specified medical and psychiatric indications. A pro-natalist policy increased family allowances and taxes on childless persons over 25 and put obstacles (including a waiting period of 6 months to a year and a fee of 3,000 to 5,000 lei) in the way of divorce. Demographic experience was transformed overnight — the decree came into force on 1 October 1966 and the 1967 birth rate leapt to 27.4 per 1,000, and was 26.7 per 1,000 in 1968. This was nor far off the prewar rate (34.1 in 1930, 29.5 in 1938), but the really remarkable element was that whereas in 1938 the rate was an average of low urban experience (18.7 per 1,000) and high rural fertility (32.6 per 1,000), the urban rate in 1967 was, at 26.9, virtually identical with the rural (27.6 per 1,000). The age-specific birth rate (i.e. standardized for the age distribution of those in the reproductive age groups) in Romania has been rather above the crude birth rate. The decline after the postwar 'baby boom' until 1966 was due more to fertility reduction than to change in the age-sex structure. The urban differential subsequently re-emerged and 1973 crude birth rates were 16.4 in towns and 19.5 in the countryside. The relativity has been constant for death rates (10.0 per 1,000 in 1967 and 10.8 in 1973 in rural zones and 8.2 and 8.3 respectively in urban), but while urban rates of infantile mortality have hardly changed (42.6 and 41.1 in the stated years), that in rural areas has dropped from 49.0 to 33.3. The age-standardized death rate in 1966 coincided exactly with that for Eastern Europe as a whole.

The mean expectation of life in 1970-2 was 68.58 years (66.27 for males and 70.85 for females), a substantial increase on that at the time of the 1956 census when respective rates were 63.17, 61.48 and 64.99 in 1956) and far longer than before the Second World War (when as already noted the average for both sexes was 42.01). The age pyramid of the 1974 census is nevertheless still abnormal, with three major indentations, viz. between the ages of 8 and 18 as a result of the recent decline in fertility, between 24 and 35 as a consequence of the fall in the birth rate during the Second World War and between 53 and 61 due to wartime deaths (the male shortfall in this group being of course greater than the female). The gross reproduction rate in 1968 was at a peak of 174 (viz. the number of females born to 100 women in their reproductive lifetimes if the current age-specific fertility rates prevail throughout that period), far above that of any other East European country, whereas in 1966 it had, at 91, been bracketed with Hungary as the lowest in the area. By 1972, however, it was (at 124) the highest of the group, and if this were to be constant over the next two decades, the projections of Table 8.1 would be realized.

Illiteracy was declared eradicated by 1955, after the educational reform and literacy drive begun in 1948, although some elderly country-dwellers are barely, if at all, literate. No nationality disparities hinder the improvement of health conditions: the substantial Hungarian and German minorities of Transylvania have the highest standards in the country and gypsies were brutally depleted by the wartime, pro-Nazi government.

III.   Health conditions

The postwar industrialization and increasing urbanization of Romania has been accompanied by a general improvement of nutrition and the extension of medical care. Before the Second World War Romania and Yugoslavia were the only European countries where pellagra (caused by a lack of vitamin B characterizing a maize-dependent diet) was endemic. This, together with diphtheria, poliomyelitis, typhoid fever and tetanus, has been brought to the point of eradication, while malaria, endemic in the Danube swamplands and delta, has been eradicated since 1962 and tularemia and relapsing fever are under control. The incidence of acute respiratory, digestive and infectious diseases has fallen but the morbidity pattern does not, at least yet, reflect that of advanced industrial countries with respect to cardiovascular diseases and cancer. The incidence of cancer is among the lowest in the continent. Occupational diseases are important, although their incidence has declined faster than the rate of manpower absorption into industries at risk. Accidental death and injury are in aggregate with the rates experienced in Western Europe but because motor car ownership is far less than the corresponding levels of the West, it is unlikely that motor accidents (on which no data are published) are as high. Complementing the lorry production initiated in the fifties, the opening of a domestic car factory in the sixties has, however, already begun to fill the roads which, while motorable, do not yet need, in traffic terms, to meet standards of Western European highways.

Mass tuberculosis detection, compulsory vaccination with BCG vaccine, immunization against diphtheria, poliomyelitis, typhoid fever and tetanus have been among the major postwar health programmes. All the conditions save tuberculosis have responded very favourably but the incidence of tuberculosis is still high because in some regions migration to towns and a lag in state-financed house construction in the fifties and early sixties caused overcrowding.

Long-run comparison of mortality and morbidity are inhibited by changes in classification. Until 1965, the Central Statistical Office used a national classification of 44 causes, and between 1966 and 1968 one of 150 causes. Data for 1960 onwards were recalculated and published.[10] From 1969, when the Ministry of Health took over compilation, a 300-cause list was introduced, closely (though apparently not precisely) following the WHO Eighth International Classification.[11] In order correctly to group mortality causes by increment or decrement, Table 8.2 shows 1955 and 1966 and Table 8.3 from 1967 to 1971.

The incidence of new tuberculosis cases was in 1967 one-third of that in 1951, but it was still seventh in the ranking of causes of death and has not greatly decreased since. The trend of leading causes of death is, however, typical of developed industrial economies; such diseases as cancer, of the cardiovascular system and of the nervous and sensory organs exhibited the sharpest rises in the decade after 1955. Diabetes, though trivial as a cause of death, had also risen substantially, and infections of the newborn, though declining, still occupy an unnecessarily high place, giving Romania the highest rate of infantile mortality in Comecon (Table 1.2). The high mortality due to cirrhosis of the liver is testimony to continuing alcoholism in a country where wine and plum brandy (*ţuică*) are home-made on every other farm.

The changing pattern of morbidity can for most causes be shown only to 1967 (Table 8.4). The most remarkable increases between 1960 and 1967 were in diseases of the respiratory system, other than influenza, the incidence of which slightly declined, and, to 1971, in parotiditis and bacillary dysentery. An epidemic of scarlet fever in 1967-8 was within a rising trend (although the incidence in 1968 of 105 was well below that of the previous epidemic − 307 in 1958), and new cases never fell below 47 per 100,000 in the sixties. Chickenpox on the other hand happened to show a slight decrease by the choice of 1967 in the Table, but has in fact shown an increasing incidence in the period.

Table 8.5 shows the reasons for physician contact in a large health centre, the Tudor Vladimirescu Polyclinic in Bucharest in 1964, broken down by adults and children.[12]

The statistics in the Table of a 1955 investigation are not necessarily from the same health centre and a comparison between the columns for intertemporal change would hence not be appropriate. Aggregates for the country as a whole are, however, published for physician and hospital consultations and treatments, and are shown in Table 8.6. The columns for 1960 and 1967 are comparable save for the trivial difference that in 1960 consultations and treatments in balneological institutions, though included in the total, are not broken down by specialization; the residual shown for 'other' in each year includes consultations in nutritional and occupational matters and in 'labour expertise' (*medic-specialise în expertiza muncii*), whose main concern is the issue of disability certificates. It is less wage-earners than collective farmers who apply for such certificates to obtain sickness benefit, for any general practitioner is authorized to sign a certificate for an employee Treatment in local dentist surgeries may be separated from all stomatological treatment as follows :

	Thousands of treatments	
	1960	*1966*
In local surgeries	860.4	2273.4
Elsewhere	6503.7	13438.5
Total	7364.1	15701.9

Source: As for Table 8.6

The 123 per cent rise in stomatological consultations is faster than the increase of 61 per cent in reported morbidity for diseases of the teeth and gums (from data underlying Table 8.4) and is partially explicable by the widening of the dental-treatment catchment area. During 1960-68 the number of dentists and stomatological surgeons in health facilities increased from 1,626 to 2,576, or from 6.5 to 8.6 per cent of the total medically qualified staff in that employment. Untreated dental conditions were certainly substantial in 1960 and are understood to be still numerous. The plenary meeting of the Communist Party Central Committee of October 1968 devoted to the health service observed that dental treatment was inadequate and laid particular emphasis on its improvement.

Part of the shortages in dental treatment can be ascribed to an attempt to raise professional standards. The training of lower-qualified dentists was stopped in 1955 in favour of recruiting to the profession only medically qualified personnel (the 'stomatological physician'). Those with the previously accepted qualifications remained, of course, in service. In 1969, to remedy the gap in available treatment, the training was resumed to the lower level (2 to 3 years training after secondary school). Because of delays and inadequacy of treatment in the free dental service many patients have opted for private treatment, which — unlike other medical services — has always remained legal, in the form of licensed cooperatives of dental surgeons working after completion of standard hours in a polyclinic. In the early sixties the private charge for a filling, or a metal tooth-plating, for example, 30 lei, may be compared to the manual worker's wage of 600 lei; gold was and remains quite extensively used for fillings (the National Bank selling gold to specially appointed dentists for this purpose, since otherwise transactions in gold other than jewellery are illegal). The cost of treatment privately and the charge in the free sector for all dental prostheses has been a deterrent to widening the circle of patients.

A similar situation exists in ophthalmological consultations and treatments which rose by 85 per cent in the seven years, compared to an increment of 53 per cent for all causes and then remained constant while the total rose by a further 21 per cent. The rise is not attributable to an increase in specialist ophthalmologists, which was in fact smaller than the rise in all medically trained staff, but to charges for spectacles; only as the incomes of prospective patients rise do they attend health facilities for treatment which would involve a purchase of the prescribed spectacles. Moreover, a member of a rural household is readier to accept poor eyesight than is an urban dweller, whose occupation may require corrected sight, and the changed attitude to eye care is correlated with urbanization. In 1967 when two-thirds of the population were living in rural areas, where only 69 polyclinics were located (against 393 in urban), the extent of untreated eye complaints was substantial.

The case of ear, nose and throat (ENT) consultations and treatment is analogous: their number increased in 1960-7 by 30 per cent, then levelled off, the number of specialists rising relatively less fast than the total of medical staff; hearing-aids are costly and the threshold of seeking treatment has been rising with urbanization. Here again the degree of untreated cases is high and may be proportionately higher than for teeth or eyes.

IV. Health service administration

The Ministry of Health included Social Welfare until 1968, when welfare services were transferred to the Ministry of Labour; it administers the national health service largely through the local authorities; certain other ministries operate their own hospitals (e.g. the Ministry of Defence for the armed services, certain industrial ministries for their production staff), sanatoria (e.g. trade unions) and factory clinics. The extent to which the Ministry of Health predominates in the furnishing of civilian inpatient facilities is indicated by the distribution of beds in Table 8.7, which also shows urban or rural location; the measure of bed capacity shows the Ministry particularly dominant (98 per cent) because its units are on average larger than those of other public agencies.

In 1969 the administration of hospitals and of polyclinics was reunited (after a separation of 18 years) under a single local government agency, the county health board (*direcţia sanitară judeţeană*), grouping all locally run health facilities whether rural or urban within the county boundary (hospitals, polyclinics, dispensaries, laboratories and pharmacies). Romania is divided into 39 counties; Bucharest ranks as a county but the other 47 towns classified as cities are subordinate to a county.

In 1959 a new category of polyclinic (*policlinici cu plată*) was established at which the patient pays for treatment, but only a few were set up in the first 10 years; now many more are being created. These apart, the facilities of the county health boards are funded by the county authorities, although they are dually subordinate to those authorities and to the Ministry of Health. A few institutions are managed centrally by the Ministry. County board and Ministry of Health institutions are shown together under 'Ministry' in Table 8.8. In 1971 9 per cent of hospitals were run by agencies other than the Ministry, including 2.5 per cent in enterprises of other ministries; 12 per cent of polyclinics were outside the Ministry of Health remit, as were 22 per cent of enterprise dispensaries and health posts.

As already explained in Section I, the Ministry of Health as well as other agencies dealing with health problems are overseen by the Higher Health Council, which is part of the Council of Social and Economic Development. Although the latter is the seat of policy-making at the highest level, the National Assembly's Standing Commission on Health, Labour and Social Insurance keeps the service under review. In particular it established a special commission on the endowment of clinical health facilities and pre-clinical training institutions with medical, research and training equipment in December 1968 (at the request of the Party Central Committee in its resolution of October) and its report was presented to the Assembly on 17 December 1969 by the vice-chairman of the standing commission.

The State Social Insurance Board is managed by the Trade Union Central Committee.

V.   Health-care facilities

Like all East European countries, Romania has a high proportion of physicians to population, although, at 630 inhabitants to one physician in 1974 (737 in 1960), it does not have the most favourable ratio of the group. The doubling of physician numbers since 1950 (when, for comparison with Table 8.9, it was 15,583) has not, however, been effected by a dilution of training (dentists excepted) and in terms of professional ability the Romanian physician is second to none in the region. The affinity of the Romanian language with French enables the average physician to read technical articles and books in French and thus to keep up with Western clinical and pharmacological developments more widely and fully than those who must rely on selected translations and abstracts or on national publications. Many Romanian physicians trained in France before and immediately after the Second World War, and there is now a reviving flow of some new students and many old contacts. The high standard of Romanian nurses — perhaps the best in Eastern Europe — and the increase of paramedical personnel has raised the number of intermediate-trained medical staff (*personal mediu sanitar*) per physician from 2.43 in 1960 to 3.32 in 1971.

The intermediate-trained staff at a special census of 15 March 1968 included 29,242 assistants of whom 8,736 were classed as medical, 3,259 as pharmacist, 1,345 as dental and 3,136 as paediatric; other substantial specialisations included obstetrical, clinical-pathological, radiological, social welfare, etc. Assistants (*asistenţi*) have two to three years' training after completion of secondary education. The more junior grade of feldsher (*felcer*) is also used in Romania, for which four years' training after primary schooling is adequate: there were 4,230 in 1968 of which 2,409 were classed as medical. Among other intermediate health staff the biggest group in 1968 was dental technicians grade I (733 persons), medical statisticians (778), social-welfare nurses grade I (*soră de ocrotire I*, 600) and dentists (437). The total number of nurses (*surori*) was 30,086 (of which 1,390 social-welfare nurses grade II) and of midwives (*moaşa*) 6,173; both are classified as intermediate staff. Other auxiliary staff in the same intermediate category included dental technicians grade II (294) and sanitary officers (*officianti sanitari*, 3,712). Of the 'elementary health' staff (*personal elementar sanitar*) shown in Table 8.9, 18,519 were nursing helpers (*infirmiere*), 18,299 were cleaners, and 2,329 orderlies; the lack of mechanised laundering is emphasized by the employment of 2,700 hospital laundresses in this group and 1,130 in other health facilities.

A medical assistant with three years' training in Romania is recognised in Britain as the equivalent of a State Registered Nurse, the highest nursing qualification; feldshers are no longer being trained. Every village with 2,500 or more inhabitants has a resident physician, and those of 700-2,500 population have a medical assistant (or, while still in service, a feldsher). Of the total of assistants and feldshers in 1968, 30,034 and 2,725 were respectively in urban areas and 7,291 and 1,505 respectively in rural areas; midwives were predominantly located in rural areas (4,039, against 2,134 in towns).

Physician contacts, as might be expected from the use of lower-qualified staff in rural areas, are much fewer in the countryside than in towns. Within national average contacts per person of 4.16 in 1960 and 5.02 in 1963, there were only 1.87 (1960) and 2.44 (1963) contacts by rural residents but 9.31 and 10.43 in the respective years by urban residents. It may be assumed that child-to-physician contacts are a high proportion of both groups, not only because all children enjoy the national school health service, but also because the norms for annual physician visits to the children (laid down by regulations of 1955) are 12 at ages below 1 year, 4 for ages 1-7 and 1 for ages 7-14.[13]

The rule for a quarter-century that only emergency services were gratis to adults overburdened casualty wards and in February 1976 the Minister of Health, Radu Păun, announced a programme for opening 20 emergency centres, *staţii de salvare*, in districts as yet without them and providing 300 new ambulances in 1976 alone; but he limited access to such centres to cases of accident and acute illness; only 20 per cent of cases hitherto treated as emergencies fell into that category. By 1980 all district hospitals would be equipped for cardiac emergencies.

There is very little practice of folk medicine or by non-qualified practitioners, but herbal self-medication is widespread in rural districts, and rural areas are much less intensively served by fully medically qualified staff than urban. In 1968 79 per cent of all physicians worked in urban areas, leaving only 21 per cent in the rural zones; distribution by district remains uneven with some counties extremely short of physicians. The continued improvement of territorial distribution (the subject of the special parliamentary commission of 1968-9) will bring considerably more morbidity into physician contact. One of the consequences of its report was the requirement that physicians remain for a time in the post to which they were appointed for final pre-graduation experience: a physician obtaining his *gradaţii* (usually directed to a rural area for the purpose) is forbidden to quit immediately, as was usually the case in the past, to find himself an appointment in town.

The recently established local medical and pharmacists' associations may also be mentioned – the *Colegii ale medicilot şi farmacistolor* – to the extent that they are likely to promote higher standards, exchange of experience and better contact between urban and rural physicians. Together with the planned stress on medical education and research, they could enhance physician demand for new medication.

Orthopaedic treatment is still relatively inconsiderable, due partly to the low incidence of automobile accidents. The number of hospital beds for orthopaedic surgery in fact declined from 1,048 in 1960 to 930 in 1965 before moving up to 1,080 in 1971 and the prosthetic industry is neither highly-developed nor dynamic (adjusted for price reductions, private purchases of medical supplies and prostheses were only 3.6 per cent larger in 1967 than in 1960).

Health problems are also changing in bacillus-carried disease. Standards of environmental sanitation are still low and the rise in morbidity from dysentery (Table 8.4) was accompanied by a rise in the number of gastro-enterological consultations and treatments (from 54,100 in 1960 to 82,000 in 1967) and much investment in sewage disposal and water purification is still needed. The irony in the traditional Bucharest song 'Dimbovița, apă dulce' ('Sweet water of the Dimbovitsa', the river flowing through the capital) can only be appreciated by those who have seen its drain-like consistency.

Under the 1975 plan more general-practice clinics (*dispensare*) were kept open throughout the day (and more were endowed with small laboratories for on-the-spot diagnosis) while there was a further increase in 'health posts' (*puncte sanitare*) in the countryside. The development and modernization of dental treatment clinics was included in the annual plan for 1975, with an experiment with the topical application of fluoride extended to primary school children in grade I in several large cities. Surgical departments for heart disease treatment and other services were to be developed, and a cancer screening programme was to be started for all women between 30 and 64 years old.[14] 1975 was the terminal year of the Five-Year Plan, which had given priority to four lines: first, increased health care of children; second, improved medical training; third, comprehensive prophylaxis, especially at the workplace and linked with better therapy for occupational diseases; and fourth, the development of medical research. The establishment of the Academy of Medical Sciences was the main contribution to the latter. Its goal for the addition of 12,400 hospital beds between 1971 and 1975 was reached as early as 1973. It has required these (and to some extent those in existing small hospitals) to be concentrated into large units, with standard hospital sizes of 300-600 beds and 900-1,000 beds. The average hospital opened in 1974 had 646 beds. To reduce overhead costs new hospitals have begun to incorporate polyclinics to service the local area. The concentration policy for small hospitals will reduce the number in rural areas and, while the local population will still be expected to make voluntary contributions towards the cost of rural health facilities, the government has promised more finance for poor villages. Common clinical laboratories (see Table 8.10) will be established for the use of both hospitals and polyclinics: until the recent reunification of these, laboratories were often somewhat wastefully duplicated.

The 1975 research plan was the first consolidated plan on medical and pharmacological research drawn up by the Academy of Medical Sciences. Over 90 per cent of all research was based on contracts and the plan contained 1,000 projects in 40 research fields. The main components of the plan were that 38 per cent of projects were on illness detection, diagnosis, treatment and recovery from chronic diseases, and 16 per cent on development of new drugs, vaccine, materials and medical equipment. Special research programmes dealt with geriatric problems, medical physiology, mother and child protection, recovery from chronic illnesses, the national anti-cancer campaign, and on mineral waters and other sources of medical treatment. Research fields for special attention were in the diagnosis and treatment of heart diseases, nervous diseases and stomach ailments.[15]

The 1976-80 Plan, as drafted in November 1974, envisaged the opening of 45 hospitals with 23,400 beds (see Table 8.11), 41 new outpatient centres and 430 dental surgeries but a revision in January 1976 raised the two latter goals to 64 and 500.

VI. Finance of health care

The health services provided free to all residents in Ministry of Health facilities are prophylaxis and anti-malarial medication (and anti-helminithic until 1967 in the regions at risk), immunization against communicable diseases, and first aid, but 93.8 per cent of the gainfully employed population (in 1968; in 1960 the percentage was 88.1), expectant and nursing mothers, children and old-age pensioners are entitled to gratis services. All those employed in government service and in nationalized industries are entitled to free inpatient and outpatient care (including all treatment, examinations and radiological and laboratory investigations) — during hospitalization medication and board are gratis; sickness benefit, varying between 50 and 90 per cent of average earnings, is payable by the Social Insurance Board of the Central Trade Union Council. Pensioners from state employment and their dependants, insured members of handicraft cooperatives and their dependants, have the same health care rights, although, while pensioners receive an undiminished pension during illness, members of craft cooperatives receive only whatever provision their cooperative makes. Children up to the age of 17 and students receive all medical care free (in- and outpatient and through school and university medical services); children of state employees and pensioners with low pensions can also obtain free balneological treatment; state employees are admitted to spas at reduced rates. Pensions were linked to earnings from January 1967.[16]

Members of cooperative farms are given free outpatient care in local general dispensaries and benefit from a 50 to 75 per cent reduction in hospitalization charges for hospitals and specialized polyclinics.[17] Virtual completions of farm collectivization in the early sixties accounted for the rise in health care coverage since 1960 noted above; 16.0 per cent of those engaged in agriculture were private farmers in 1960 but the percentage had fallen to 9.9 by 1968. Artisans outside cooperatives were enrolled in the cooperative insurance scheme in 1968 (when they constituted 1.2 per cent of the industrial workforce and 1.4 per cent of manpower in construction). Private farmers and those in the liberal professions and arts (if not employed by state institutions) are not eligible for free or reduced-rate care. A now minor population group — political prisoners of the pre-1944 administration and wartime deportees — are provided with all care gratis. Employment status did not until 1968 determine eligibility for spouses or dependants, but since about that time both territorial and enterprise out-patient services seem to have been made available without charge to the spouses or parents of insured persons. A corresponding extension of the free medical provision to cooperative farmers seems also to have begun in 1973.[18]

Pharmaceuticals are supplied free against medication registers for all hospitalized patients and are dispensed free to outpatients in specified categories (pregnant and post-partum women, schoolchildren, students and certain pensioners); ambulatory prescriptions, paid or not, must be made out on standard forms.[19] Free provision is also applied to those suffering from specified diseases: the list numbers nearly 100 and includes tuberculosis, cancer, certain forms of rheumatism and of mental illness, and diabetes. No commitment has been made by the government to add to the categories entitled to free prescriptions, and official concern on over-prescribing makes extension unlikely. Priority for child care over the next decade and government pro-natalist policy should, however, increase the costs for those groups already on the gratis schedule. Some reduction is made for the purchase of prosthetic devices — the rebate being greater for state employees than for members of cooperatives — and they are in a few cases available free of charge, where the recipient has a low income; Since 1968, the government is said to have been considering imposing hospitalization charges on insured workers, but no decision has in the event been made.

Private practice, though discountenanced, was tolerated under what a political scientist has interpreted as a 'truce' with former bourgeois doctors provided that they absorbed themselves in the programmes of planned development launched with the one-year plans of 1949 and 1950.[20] It has been forbidden since 1959, but since then physicians after specified duty in a post in the gratis sector may attend payment-clinics or make domiciliary visits to paying patients, though both services are within the state system, which shares the fees. During the sixties for a consultation at the polyclinic (or hospital in the case of a professor) the fee was 30 lei for a physician and 50 lei for a professor, divided between the physician, his paramedical assistant or nurse and the government (which provides the consulting room and equipment), but in 1970 they were increased as shown in the table on p. 250.

Even a specialist of professorial or senior status (*medic primar*)

1. Tariff for consultations at the special payment-clinics		
Professors, readers and docents	60 lei	
Senior registrars (*medici primari*)	50 lei	
Specialist physicians	40 lei	
Dental surgeons	30 lei	

2. Fees charged for domiciliary visits	Day	Night
Professors, readers, docents	80 lei	120 lei
Senior registrars	50 lei	70 lei
Specialist physicians	40 lei	60 lei
General practitioners	30 lei	40 lei

3. Other provisions		
Transportation expenses to the patient's home –	supplement of	20 lei
For physicians travelling in localities other than that of their permanent homes —	supplement of	40 lei

4. Fees for other domiciliary services	
Injections	5 lei
Other treatment	10 lei
Nurses	3.5 lei per hour, both day and night

Source: *Buletinal official al RSR*, Part I, No. 70

cannot of right dispose of beds in his department, although informal payments were quite frequently offered until a strict control of 'illicit incomes' was introduced (1968) and tax increases were imposed on self-employed earnings (1970). A new salary scale for physicians of November 1970 was a partial compensation for the tighter rein on private earnings, but medical personnel had never been ill-paid in comparison with other earners, as Table 8.12 shows.

Health facilities which serve the local population aré dually subordinate to the Ministry of Health and to the local authority, and their finance is consequently a compound of support from local taxes and from general government revenue. They are not permitted to transfer budget outlays from one head to another: thus underspending within an annual budget on wages does not justify equivalent overspending on, say, pharmaceuticals. The standard budget heads for a hospital (with percentages for the Bucharest group of hospitals, but excluding out-patient departments) are salaries (40), pharmaceuticals and medical supplies (25), food (15), maintenance (11) and other costs (7); the capital budget is separate and includes for existing health facilities entries for purchase and repair of medical equipment. For a new facil-

facility, the Ministry of Health classifies its project-budget as follows (with percentage for a polyclinic costing approximately 10 million lei): construction and assembly (80), of which framework and sanitary and electrical installations (60), equipment and furniture (15), labour protection (1), site organization (3) and site management (1). Rather more than one-third of the budgetary classification, 'Social and Cultural Expenditure' is financed from local authority revenue and forms rather more than half of their total outlay (55 per cent in 1971).[21] That budget head is only subdivided in published statistics for the combined outlays, of which the sections relating to health care are extracted in Table 8.13. The entry 'Social insurance' covers all payments to insured persons and was formerly covered by premium income (3,574 million lei in 1960), but came to represent a net subsidy from general revenue (1968 premium income was 7,378 million lei, viz. 2,130 million lei short of outpayments). The government has on occasion considered raising the employer contribution in order to balance outlays.

In 1975 expenditures on state social insurance and family allowances were to be 25,900 million lei. The Social Insurance Board in that year covered 6.4 million people working on the basis of a labour contract, to which 1.5 million pensioners were added; other types of social insurance exist for craft cooperatives, cooperative farmers, the army, lawyers, writers and for other smaller categories of people. Over 12 million people were covered by all kinds of social insurance,[22] or 57 per cent of the end-1974 population. Premiums paid by the employee are 2 per cent of earnings and on a sliding scale 15 to 5 per cent of payroll by the employer. The employee contribution is paid into a separate fund from which a retirement pension is paid graduated by years and size of contribution. The ordinary pension, financed from the employer contribution, varies with salary paid during the 5 years preceding retirement. Outlays are administered by the State Social Insurance Board of the Central Trade Union Council. The 'social welfare' spending in Table 8.13 includes pensions paid to the non-insured, and, although no government spending on health has been so funded, that on physical culture and sport has since 1959 been very substantially supplemented by the profits of 'Loto-Pronosport', the football-pool and betting enterprise run by the State. Voluntary contributions to hospital and health centre construction in 1960 amounted to 3 million lei and to 4 million in 1965.[23] An estimate of 10 million is written into the 1968 column of Table 8.14 because of a campaign to build creches and maternity homes in rural areas and housing for medical staff transferred to the countryside, when urgent needs arose after the rise in the birth rate. Although no data are published on social insurance and enterprise spending on health care,

the share of the Ministry and local authorities is so high as to indicate
a low figure. In putting a 1968 estimate into Table 8.15, the proportion
was borne in mind that they ran 98.1 per cent of the therapeutic beds,
100 per cent of the prophylactic beds and 99.6 per cent of beds classified as 'in other units', as well as 94.6 per cent of the polyclinics (including all but one enterprise polyclinic), 93.6 per cent of the enterprise dispensaries and 97.5 per cent of enterprise 'health posts'.
Facilities run by the Social Insurance Board for strictly health purposes
could, with such proportions, not be more than one per cent of the
Ministry's recurrent spending (making 56 million lei in 1968), while
those run by enterprises could have been scarcely more than double
that sum (say 110 million lei in that year). To these are added, in Table
8.15, the non-government capital outlays shown in Table 8.14.

Private payments in Table 8.15 are drawn from Tables 8.14 and
8.16; payments in 'paying polyclinics' were estimated on the assumption that about one in ten of the 39.69 million consultations in
territorial-services polyclinics[24] were paid for at the fee, already mentioned, of 30 lei each. Table 8.15 puts government funding at just on
80 per cent of total health care outlay. Of government outlay 6.7
per cent was capital investment.

Mention has already been made of President Ceauşescu's public
complaint of October 1975 that the tripling of pharmaceutical consumption between 1960 and 1975 had been excessive.[25] At the beginning of 1975, a national network for Pharmacology-Vigilance (*Farma-
covigilenţă*) was set up by the Ministry of Health to moderate
self-medication and to prevent excessive use of pharmaceuticals. This
special service became a member of the WHO international centre dealing with drug abuse.[26] Pharmaceutical supply for human use in domestic currency was 2,085 million lei (Table 8.16), or 106 lei per head, or
US $4.20 at the 25.2 lei rate indicated by a Ministry of Health survey.

Expenditure under the pro-natalist policy is large: in 1975 family
allowances, aggregating 7,240 million lei, accounted for 13 per cent of
all 'social and cultural' outlay in the Budget. At that time payments to
encourage childbirth comprised family allowances for wage-earners of
60 to 240 lei per month (decreasing with paternal income but increasing per successive child), for cooperative farmers of 50 lei per month,
and for others with effect from the fourth birth, and a bounty of 1,000
lei as maternity grant on the birth of a third or subsequent child. A
mother of eight would have a supplementary grant of 200 lei per month
and the Order of Maternal Glory, second class, carrying an income-tax
rebate of 40 per cent.[27]

REFERENCES

1.   N. N. Constantinescu (ed.), *Situaţia clasei muncitoare din România 1914-1944*, Bucharest, 1966, pp. 208, 256, 326, 372-3
2.   Ibid., p. 287
3.   Ibid., p. 443
4.   M. Kaser, 'Romania', in H. H. Höhmann, M. C. Kaser and K. C. Thalheim (eds.), *The New Economic Systems of Eastern Europe*, London, 1975, p. 188; on the general reforms, ibid., pp. 172-4, 187-8 and I. Spigler, *Economic Reform in Romanian Industry*, London, 1973, pp. 27-71
5.   *România Libera*, 27 October 1975, p. 2
6.   Ibid.
7.   *Scînteia*, 24 July 1975
8.   Ibid., 27 October 1968
9.   H. P. David, *Family Planning and Abortion in the Socialist Countries of Central and Eastern Europe*, New York, 1970, pp. 128-36
10. 'Notă metodologică', *Breviar de statistică medico-sanitară* (hereafter, *Health Statistics*), *1968*, p. 217
11. 'Notă', *Health Statistics, 1971*, p. 90
12. V. Coroi, Th. Ilea, D. Enăchescu, T. Hussár, *Igiena* (Bucharest), No. 8, 1965
13. Th. Ilea *et al.*, *Sănătate publică*, Bucharest, 1966, pp. 402-9
14. *România Liberă*, 22 January 1975, pp. 1, 5
15. Ibid., 15 January 1975, pp. 1-2
16. *Dezvolterea economică a Romînei, 1944-1964*, Bucharest, 1964, pp. 655-8
17. I. Rădulescu, *Funcţia economică-organizatorică a statului socialist*, Bucharest, 1967, p. 241
18. *Satul socialist*, 7 February 1973, pp. 1, 4
19. *Produse farmaceutice în practica medicala*, Bucharest, 1969, p. 9
20. Gh. Ionescu, *Communism in Rumania, 1944-62*, London, 1964, pp. 173-6
21. *Health Statistics, 1971*, p. 284
22. *România Liberă*, 27 January 1975, pp. 1, 5
23. *Investiţii-construcţii in RSR*, Bucharest, 1966, p. 94
24. *Health Statistics, 1971*, p. 149
25. *România Liberă*, 27 October 1975, p. 2
26. Ibid., 20 January 1975
27. *Romania Today*, No. 3, 1976

TABLES

8.1 Demographic projections for Romania

	1971	1981	1996
Total population (millions)	20.47	22.47	25.34
Per cent aged 0-14	25.6	27.0	24.5
15-39	38.0	34.2	35.4
40-64	27.6	28.7	28.4
65 and over	8.8	10.1	11.7
Median age	31.1	31.0	31.7
Males per 100 females	96.6	97.4	98.5
Dependants (children under 15 and persons aged over 64) per 1,000 aged 15-64	34.4	37.1	36.2

Source: Projection B (constant gross reproduction rates) from P. F. Myers in US Congress Joint Economic Committee, *Reorientation and Commercial Relations of the Economies of Eastern Europe*, Washington, D.C., 1974, p. 430

NOTE: Variant IIb (assuming a constant life-table experience and specific fertility of 1971) in I. Hristache, 'Population Forecast in Romania until 1990', *Economic Computation and Economic Cybernetics* (Bucharest), No. 2, 1975, p. 93, gives 22.35 million for 1981 and 24.12 million for 1991

8.2 Causes of death in Romania 1955-66

	No. of cases		Per 100,000 population in
	1955	*1966*	*1967*
1. Group of causes exhibiting an increase			
Neoplasms	12050	23175	121.1
Diabetes mellitus	250	536	2.8
Diseases of the nervous and sensory organs	10567	25014	130.7
Diseases of the cardiovascular system	35035	47531	248.3
Diseases of the respiratory system (including influenza)	22236	25601	133.7
2. Group of causes exhibiting a decrease			
Infectious and parasitic diseases (except tuberculosis, syphilis, influenza)	2979	1603	8.4
Tuberculosis	7785	4239	22.1
Diseases of the digestive system	9016	7887	41.2
Diseases of the genito-urinary system	3488	3337	17.4
Diseases of pregnancy, delivery and confinement	388	235	1.2
Congenital malformations and specific diseases of infancy	11588	4584	23.9
3. Total deaths	167535	157445	822.5

Source: *Vademecum of Medico-Sanitary Statistics, 1968*, pp. 26-9

8.3 Leading causes of death in Romania 1967-71

	1967	per 100,000	*1969*	per 100,000	*1971*	per 100,000
1. Causes exhibiting an increase						
Diseases of the circulation	74409	385.8	93905	469.3	96415	471.0
of which cerebrovascular	24522	127.2	27030	135.1	26590	129.9
Neoplasms	23306	120.9	25018	125.0	25968	126.9
of which malignant	22625	117.7	24425	122.1	25152	122.9
Diabetes mellitus	574	3.0	721	3.6	685	3.3
Diseases of pregnancy, delivery and complications	481	(91.1) [a]	491	(105.4) [a]	522	(130.5) [a]
2. Causes exhibiting a decrease						
Diseases of the respiratory system	32986	171.0	37617	188.0	33211	162.2
of which influenza	837	4.3	1692	8.5	1596	7.8
pneumonia, bronchial pneumonia	12429	64.4	18367	91.8	14816	72.4
Diseases of the digestive system	8507	44.2	7553	37.7	7336	35.8
Tuberculosis	4349	22.6	4119	20.6	3491	17.1
Diseases of the genito-urinary system	3405	17.7	3755	18.8	3154	15.4
Infections, parasitic diseases (excluding influenza, tuberculosis, syphilis)	1710	8.6	4634	23.2	2936	14.3
of which typhoid and paratyphoid	13	0.07	30	0.1	47	0.2
scarlet fever	14	0.07	3	0.01	7	0.03
whooping-cough	83	0.4	177	0.9	6.9	0.3
diphtheria	7	0.04	1	0.005	2	0.009
measles	222	1.2	443	2.2	217	1.1
Congenital anomalies	1784	9.3	1919	9.6	1626	7.9
Nephritis and nephrosis	1612	8.4	..	..	1390	6.8
Total deaths	179129	928.8	201225	1005.6	194306	949.2

Source: *Breviar de statistică medico-sanitară* (hereafter, *Health Statistics*), *1968*, pp. 84-7; *1971*, pp. 90-3

a   Per 100,000 live births

NOTE: The source for Table 8.2 is an English translation of the above for 1968 but includes data only to 1966

8.4 Morbidity in Romania

New cases per 100,000 inhabitants

	1960	1967	1971
1. *Causes exhibiting an increase*			
Diseases of the respiratory system other than influenza	15409.2	21973.3	..
Diseases of the teeth and gums	6638.3	10206.9	..
Endemic hepatitis	280.2	212.2	285.4
Bacillary dysentery	55.9	71.8	106.9
Parotiditis	272.4	248.0	385.8
Chickenpox	276.1	257.8	369.4
Scarlet fever	58.0	97.7	66.2
Q fever	0.2	0.5	0.3
2. *Causes exhibiting a decrease*			
Infections other than tuberculosis and syphilis	4674.9	3581.4	..
Malignant neoplasms	85.7	79.5	..
Diseases of the circulatory system	1773.4	1171.4	..
— of which acute arthritis	250.7	108.3	..
of the heart	532.2	290.1	..
arterial hypertension	663.1	456.2	..
Influenza	1670.6	1476.7	..
Diseases of the digestive system	5222.6	4708.3	..
— of which ulcerative	265.3	144.1	..
of the liver and biliary ducts	648.7	445.9	..
Diseases of the genito-urinary system	1863.0	1669.6	..
— of which in women	1153.3	901.1	..
Rheumatic diseases other than acute rheumatism	1773.5	1519.5	..
— of which muscular rheumatism	1359.0	1086.9	..
Congenital malformations	20.1	10.7	..
Tuberculosis	333.4	148.5	133.9
Syphilis	51.4	27.2	38.4
Malaria	0.4	–	–
Anthrax	1.6	0.7	0.5
Leptospirosis	1.5	2.2	1.1
Botulism	0.01	–	–
Brucellosis	0.14	0.05	0.15
Diphtheria	4.4	0.16	0.04
Typhoid	10.8	2.3	1.45
Paratyphoid	1.7	0.10	0.09
Poliomyelitis	5.9	0.14	0.10
Rabies	0.1	0.04	0.01
Measles	662.0	487.1	474.3
Tetanus	4.6	0.8	0.42
Whooping-cough	650.6	107.2	86.1

Source: *Health Statistics, 1968*, pp. 52-71; *1971*, pp. 114, 118, 126-7

8.5 Reason for physician consultation in Bucharest

Percentage of total

	All consultations	Adults	Children
	1955	*1964*	*1964*
Internal medicine	3.50	14.0	16.0
of which cardiological	..	2.5	1.5
endocrinological	..	2.0	2.0
rheumatological	..	1.5	2.5
gastroenterological	..	1.0	0.0
medical-physical culture	..	2.0	8.0
parasitological	..	—	2.0
other	..	5.0	—
Surgical	15.6	12.5	8.0
— of which orthopaedic	..	1.5	3.0
urological	..	2.0	0.0
other	..	9.0	5.0
Otorhinolaryngological	2.6	8.0	10.0
Ophthalmological	4.2	7.0	9.0
Dermato-venereological	3.4	6.0	3.0
Obstetric and gynaecological	5.0	11.0	—
Neurological	2.1	6.0	6.0
Tuberculosis	3.0	10.0	9.0
Paediatric	17.2	—	16.0
Stomatological	11.3	22.0	23.0

Source: Th. Ilea *et al., Sănătate publică*, Bucharest, 1966, p. 404

8.6 Breakdown of consultations and treatments in health facilities of the Romanian Ministry of Health

	Per 100 inhabitants			Thousands	
	1960	*1967*	*1971*	*1967*	*1971*
Cardiological	1	3	3	508.1	539.1
Surgical	17	24	23	4556.8	4746.0
Dermato-venereological	8	13	14	2500.9	2790.2
Endocrinological	2	2	2	444.5	453.5
Tuberculosis	16	15	14	2886.4	2848.9
Gastroenterological	< 1	< 1	< 1	82.2	55.3
Internal n.e.s.	14	23	23	4353.5	4632.9
Sport medicine	2	4	5	776.2	1013.8
Neuro-psychiatric	4	11	12	2149.6	2447.8
Obstetric and gynaecological	15	21	18	4112.9	3711.3
Ophthalmological	10	18	18	3462.2	3653.5
Oncological	< 1	1	2	285.6	354.8
Otorhinolaryngological	12	19	19	3612.5	3848.3
Orthopaedic	1	2	2	310.9	409.4
Urological	1	2	2	305.7	264.3
Paediatric	6	12	19	2290.4	3800.5
Stomatological	40	85	120	16440.5	24543.8
Other	27	35	40	68256.1	81913.2
Total	42	61	69	117336.8	142067.9

Source: *Health Statistics, 1968*, pp. 84-7; *1971*, pp. 152-3

8.7 Bed numbers in all types of health facility (excluding military hospitals) in Romania

		Urban	Rural	All areas
Ministry of Health	1967	105756	44572	150328
	1971	129080	39995	169075
Other civilian agencies	1967	2986	15	3001
	1971	3685	536	4221
Total	1967	108742	44587	153329
	1971	132765	40531	173296

Source *Health Statistics, 1968*, p. 125; *1971*, p. 209

8.8 Number of health facilities run by Ministry of Health and by other public agencies in Romania

| | Urban | | | | Rural | | | | All areas | | | |
| | Ministry | | Others | | Ministry | | Others | | Ministry | | Others | |
	1967	1971	1967	1971	1967	1971	1967	1971	1967	1971	1967	1971
Hospitals	327	350	19	23	258	214	–	4	585	564	19	27
University clinics	–	–	13	16	–	–	–	–	–	–	13	16
Enterprise hospitals	48	29	3	12	28	9	–	4	76	38	3	16
Polyclinics	318	275	24	35	72	30	–	6	390	305	24	41
Tuberculosis sanatoria	..	..	–	–	..	..	–	–	52	40	–	–
Preventoria	..	..	–	–	..	..	–	–	7	26	–	–
Tuberculosis dispensaries	147	–[a]	–	–	56	–[a]	–	–	203	–[a]	–	–
Dermato-venereological dispensaries	145	–[a]	1	–	20	–[a]	–	–	165	–[a]	1	–
Children's homes	..	..	..	–	..	..	–	–	34	46	–	–
Local health centres	1052	1190	–	–	3001	2710	–	–	4035	3900	–	–
Local children's clinics	..	..	..	–	..	..	–	–	446	426	–	–
Local clinics for adults	..	..	..	–	..	..	..	–	59	41	2	–
Maternity homes	..	..	..	–	..	..	..	–	1901	1621	–	–
Public health inspection offices	..	..	..	–	..	..	..	–	121	40[b]	6	–
Enterprise dispensaries with physician	484	766	42	263	199	152	2	81	683	918	44	344

Health posts with medical assistant	656	518	17	144	707	398	8	41	1363	916	25	185
Creches	..	..	..	..	..	..	..	..	306	436	7	11
Pharmacies
— retail	571	647	—	—	591	549	—	—	1162	1196	—	—
— within health facilities	420	442	18	35	119	87	—	3	539	529	28	38
Pharmacy points ^{c}
— category I	..	..	—	—	..	..	—	—	370	467	—	—
— category II	..	..	—	—	..	..	—	—	3635	3409	—	—
Blood collecting stations	..	..	—	—	..	..	—	—	32	31	—	—
Air ambulance units	..	..	—	—	..	..	—	—	19	22	—	—
Malaria and helminthiasis stations	..	— d	—	—	— d	— d	—	—	30	— d	—	—

Source: *Health Statistics, 1968*, pp. 110-19; *1971*, pp. 190-7

a From 1970 included with polyclinics as a subordinate dispensary
b Reduction due to new county structure introduced in 1968
c Distributive 'kiosks' (category I) and other outlets (category II)
d Abolished in 1968

8.9 Medical staffing of Romanian health facilities on 31 December 1960 and 1971 and 15 March 1968

			Local authorities	Ministry of Health	Other public bodies	Total
1.	Higher-qualified					
1.1	Physicians					
	Hospitals	1960	5586	213	—	—
		1968	7215	631	—	—
		1971	7185	256	—	—
	Polyclinics	1960	4241	140	—	—
		1968	5444	166	—	—
		1971	6713	144	—	—
	Tuberculosis sanatoria	1960	214	181	—	—
		1968	211	178	—	—
		1971	271	54	—	—
	Public-health laboratories	1960	722	3	—	—
		1968	883	4	—	—
		1971	447	4	—	—
	Medical research institutes	1960	—	453	—	—
		1968	—	843	—	—
		1971	—	785	—	—
	Total	1960	18823	2859	3302	24984
		1968	22079	2071	5850	30000
		1971	24134	1347	5765	31246
1.2	Pharmacists	1960	—	—	—	4797
		1968	—	—	—	4885
		1971	—	—	—	4338
1.3	Chemists	1960	—	—	—	971
		1968	—	—	—	1109 [a]
1.4	Toxicologists	1960	—	—	—	99
		1968	—	—	—	167
1.5	Psychologists	1960	—	—	—	30
		1968	—	—	—	78
1.6	Social specialists	1960	—	—	—	120
		1968	—	—	—	118
2.	Intermediate-trained	1960	—	—	—	60648
		1968	—	—	—	89892
		1971	—	—	—	103593
3.	Elementary staff	1960	—	—	—	32727
		1968	—	—	—	52111
		1971	—	—	—	57076

Source: *Health Statistics, 1968*, pp. 172-80; *1971*, pp. 260, 261, 263

a   31 December 1966

8.10 Public clinical laboratories in Romania

	1960	1968
Number of laboratories	439	660
Number of clinical procedures (thousand)	19501	48981

Source: Direct communication from Ministry of Health

8.11 Romanian plans for hospital capacity

	Thousand beds	Incremental bed to hospital ratio
1970	168.1	..
1971	173.3	..
1972	179.4	..
1973	186.2	..
1974	191.9	646
1975 Plan	180.5	..
1976-80 Plan	..	520

Source: *Statistical Yearbook, 1975*, p. 489; *România Liberă*, 11 February 1975, p. 3; *Directives on Five-Year Plans*

8.12 Salaries of personnel in Romanian health, social welfare and physical education services

	1950	1960	1970	1971	1974
Monthly average (lei)	336	801	1339	1375	1542
as per cent of average					
− in industry	90.6	90.3	93.5	94.1	92.9
− for all employed	91.8	93.8	93.4	93.5	92.7

Source: *Statistical Yearbook, 1975*, p. 76

8.13 Government and Social Insurance expenditure on health and social welfare in Romania

Millions of lei

	Health	Social Insurance	Social welfare
1950	645	827	352
1960	2955	3540	990
1968	5965	9508	1194
1970	6930	11263	1250
1974	9178	16674	1548

Source: *Health Statistics, 1971*, pp. 282-3; *Statistical Yearbook, 1975*, p. 417

8.14 Estimates of Romanian capital investment in health and social welfare

Millions of lei at 1963 prices

		1960 [a]	1965	1966	1967	1968
1.1	Health	232	214	495	..	398
1.2	Physical culture and social welfare	145	304	319	..	337
1.3	Total	377	518	814	692	735
1.4	of which from government funds	368	501	788	659	705
1.5	from other funds	9	17	26	33	30
2.1	Government central investment in health, welfare and education					
2.2	Plan	..	..	1180	1180	1420
2.3	Plan: health only	..	..	445	..	535
2.4	Local and central government expenditure in health, welfare and education	932	1200	1679	1664	1962
3.1	Equipment and furniture element in health outlay	72	72	166	..	133

8.14 (cont)

Source: Row 1.1 estimated from data in *Scînteia*, 27 October 1968; for row 2.3
while total investment in health, welfare and education (row 2.2) was to have
risen by 20.3 per cent in 1966-8 (plan) (from *Scînteia*, 1 July 1966), health
and welfare actual spending dropped by 10.5 per cent over those three years
(row 1.3) (although that of the budget group including education (row 2.4)
had risen by 17 per cent); it was assumed that in 1968 the average planned expenditure was under-fulfilled in the proportion of the entire group (ratio of
row 2.4 to row 2.2); row 1.2 was derived by difference and extrapolated back
to 1960 and 1965 on the basis of actual spending in these fields (*Health
Statistics, 1968*, p. 184); rows 1.3, 1.4 and 1.5 were from *Statistical Yearbook, 1969*, pp. 456-9; row 3.1 from proportion of investment outlays on
health and social welfare spent on equipment and furniture in 1960 (31.4 per
cent) and in 1965 (33.6 per cent) from *Investiţii-Construcţii in RSR*, Bucharest, 1966, pp. 88-9

a   Prices fell 1 per cent in 1963

8.15 Estimate of Romanian health-care expenditure in 1968

Millions of lei

1. Government		
1.1 Health facilities and salaries		5965
1.2 of which investment	398	
1.3 Subsidy to social insurance	2130	
2. Social insurance		
2.1 Premiums spent	7378	
2.2 Total outlay through social insurance	9508	
2.3 of which on health		56
3. Enterprises		
3.1 Recurrent	100	
3.2 Capital	20	
		120
4. Direct (including cooperatives)		
4.1 Purchase of pharmaceuticals	924	
4.2 Purchase of other health-care products	44	
4.3 Voluntary contributions	10	
4.4 Payments for private practices in polyclinics	400	
		1378
Total		7519

Source: See text (p. 252)

8.16 Romanian domestic sales of health products

Millions of lei

	1960	1965	1967	1968
Pharmaceuticals				
1.1 Purchased through retail shops	613	743	826	924
1.2 Free prescriptions and uses in hospitals		545		
1.3 Free prescriptions and uses for out-patients	383	347	1074	1161
1.4 Veterinary	39	55	61	65
1.5 Total pharmaceutical sales	1035	1690	1961	2150
Medical supplies and prostheses				
2.1 Purchased through retail shops	44	37	43	44
2.2 Purchased for use in hospitals and other institutions	192	223	..	243
2.3 Total medical-supply sales	236	260	..	287

Source: Row 1.1: 1960 and 1965 from *Health Statistics, 1968*, p. 189. 1968 from percentage of pharmaceuticals in total non-food retail turnover in *Statistical Yearbook, 1969*, p. 531. Free prescriptions increased by 630 million lei between 1960 and 1967 according to the Deputy Minister of Health, Dr Eugen Mares, in an interview in *Rumania Today*, April 1969, p. 29; drugs supplied by the Ministry of Health rose from 996 million to 1,900 million lei in 1967 (*Scînteia*, 27 October 1967); deducting this from the sum of rows 1.1 and 1.5 yielded row 1.4. An extrapolation of row 1.4 to 1968 on the 1960-7 rate of 6.6 per cent per annum yielded the 1968 figure of 65 million lei. This and row 1.1 was then deducted from row 1.5 to yield the sum of rows 1.2 and 1.3. Row 1.4 was interpolated for 1965 to check the following calculation for rows 1.2 and 1.3 for 1965, for which the sum was (by subtraction of row 1.1 + 1.4 from 1.5) 892 million lei. It was stated by Th. Ilea *et al., Sănătate publică*, p. 460, that pharmaceutical outlay per hospitalized day was 16 lei in 1964, when there were 34.49 million such days, viz. 552 million lei. Outlays per day were assumed unchanged in 1965 when there were 34.06 million days, viz. 545 million lei. The Ministry of Health (in a direct communication to the writer) stated that 60 per cent of free prescriptions are for inpatients and 40 per cent for outpatients: applying the former percentage to the 1965 figure in row 1.2 yields a notional 908 million total free prescriptions in Ministry of Health hospitals, which was a course consistent with the derived 892 million, of which 40 per cent is 356 million, close to the estimate derived by difference of 347 million. Row 1.5: direct communication to writer from Ministry of Health. Row 2.1: as for row 1.1. Row 2.2: estimated from 1967 proportion of institutional expenditure in Poland applied to expenditure on pharmaceuticals and worked back to 1960 and forward to 1968 on rate of increase of hospitalized days (3 per cent per annum)

9 INTERNATIONAL ECONOMIC LINKS WITHIN COMECON

Comecon's exchanges of pharmaceuticals and of medical equipment (there is little trade in prosthetic and hospital supplies) have constituted the organization's chief part in collaboration among its members' health care services, but more recently it has come to contribute in other spheres.

A Working Group (*Rabochaya gruppa*) on the Pharmaceutical Industry was established in 1957 among the very first of the Council's regular organizations. The constitution of eleven Permanent Commissions at the Council Session of May 1956 endowed the organization with agencies for a specialized collaboration among member states which its previous *ad hoc* nature had precluded. The Permanent Commission on the Chemicals Industry was set up in Berlin, and the GDR Minister of the Chemicals Industry has by convention always been its chairman. A corresponding Department of the Chemicals Industry was formed, and has so remained, within the Secretariat in Moscow. The launching in 1958 by the Soviet government of an ambitious national programme for the increased utilization of chemicals reflected general and rapid development of this branch of industry among Comecon members, but, because it was a spearhead of domestic modernization and potentially a major export sector, national competitiveness hindered collaboration.[1]

Each member government in the interests of broad self-sufficiency was already determined to create a pharmaceutical industry (Bulgaria, Czechoslovakia and Romania) or greatly to develop its prewar sector (the USSR, GDR, Hungary and, to a lesser extent, Poland). The world's pharmaceutical production was concentrated in the United States and five countries of Western Europe, partners on whom at the time of the Cold War continued reliance was not desired.

The Comecon Working Group on the Pharmaceutical Industry was provided with offices and a small staff in Budapest by the Hungarian Pharmaceutical Manufacturers' Union and given the task of elaborating recommendations for inter-member specialization, whereby one or a few states would concentrate on specified products and on associated research and development. The lower-cost and higher-quality pharmaceuticals thus obtained would be supplied to non-producers, who in turn would be allocated other special lines of output and research. Collaboration in the supply of crude chemicals and semi-manufactures, and joint work on the experimental and semi-commercial stages of development were also foreseen.[2] Some broad international division of labour was achieved, in that Bulgaria concentrated on antibiotics and Hungary specialized in the purchase of foreign licences and a counter-supply of its own innovations, while the USSR stood ready to use internally any available export supplies. The USSR itself was a large enough manufacturer (equal to the rest of Comecon put together) in its Glavkhimfarmprom (38 out of 66 enterprises in 1956) to undertake its own rationalization and specialization programme. Investment in 1956-8 was limited to existing plants and specialization was the keynote of the 1959-65 Plan.[3] But international collaboration did not greatly develop, and never as far as in other Comecon industries where an international economic organization brought together all the national associations as producers.

The Group's first *Compendium Medicamentorum*, a register of all pharmaceutical preparations manufactured in member states, was published in the GDR in 1971. The previous year an inter-Comecon economic association, Interchim, was founded in Halle (GDR) to co-ordinate production of chemicals with a high value to volume ratio. Rather more success attended a consortium of Comecon manufacturers of medical equipment, Medunion, which from an office in Budapest has acted as a focus for marketing policies over the past decade.

A trilateral coordination of the GDR, Czechoslovakia and Polish pharmaceutical industries was started in 1956, including the respective national Planning Commissions and Ministries of Health. Bilateral cooperation between GDR and Polish firms has particularly developed since 1967.[4] The USSR has provided equipment and technical assistance for pharmaceutical plants in Bulgaria, Czechoslovakia and Romania; Czechoslovakia, the GDR and Hungary have undertaken collaboration in the medical-equipment as well as pharmaceutical industries under Comecon auspices.[5]

The close political relations of Comecon members have fostered contacts among scientists and applied researchers since the changes of administration in the postwar years. The present Minister of Health of the USSR, Boris Petrovsky, was involved at an earlier stage of his career, spending two years (1949-51) as visiting professor of military medicine in Budapest University.[6] Collaboration of research institutes and learned societies has in general been accelerated by the creation of Comecon's Standing Commission for the Coordination of Scientific and Technical Research, founded in June 1962 with headquarters in Moscow (and raised in status to a Committee in January 1972). A working group to study the diffusion of innovation had brought together chairmen of national scientific-coordination bodies in June 1970. The establishment of professional organizations in the USSR promoted contacts at other levels. The trade union for medical staffs, Medsantrud, which had been dissolved in 1934 into sixteen Union-

Republican units (that for the Russian Federation being further broken up, into five regional sections, in 1939) was re-established in 1949; an All-Union Pharmacological Society was set up in 1964. Both have played their part in links among corresponding bodies elsewhere in Comecon, although no specific international links seem to have been forged.[7]

In 1971, Bulgaria, Czechoslovakia, the GDR, Hungary, Poland, Romania and the USSR concluded an 'Agreement on Scientific and Technological Collaboration in the Creation of a Biomedical Technology for Scientific Research and Clinical Medicine'. One of its provisions was the establishment of a Coordinating Centre for the Development of Medical Technology of the Member States of Comecon, located in the All-Union Research and Experimentation Institute for Medical Technology of the USSR Ministry of Health. It is run by a Plenipotentiary Council representing all members with the advice of an international scientific-technical board. Its Director, R. Utyambyshev, is also the Director of the All-Union Institute. Studies for the coordination of research, design and production of medical equipment have already involved over fifty industrial ministries and departments of state and more than 500 scientific and industrial organizations in the seven member countries. Among schemes of collaboration noted at the 1975 meeting of the Plenipotentiary Council (which set coordination targets for 1975-80) may be cited those of RFT of the GDR, Tesla and Chirana of Czechoslovakia and Medicor of Hungary on equipment for intensive-care units, between the Dresden Medical Academy (GDR) and the All-Union Institute in the USSR for complex automated diagnostic systems, between Polish and Soviet specialists for the development of polymers with medical applications, and of a six-channel electrocardiograph between the Czechoslovak Chirana and the USSR Ministry of the Medical Industry.[8] An electronic thermometer has been developed with Romania,[9] but, following a national policy since 1964 of less than full collaboration within Comecon, least action has ensued with respect to that country.

Medical education has been part of the activity of Comecon's Permanent Working Group on the Preparation and Past-Experience Training of Scientific Staffs, which has produced a 'Handbook' compiling and analysing the composition of highly skilled personnel in Comecon member states, and has evolved a nomenclature.[10]

Work began in August 1974 (pursuant to a resolution of the 36th meeting of the Standing Commission of Standardization of Comecon) to define international legal standards for the incorporation into manufacturing processes of norms on standard criteria of health production and labour safety: the novelty of the approach was to seek to ensure that at the research stage of evolving a new process proper account is taken of such factors as protection from industrial accidents or occupational disease and the minimization of environmental damage. Some norms along these lines were established in a joint GDR-USSR agreement which took effect on 1 October 1975.[11]

These strands of collaboration were at length coordinated by the creation in October 1975 of a Standing Commission on Collaboration in Health Protection which brings together Ministers of Comecon member states and provides, in Moscow, a permanent secretariat. Its terms of reference, resolved by Comecon's Council (Budapest, June 1975) and approved by the Executive Committee (Moscow, January 1976) are 'the field of health protection, medical science and technology'.[12] Table 9.1 may indicate why its establishment came some 25 years after Comecon's own foundation and the organization of national health services in each of the member states. It is only in the past few years that those services have become fully comprehensive. Four of the countries now furnish medical care as a civic right. To all intents and purposes this had come with the Constitution of 1936 in the USSR, when the social-insurance basis was liquidated and an All-Union Ministry of Health was established. But, as Chapter 2 shows, the rural services were differentially treated until the sixties and full parity awaited the Health Law of 1969. The Bulgarian Constitution of 1971, the Czechoslovak Health Law of 1966 and the Hungarian Social Insurance Law of 1975 similarly formalized cover for all citizens. The considerable extensions to those outside state employment in the GDR and Romania (1968) and in Poland (1971) have brought these countries *de facto* into line. In consequence, the Ministers of Health concerned must now be facing very similar issues of research, administration and finance. A quarter-century of diverse means has been concluded and more uniformity may now the better achieve the common end of inexpensive, but comprehensive, health care for the totality of Comecon's population.

REFERENCES

1.   M. Kaser, *Comecon: Integration Problems of the Planned Economies*, 2nd edn. London, 1967, pp. 75, 114-15
2.   A. G. Natradze, *Ocherk razvitiya khimiko-farmatsevticheskoi promyschlennosti SSSR*, Moscow, 1967, pp. 182-3; B. V. Petrovsky (ed.), *50 let sovetskogo zdravookhraneniya*, Moscow, 1967, pp. 174-5
3.   Natradze, op. cit., p. 173
4.   Ministry of Health (Poland), *Dzialalność w 1967 roku*, Warsaw, 1968, p. 167
5.   Petrovsky, op. cit., p. 174
6.   Biography, *Bol'shaya sovetskaya entisiklopediya*, 3rd edn, Vol. 19, Moscow, 1975, p. 487

7.   Petrovsky, op. cit., pp. 182, 215, 216
8.   R. Utyambyshev, 'In the Service of Health', *Ekonomicheskoe sotrudni-chestvo stran-chlenov SEV* (Comecon Secretariat, Moscow), No. 2, 1975, pp. 49-50
9.   A. Munteanu, 'Medical Technology for the Good of Mankind', ibid., pp. 51-3
10. B. Toth, Chairman of the Working Group, ibid., pp. 63-4
11. U. Rieger, *Die Wirtschaft*, No. 18, 13 September 1975
12. *Ekonomicheskoe sotrudnichestvo stran-chlenov SEV*, No. 3, 1975, p. 3

TABLE

9.1 Introduction of comprehensive health care in Comecon states

	Date of enactment	Percentage cover immediately prior to enactment
Introduction as civic right		
USSR	1936; 1969	100
Bulgaria	1971	100
Czechoslovakia	1966	87
Hungary	1975	99
Extension of social insurance		
GDR	1968	71 [a]
Poland	1971	79
Romania	1968	94 [b]

Source: Preceding chapters; compiled for comparison with Table 1 in A. Maynard, *Health Care in the European Community*, London, 1975, p. 251

a   Social Insurance Fund of trade unions, excluding other funds, as percentage of total gainfully-occupied population
b   As percentage of gainfully-occupied population

INDEX

273

For Product Safety Concerns and Information please contact our EU
representative GPSR@taylorandfrancis.com
Taylor & Francis Verlag GmbH, Kaufingerstraße 24, 80331 München, Germany